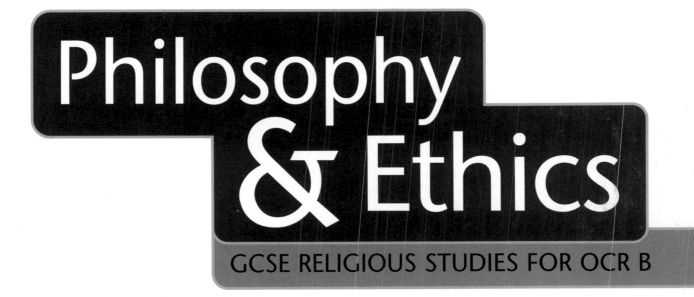

Philosophy & Ethics

GCSE RELIGIOUS STUDIES FOR OCR B

Michael Keene

Folens

Acknowledgements

ACE STOCK LIMITED/Alamy, 73; Alex Keene/The Walking Camera: 6, 7, 8, 9, 10, 11, 16 (both), 17, 20, 21, 24, 26, 27, 34, 35, 36, 37, 38 (both), 39, 40, 42, 43, 44, 45 (both), 47, 49, 50, 51, 52 (top), 54, 55 (both), 57 (top), 60 (both), 61, 64, 65, 66 (all), 79, 80, 81, 84, 99, 101, 105, 110, 123 (both), 129, 134, 138, 139, 140, 146, 147 (both), 148, 151, 154, 155, 162, 168, 176, 183, 200, 207, 229 (both), 231, 232, 234, 241, 244 (all), 246, 257, 261, 267; Corbis: 15 (both), 93, 115, 130, 153, 178, 210, 223, 265, 278; Design Pics Inc/Alamy, 133, 228; Israel images/Alamy, 181, 186; jackhollingsworth.com/Alamy, 171; Pat Behnke/Alamy, 252; POPPERFOTO/Alamy, 224; Sally and Richard Greenhill/Alamy, 177; Serge Kozak/Alamy, 53; TIM GRAHAM/Alamy, 175; World Religions Photo Library/Alamy, 52 (bottom), 57 (bottom), 89, 136, 222, 237.

United Kingdom: Folens Publishers, Apex Business Centre, Boscombe Road, Dunstable, LU5 4RL.
Email: folens@folens.com

Ireland: Folens Publishers, Greenhills Road, Tallaght, Dublin 24.
Email: info@folens.ie

Poland: JUKA, ul. Renesansowa 38, Warsaw 01-905

Editor: Nina Randall

Layout artist: Jason Billin

Illustration: Mike Lacey

Cover design: Jason Billin

Cover image: Alex Keene

First published 2005 by Folens Limited.

British Library Cataloguing in Publication Data. A catalogue record for this publication is available from the British Library.

ISBN 1 84303 779 3

CONTENTS

TOPIC 1
The Nature of God   **4**
- Introduction   4
- CHRISTIANITY   6
- HINDUISM   14
- ISLAM   20
- JUDAISM   24
- Exam Help   30

TOPIC 2
The Nature of Belief   **34**
- CHRISTIANITY   34
- HINDUISM   48
- ISLAM   56
- JUDAISM   62
- Exam Help   68

TOPIC 3
Religion and Science   **72**
- Introduction   72
- CHRISTIANITY   75
- HINDUISM   82
- ISLAM   86
- JUDAISM   88
- Exam Help   94

TOPIC 4
Death and the Afterlife   **98**
- CHRISTIANITY   98
- HINDUISM   106
- ISLAM   112
- JUDAISM   118
- Exam Help   124

TOPIC 5
Good and Evil   **128**
- CHRISTIANITY   128
- HINDUISM   136
- ISLAM   142
- JUDAISM   150
- Exam Help   156

TOPIC 6
Religion and Human Relationships   **160**
- CHRISTIANITY   160
- HINDUISM   170
- ISLAM   176
- JUDAISM   182
- Exam Help   188

TOPIC 7
Religion and Medical Ethics   **192**
- Introduction   192
- CHRISTIANITY   196
- HINDUISM   204
- ISLAM   208
- JUDAISM   212
- Exam Help   216

TOPIC 8
Religion and Equality   **220**
- Introduction   220
- CHRISTIANITY   220
- HINDUISM   230
- ISLAM   236
- JUDAISM   242
- Exam Help   248

TOPIC 9
Religion, Poverty and Wealth   **252**
- Introduction   252
- CHRISTIANITY   254
- HINDUISM   260
- ISLAM   264
- JUDAISM   268
- Exam Help   272

TOPIC 10
Religion, Peace and Justice   **276**
- CHRISTIANITY   276
- HINDUISM   284
- ISLAM   288
- JUDAISM   292
- Exam Help   296

GLOSSARY   **300**

INDEX   **305**

INTRODUCTION

Not everyone, of course, believes in God. There are people who believe that God does not exist and they are called **atheists** (meaning 'no god'). Some people find that their belief in God fluctuates at different times between faith and doubt. They may believe in God, for example, but then some experience of suffering shakes their faith. They may, of course, later regain that faith. Many people simply do not think that it is possible to know for certain in this life whether God exists or not. These people are called **agnostics** (meaning 'not knowing'). We can sum up the beliefs of atheists and agnostics in this way:

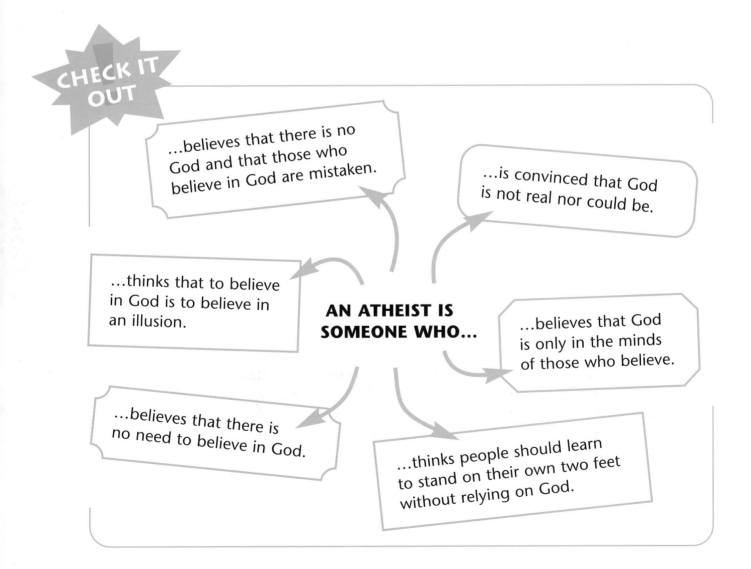

CHECK IT OUT

...believes that there is no God and that those who believe in God are mistaken.

...is convinced that God is not real nor could be.

...thinks that to believe in God is to believe in an illusion.

AN ATHEIST IS SOMEONE WHO...

...believes that God is only in the minds of those who believe.

...believes that there is no need to believe in God.

...thinks people should learn to stand on their own two feet without relying on God.

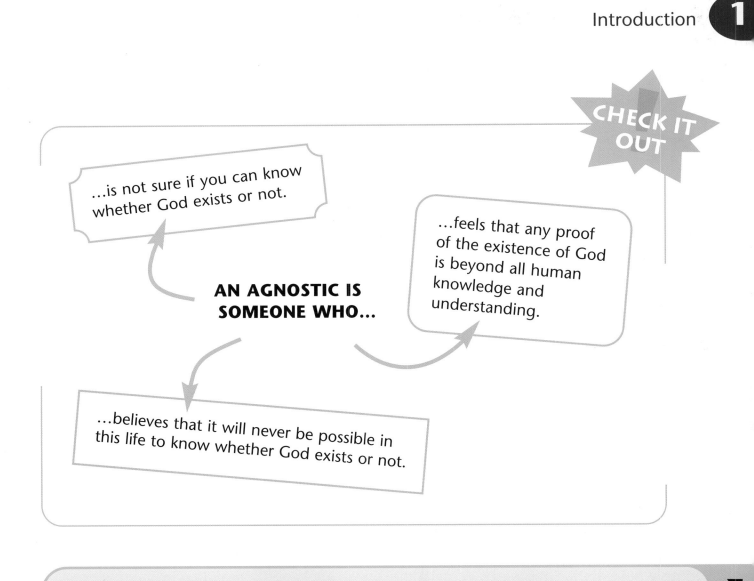

CHECK IT OUT

...is not sure if you can know whether God exists or not.

...feels that any proof of the existence of God is beyond all human knowledge and understanding.

AN AGNOSTIC IS SOMEONE WHO...

...believes that it will never be possible in this life to know whether God exists or not.

TASK 1

1. What is an atheist?
2. What is an agnostic?
3. Explain the differences between a believer, an atheist and an agnostic.

In this book, we are going to look at four different religions – Christianity, Hinduism, Islam and Judaism. About three billion people worldwide belong to one of these religions. That is almost 50% of the world's population. The followers of all four religions are called **monotheists**, which means that they believe in one God. They believe this God to be unique and quite unlike any other kind of being.

CHRISTIANITY

What you will learn about in this section:

1. Why Christians believe in God
2. What Christians believe about God
3. The Bible and its authority for Christians
4. The ways in which God can be known

1. Why Christians believe in God

Reason 1 The world in which we live could not possibly exist without an all-powerful God who created it. In the eighteenth century, a Christian thinker, William Paley, said that the world was like the intricate machinery of a watch. If you take the back off a watch, you find a finely balanced arrangement of wheels and cogs. Can anyone seriously believe that this watch came about by accident – perhaps by an explosion in a watch factory? No. There is only one sensible explanation. Only a highly skilled watchmaker could create a watch and make it work.

The universe is much more complicated than a watch. Only someone as powerful as God could have created this beautiful universe and the world in which we live. This is called the 'argument from design' and it has persuaded many people over the centuries to believe in God.

▲ Christians believe that God mainly communicates with people while they are reading the Bible.

Reason 2 Everyone knows the difference between right and wrong because we all have a conscience. Christians believe that their conscience comes from God and reflects the standards of behaviour that God expects of them. The conscience may be stronger in some people than in others but it is there in all of us and that leads many people to believe in God.

Reason 3 Many people believe that they have met God and they cannot all be wrong. They may have seen a miracle or have been miraculously healed from a serious illness. Some may have felt God to be close to them while they have been reading the **Bible**. They may have had an experience of God while worshipping Him or had a divine inner feeling of love and peace while sitting on their own in an empty church. Others have experienced an overwhelming sense of natural beauty. The exact circumstances of the experience are not important. What matters is that millions of people cannot have been mistaken. If people experience God, then God must exist.

Many people have found God through becoming part of a worshipping community.

Reason 4 Some people have been brought up in a home by parents who believe in God. The family has read the Bible and prayed together. They cannot remember a time when they didn't believe in God or go to church. They do not need to be convinced that God exists – they simply 'know'.

Many people, however, argue that these are not persuasive arguments for believing in God:

- The scientist, for example, would argue that the universe came about through a 'Big Bang' a very long time ago, while a very long process of evolution brought human beings into existence.

- It can be argued that we gain our sense of right and wrong from the many different influences which play a part in our lives – our parents, our school, our friends, the books we read, the society in which we live and so on.

- The claim of many people to have experienced God is open to doubt. It is very easy to misunderstand these experiences. They might have a totally natural explanation.

- When we are overwhelmed by the beauty of nature, we do not need to believe in God to make sense of it. Nature might just be beautiful in itself.

TASK 1

1. Write down three reasons that a Christian might give for his or her belief in God.

2. Write down three reasons that a person might give for questioning these reasons.

2. What Christians believe about God

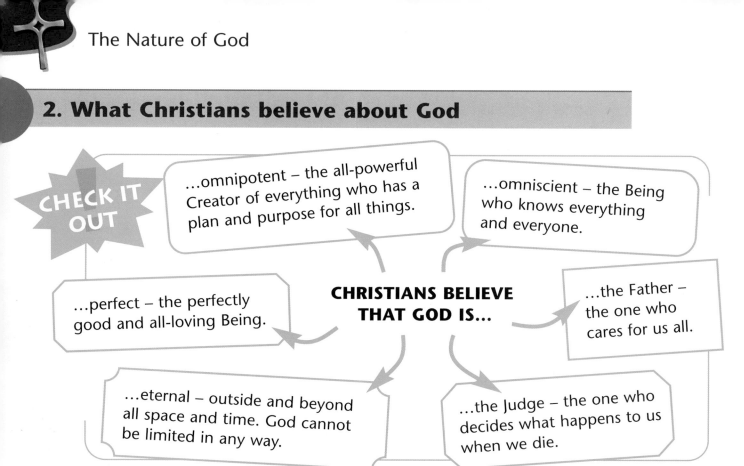

CHECK IT OUT

CHRISTIANS BELIEVE THAT GOD IS...

...omnipotent – the all-powerful Creator of everything who has a plan and purpose for all things.

...omniscient – the Being who knows everything and everyone.

...perfect – the perfectly good and all-loving Being.

...the Father – the one who cares for us all.

...eternal – outside and beyond all space and time. God cannot be limited in any way.

...the Judge – the one who decides what happens to us when we die.

The Trinity

Christians believe that Jesus is the best way for people to know about God. Jesus was the Son of God. The death of Jesus on the cross and his resurrection from the dead are both powerful reminders of God. Christians believe that God is one but is known or experienced through three distinct Persons – God the Father, God the Son and God the Holy Spirit. They call this belief the **Trinity**.

Christians do not pretend that this belief is easy to understand. Over the centuries, however, many analogies have been suggested to help worshippers understand the Trinity. Water, or H_2O, provides us with one of the most helpful illustrations. We can experience water in one of three different forms:

● as water when it is in liquid form;

● as ice when it is a solid;

● as steam when it is a gas or vapour.

Water, ice and steam are three different forms but they are all H_2O. It is only the nature in which they are experienced that changes.

▶ The death of Jesus on the cross reminds Christians that he was a real human being. This belief is called the **Incarnation**.

It is the same with the Christian belief in the Trinity. While there are three separate 'Persons', they remain 'God-in-one'. Each of the three Persons is an aspect of God's nature that human beings are able to understand.

So, what do Christians really mean when they speak of the Trinity?

God the Father

Calling God his 'Father' was a favourite expression of Jesus and he encouraged his disciples to refer to God in the same way. This was a way of teaching them that God cared for them and loved them – just as a good human father cares for and loves his own children.

God the Son

Christians believe that the most complete revelation of God has come to them through Jesus. They believe that he was God's Son, born to the **Virgin Mary**, and yet a full human being in every way – 'God in flesh'. This was how he was able to show people something of the true nature of God. While on earth, he taught people about God by showing them what He was really like. He died on a cross so that the sins of people could be forgiven. Christians believe that God brought Jesus back from the dead (an event known as the **Resurrection**) before he returned to his Father in heaven (the **Ascension**).

▶ *There are many images of the Virgin Mary in Christian churches, especially Roman Catholic churches.*

This is how the **New Testament** describes the death of Jesus:

❝ *For God so loved the world that he gave his one and only Son, that whoever believes in him shall not perish but have eternal life.* ❞
(John 3.16)

FROM THE SCRIPTURES

God the Holy Spirit

Christians believe that after Jesus returned to heaven, he sent his **Holy Spirit** to guide his followers into all truth. It is the same Holy Spirit who has continued to guide the Christian Church ever since.

In stained-glass windows and church banners, the Holy Spirit is usually shown as a dove – the bringer of God's peace into the world.

TASK 2

1. Make a list of the main words that Christians use to describe God and write a sentence to show that you understand what each of them means.

2. Describe what Christians mean when they speak of God being a Trinity.

3. What do Christians mean when they speak of:
    a. God the Father? **b.** God the Son? **c.** God the Holy Spirit?

❋ TO TALK ABOUT

Discuss each of these four questions in a small group. Write up the findings of your group.

1. What are the main reasons that a person might put forward for:
    a. Believing in God?
    b. Believing that God does not exist?
    c. Suggesting that we cannot be sure whether God exists or not?

2. Which of these three positions best describes what you believe?
    If someone challenged your position, how would you answer them?

3. The Bible and its authority for Christians

The Bible is divided into two parts – the **Old Testament** and the New Testament.

The Old Testament

The early Christians were almost all Jews and the Jewish Scriptures were particularly important to them. These Scriptures contained 39 different books that told the story of the Jewish people. They started with the creation of the world, moved through such important Jewish figures as **Abraham** and **Moses** and ended with the disintegration and dispersal of the Jewish people among other nations. When the Christians collected together the different books to form the Bible in the fourth century CE, they included all of the Jewish Scriptures as the Old Testament.

The New Testament

There are 27 books in the New Testament, starting with the four **Gospels** written by Matthew, Mark, Luke and John. Although these books come at the beginning of the New Testament, they were almost the last books of the Bible to be written. So, too, was the Acts of the Apostles, which describes the history of the early Christian Church. Many of the books of the New Testament are **epistles** (letters) and most of these were written by one man – **Paul**. Paul was the dominant personality in the early Church – a tireless traveller, missionary and letter-writer. He died in 64 CE.

▲ Most Christians read the Bible regularly. They believe that is the way that God speaks to them and guides them in their everyday lives.

The authority of the Bible

Christians do not believe that the Bible is like any other book – it carries a unique authority. They believe that, in some way, God was responsible for guiding those people who wrote the different books in the Bible. This is why its teachings help them to know the way in which God wants them to lead their lives. Even though times have changed a great deal since the Bible was first written, it lays down the principles that should guide and direct each Christian today. There are Bible readings in almost every church service. These help those people who go to church regularly to become more and more familiar with its teachings.

Understanding the Bible

There are two different approaches which Christians take to the holy book:

- The literal approach: many Christians believe that everything happened in the Bible in exactly the way in which it is recorded. So the world was created by God in six days; Adam and Eve were tempted by a serpent and ate the fruit in the Garden of Eden; everyone was destroyed by the Great Flood except Noah and his family and so on. Literalists say that to be a true Christian, a person must accept everything as it is found in the Bible – and follow its teachings.

- The non-literal approach: many Christians believe that there are different kinds of 'truth' in the Bible. There are accurate records of events but there are also 'myths' which do not record actual events but contain a spiritual 'truth' – just as the **parables** of Jesus are intended to teach an important spiritual lesson. The problem is knowing which is which and that is where the Bible needs to be studied very carefully.

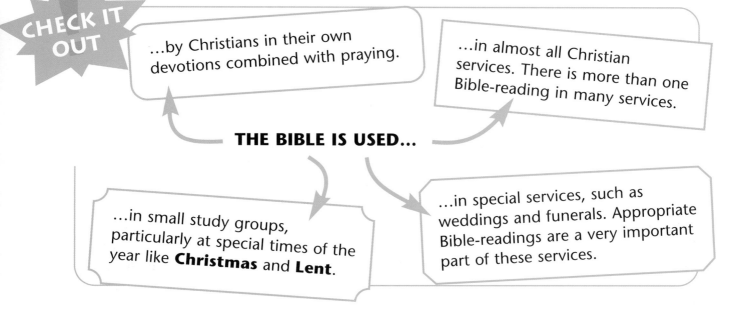

CHECK IT OUT

THE BIBLE IS USED...

...by Christians in their own devotions combined with praying.

...in almost all Christian services. There is more than one Bible-reading in many services.

...in small study groups, particularly at special times of the year like **Christmas** and **Lent**.

...in special services, such as weddings and funerals. Appropriate Bible-readings are a very important part of these services.

4. The ways in which God can be known

The Bible tells us that God created the world in the beginning and that He continues to be active in the world today. He is active in two important ways:

Through Jesus

Christians believe that God showed that He cared for the world and loved it by sending His only Son, Jesus, into it. One writer in the New Testament described this event like this:

FROM THE SCRIPTURES

> 66 *The Word (Jesus) became flesh and made His dwelling among us. We have seen His glory, the glory of the One and Only, who came from the Father, full of grace and truth.* 99
> *(John 1.14)*

Jesus came into the world to share its hopes and sadness – and to show it just what God was like. He left behind the teachings that would allow people who followed also to know what God is like – as they can read in the Bible.

This is why reading and studying the Bible is a very important part of being a Christian. Most Christians set time aside regularly, often daily, to do this. Christians believe that the Bible has a spiritual power all of its own:

> 66 *The word of God is living and active. Sharper than any double-edged sword, it penetrates even to dividing soul and spirit...* 99
> (Hebrews 4.12)

Through miraculous events

Some Christians believe that God continues to act in the world today through miraculous acts – just as Jesus did when he was on earth. The New Testament records Jesus healing the blind and dumb; feeding a large crowd with only a small amount of fish and bread and even bringing the dead back to life. Some claim that they have been healed miraculously today from a serious or terminal illness through prayer. Some Christians, especially Roman Catholics, claim that the Virgin Mary has appeared in such places as Lourdes, Santiago de Compostela and Walsingham and that miracles continue to happen there today. Other Christians, however, are far from sure that miracles like these do happen today.

✳ TO TALK ABOUT

Discuss in a small group whether you believe that miracles do happen in the modern world. Can anyone bring forward an example of any event that appears to demand a miraculous explanation? Each member of the group should explain why they are, or are not, inclined to believe that miracles do still take place.

---

1. Describe what you understand by:
   a. The Old Testament   **b.** The New Testament
2. **a.** What authority does the Bible carry for Christians?
   b. What use do Christians make of the Bible?
3. What are the two different ways in which Christians might understand the Bible and what is the main difference between them?
4. How do Christians believe that God is active in the world today?

TASK 3

HINDUISM

What you will learn about in this section:

1. Hindu beliefs about the nature of God
2. The sacred writings of Hinduism

1. Hindu beliefs about the nature of God

You will often hear it said that Hindus believe in millions of different gods. That is not true. They believe in one God who takes on millions of different forms so that people can understand Him better. Perhaps the best way of understanding this is to think of light passing through a prism and coming out on the other side. Light entering the prism (the one spirit – **Brahman**) splits into the colours of the rainbow when it leaves the prism (the many gods and goddesses). Of course, there are only seven colours in the rainbow but there are said to be about 200 million gods and goddesses in Hinduism.

Why do Hindus believe in God?

There are three main reasons why Hindus believe in God, although it must be remembered that there are many Hindus who do not believe in God.

CHECK IT OUT

Hindus believe that they are part of the universe and that everything in the universe hangs together. This is the teaching of Hinduism.

Hinduism is part of the heart of Indian society. India is where 450 million of the world's 550 million Hindus live. Hindu children are brought up from birth as part of the Hindu way of life, with its beliefs, ceremonies and dietary restrictions.

WHY HINDUS BELIEVE IN GOD

Hindus pray and worship in their homes and in the temple. Here they pray and meditate and this gives them a feeling of closeness to God. Believing in God is part of their fabric of life. The vast majority of Hindus do not question it.

This story is often told to explain the idea of the Supreme Spirit, Brahman, and the many gods:

> **"**Five blind wise men (sages) discover an elephant for the very first time in their lives. Each sage touches a different part of the elephant and then calls out to tell the others what an elephant is like. The one touching the tail says, 'I am certain that an elephant is like a piece of rope.' The sage touching the leg says, 'I am certain that an elephant is like a tree trunk' and the third, touching the side, says, 'You are both mistaken, an elephant is like a great wall.'
> The fourth, touching an ear, says, 'How can you all be so wrong? An elephant is like a sail on a boat.' The last blind sage, touching the tusk, says, 'An elephant is like a smooth rock.'**"**

Brahma, Shiva and Vishnu

Although Brahman is the Supreme Spirit, there are three main, powerful deities worshipped by Hindus. They are known as the **Trimurti**.

Brahma This is the many-faced Creator god. Brahma has few followers today.

▲ This is Brahma, the god who created the world.

Shiva Although Shiva (the destroyer god) may appear to many people to be dangerous and frightening, such destruction is necessary to allow new things to happen. Hindus know Shiva as the Lord of the Dance because most of his statues show him dancing in a circle of fire, which portrays the endless cycle of life.

▲ This is Vishnu, the god who preserves everything that is good on earth.

Vishnu Vishnu is the preserver god. He has four arms and holds a conch shell. From age to age, he visits the earth to remove evil and let good flourish. The Hindu holy books have stories that tell of Vishnu visiting the earth nine times and they expect him to visit it once more in the future. The form in which he visits the earth, as a person or an animal, is called an **avatar**.

The nine avatars of Vishnu so far have been as:

1. Matsya – a giant fish who saved the world from a flood.
2. Kurma – a tortoise who carried the whole world on its back.
3. Varaha – a boar who lifted the world out of deep waters using his tusks when it was in danger of being sent to the depths by a demon.
4. Narasinha – a half-man and half-lion who killed a demon by tearing him to pieces.
5. Vamana – a dwarf who saved the world from an evil demon king.
6. Parasurama – known as Rama with an axe.
7. Rama – a prince who had many adventures and appears in an epic story called the Ramayana.
8. Krishna – a prince who had many adventures from the moment he was born.
9. Buddha – the prince who gave up his wealth and started Buddhism.

Kalki, the expected tenth avatar, will come as a warrior on a white horse to end the present age of darkness.

Hindus pray regularly to the different deities that can help them to live their lives. They can do this in front of their shrine at home or in the local temple.

▲ The Buddha, whose teachings are at the heart of Buddhism, is believed to have been the ninth avatar of Vishnu.

▲ Krishna is one of the best loved of all Hindu gods. He is often shown playing the flute.

Two other important Hindu gods

Krishna

Krishna is the eighth avatar of the god Vishnu. There are numerous stories about this god, many of which are in the Bhagavad Gita, an important holy book. The image of Krishna can take many forms – including a mischievous baby, a young child spilling a butter jar, a young man playing the flute and a mighty prince looking after cows or dancing with milkmaids. Sometimes he is shown with his loved one, Radha, and sometimes he is seen as a warrior or chariot-driver.

Ganesha is a very important Hindu god.

Ganesha

Ganesha, a much-loved Hindu god, is considered to be the son of Parvati and Shiva. He is very important because before any worship can be made to the other gods, he must be worshipped. He removes any objects and obstacles that get in the way of real worship. Before undertaking any new projects, Hindus approach Ganesha to seek his help to overcome any problems or obstacles. The **murti** of Ganesha shows him with an elephant's head and, often, with a snake around his waist.

TASK 1

1. Give three reasons why most Hindus believe in God.
2. Write two sentences describing the importance to Hindus of Brahma, Shiva or Vishnu.
3. What else can you discover about Krishna and Ganesha? What traditional Hindu stories do they feature in?

2. The sacred writings of Hinduism

There are many holy books in Hinduism. They are used extensively for personal devotions and acts of worship (**puja**) carried out at home in front of the family shrine and in the **mandir** (temple). The holy books also play a prominent part in Hindu festivals and in ceremonies, such as the **Sacred Thread**. Hindus teach stories from the holy books to their children from a very early age and scenes from them are often acted out in the mandir.

Hindus believe that a deep knowledge of the Scriptures is very important, since this will provide them with answers to the most important questions in life. Nothing could be known, for instance, about God or the **Atman** (soul) unless it were revealed in one of the holy books. Two of them, the **Vedas** and the **Upanishads**, are believed to record the actual words of God. The holy books also provide answers to some of the practical questions of life, such as how other forms of life should be treated.

Smriti and shruti

Hindu holy books fall into two groups – smriti and shruti:

- **Smriti** ('that which is heard') – these are books believed to have been received directly by holy men from God. Such books, which include the four Vedas and the Upanishads, are eternal and go back into the very distant past. This is what gives these books their very special authority.
- **Shruti** ('that which is remembered') – these are books based on recollections of God's message. They are later books and are considered to be less important than the smriti. They do, however, contain some of the best-loved Hindu books.

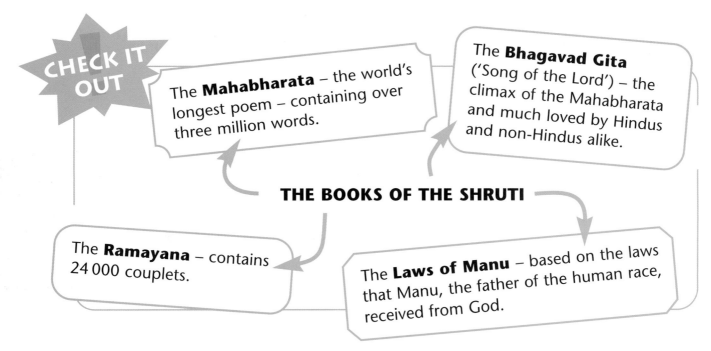

CHECK IT OUT

The **Mahabharata** – the world's longest poem – containing over three million words.

The **Bhagavad Gita** ('Song of the Lord') – the climax of the Mahabharata and much loved by Hindus and non-Hindus alike.

THE BOOKS OF THE SHRUTI

The **Ramayana** – contains 24 000 couplets.

The **Laws of Manu** – based on the laws that Manu, the father of the human race, received from God.

The sacred writings of Hinduism

The Vedas

The word 'veda' means 'knowledge' and the Vedas form a collection of four holy books.

1. The Rig Veda – the oldest Hindu book, which is at least 2300 years old. It is written in Sanskrit and contains more than 1000 **hymns**, of which the most well known is the **Gyatri Mantra**.
2. The Yajur Veda – a collection of special words that Hindu priests use when they perform Hindu rituals.
3. The Sama Veda – contains words that can be set to music and chanted to the Hindu gods.
4. The Atharva Veda – describes magic charms, herbs for treating illnesses and spells for banishing evil spirits.

The Upanishads

The word 'Upanishad' means 'sitting at the feet of the teacher'. This holy book explains discussions between religious teachers (**gurus**) and their pupils.

The Bhagavad Gita

This holy book, part of the much longer Mahabharata, tells the story of the god Krishna and a warrior leader called Arjuna. Krishna explains to Arjuna why it is important for him to do his duty, even above his responsibility to other members of his family. In doing so, he shows Arjuna a vision of God. The book teaches that the battle that Arjuna, and all Hindus, must fight is against the temptations of this world.

The most important stories and ideas of Hinduism are not only kept alive in the holy books, but also by word of mouth, passed down from generation to generation. This is a very important part of the Hindu religion as parents seek to pass on that which is sacred to their children.

✳ TO TALK ABOUT

Discuss with other members of your group the importance that the Hindu religion places on conveying spiritual truth by word of mouth. Describe one benefit of this and one danger.

TASK 2

1. Explain the difference between smriti and shruti.
2. Write two or more sentences about each of the following:
   a. The Vedas
   b. The Upanishads
   c. The Bhagavad Gita
3. Why are the Vedas and the Upanishads thought to be more important than other Hindu holy books?
4. Explain how the Hindu holy books are used.

ISLAM

What you will learn about in this section:

1. Why Muslims believe in Allah

2. The Muslim belief in Allah

3. The authority of the Qur'an

4. The activity of Allah in the world

1. Why Muslims believe in Allah

There are several reasons why Muslims believe in Allah.

1. Muslims believe that Allah created the world in the beginning and placed all good things in it for them to enjoy. He also provided them with their holy book – the **Qur'an**. It is through appreciating the beauty of the world and studying the teachings of the Qur'an that Muslims can come to know the one true God, **Allah**.

▲ *Muslims begin to read the Qur'an at a young age.*

2. Muslims believe that Allah created human beings. Human beings can worship and serve Allah unlike other forms of creation. They are Allah's agents or representatives on earth.

3. Down the centuries, Allah has spoken to the people though many **prophets**, the Prophet **Muhammad** ﷺ being the last and the greatest of them. There have been 124 000 prophets altogether, of which just 25 are mentioned in the Qur'an including Abraham, Moses, Jesus and the Buddha. Muhammad ﷺ is called 'the Seal of the Prophets' as he completed the message delivered by the others. There are no more prophets to come.

TASK 1

If you were to ask a Muslim why he or she believes in Allah, what do you think they would say?

2. The Muslim belief in Allah

The first and the most important belief in Islam is the doctrine of the Oneness of Allah. This belief is called the **tawhid**. This is made clear in the **Shahadah**, the first Pillar of Islam, which states that, 'There is no god except Allah, Muhammad ◉ is the Messenger of Allah.' The Prophet Muhammad ◉ attacked all forms of belief in Allah that denied his Oneness and Unity. A Muslim is someone who has submitted himself or herself to the will of Allah. Since Allah is beyond all human understanding, so human beings cannot describe Him.

FROM THE SCRIPTURES

> **❝** *Say: He is Allah, the One and Only;*
> *Allah, the Eternal, Absolute;*
> *He begetteth not, nor is He begotten;*
> *And there is none like unto Him.* **❞**
>
> *(Surah 112.1–4)*

Muslim tradition teaches that Allah has 99 different names that describe His character and nature. Muhammad ◉ said about these names:

> **❝** *There are ninety-nine names that are Allah's alone. Whoever learns, understands and enumerates them enters Paradise and achieves eternal salvation.* **❞**

Among the names of Allah are the Lord of all Spheres and Realms: the First and the Last; the Originator of all Things; the Sustainer; the Truth; the Compassionate and the Merciful.

Allah has always existed and will always exist. No one brought Allah into being. He is the only one who exists by necessity – everything and everyone else exists by Allah's permission.

All of these names suggest two sides to the character of Allah:
- Allah is the Overpowerer, the Abaser, the Humiliator, the Watcher, the Giver of Death, the Powerful and the Avenger.
- Allah is Welcoming, the Compassionate and Gracious One.

▲ *Muslims use these prayer beads to help them to remember the 99 names of Allah.*

Allah is 'nearer to man than his neck-vein' but does not remotely come within reach of human understanding. Male Muslims remember the 99 names of Allah daily by passing the 33 beads on a rosary through their fingers three times. These beads are called the **misbeha**.

---

1. Describe what a Muslim believes about Allah.
2. What does the tawhid tell a Muslim about Allah?
3. How do Muslims believe that Allah has made Himself known to the human race?

TASK 2

3. The authority of the Qur'an

Allah's revelations

The holy book of Islam is the Qur'an and its name means 'that which is read or recited'. This holy book contains the many revelations that Allah passed on to the Prophet Muhammad ⬡ over many years. They began when Muhammad ⬡ was 40 years old when he was meditating in a cave in Hira. The angel Jibril appeared to him and ordered him to read. Muhammad ⬡ replied that he could not read. The same thing happened three times. Eventually, the angel told him:

> **❝** *Proclaim! (or read!) in the name of thy Lord and Cherisher,*
> *Who created –*
> *Created man, out of a (mere) leech-like clot of congealed blood:*
> *Proclaim! And thy Lord is most Bountiful –*
> *He who taught (the use of) the Pen –*
> *Taught man that which he knew not.* **❞**
> (Surah 96.1–5)

Every copy of the Qur'an contains the words of the revelations just as they were spoken to the Prophet.

Collecting the Surahs together

Muhammad ⬡ repeated the words that he had received from the angel to his secretary, Zaid bin Thabit. They were not gathered together, however, until after the Prophet's death. The chapters (surahs) are not recorded in the Qur'an in the order in which they were revealed to Muhammad ⬡, but in the order in which they were collected together under the instructions of Khalifah Uthman (644–656). Within 20 years of the death of Muhammad ⬡, the Qur'an was complete. The most familiar of the 114 surahs, the first, is called 'The Opening' and is the **Al-Fatihah**, which is recited by Muslim worshippers each time they pray.

The contents of the Qur'an

The Qur'an is believed to be the actual word of Allah, which was revealed by the angel Jibril from the original in heaven. Because of this, the holy book is beyond all criticism and carries a unique authority. It cannot change or be changed. It is the final and complete book of guidance on all matters and is to be obeyed at all times. Muslims do not question what they read in the Qur'an and they treat the holy book with the greatest possible respect.

The Qur'an teaches Muslims how they should prepare themselves to appear before Allah on the Day of Judgement. To help them in this preparation, Muslims are given guidance about matters such as drinking alcohol and gambling; marriage and divorce; the treatment of widows and orphans and the lending of money with interest (usury).

1. What do you think that Muslims mean when they speak of the Qur'an being revealed by Allah?

2. Describe how the revelations were made to the Prophet Muhammad 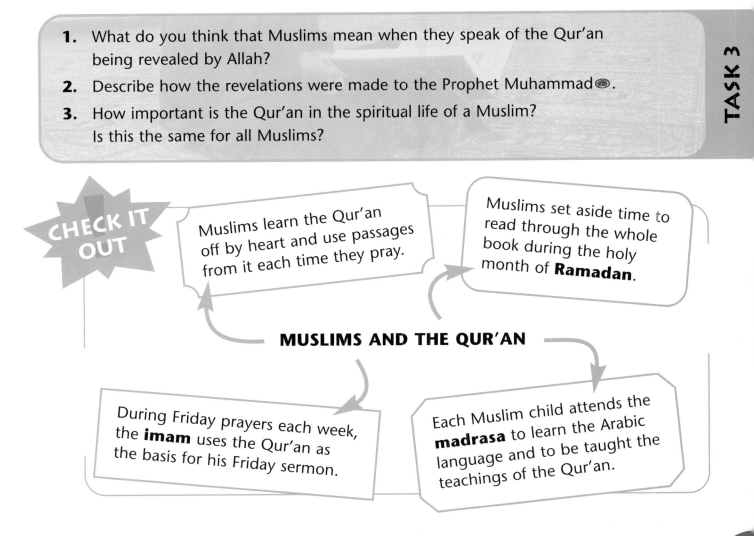.

3. How important is the Qur'an in the spiritual life of a Muslim? Is this the same for all Muslims?

CHECK IT OUT

Muslims learn the Qur'an off by heart and use passages from it each time they pray.

Muslims set aside time to read through the whole book during the holy month of **Ramadan**.

MUSLIMS AND THE QUR'AN

During Friday prayers each week, the **imam** uses the Qur'an as the basis for his Friday sermon.

Each Muslim child attends the **madrasa** to learn the Arabic language and to be taught the teachings of the Qur'an.

4. The activity of Allah in the world

There are no miracles associated with the Prophet Muhammad . There are two occasions in the life of the Prophet, however, when Allah is believed to have intervened:

1. At the time of his birth, a great star appeared in the sky. By this time, his father had died and his grandfather, Abd al-Muttalib, asked that he might have six days to choose a name for the child. Both his grandfather and mother were told in a dream that he should be called Muhammad – the 'Praised One'.

2. Al-Mi'raj – the Ascent. Muslims believe that Muhammad was taken to Jerusalem on a horse with wings – called Buraq – where he met the prophets Adam, Ibrahim, Musa, Isa and Harun. He then travelled through the heavens until he appeared before Allah.

JUDAISM

What you will learn about in this section:

1. Why Jews believe in G-d
2. Jewish beliefs about G-d
3. The authority of the Torah and the Talmud
4. The activity of G-d in the world

1. Why Jews believe in G-d

Although people can convert to become Jews, this is very unusual. The vast majority are born Jews. Most Jewish people throughout the world belong to the Orthodox faith and this group traces a person's Jewishness through his or her mother. If you have a Jewish mother, then you are a Jew. This is the main reason why people grow up believing in one G-d and belonging to the Jewish community. Even if a Jew does not believe in G-d, he or she is likely to value greatly the traditions and customs of the community into which they are born.

The belief in G-d, which is at the very heart of Jewish religious life, is expressed in the **Shema**, the most important Jewish prayer. The Shema brings together three different passages in the Jewish Scriptures. It is the custom in Jewish families to teach the first words of the Shema to a child as soon as he or she begins to talk. From then onwards, saying it is an essential part of every day. It expresses the legacy that every Jew enjoys and the main reason why he or she believes in G-d. A Jewish man covers his eyes, as a mark of respect to G-d, as he says the words.

▶ *Saying the Shema is one of the most important acts of Jewish worship.*

The words of the Shema:

> 66 *Hear, O Israel: The LORD is our G-d, the LORD is the One and Only. You shall love the LORD, your G-d, with all your heart, with all your soul, and with all your resources. And these matters that I command you today shall be upon your heart. You shall teach them thoroughly to your children and you shall speak of them while you sit in your home, while you walk on the way, when you retire and when you arise. Bind them as a sign upon your arm and let them be ornaments between your eyes. And write them on the doorposts of your house and upon your gates.* 99
>
> *(Deuteronomy 6.4–9)*

2. Jewish beliefs about G-d

It is very difficult to imagine someone being a Jew without believing in G-d, yet for many Jews, this belief is a problem. Many Jews have abandoned the traditional Jewish understanding of G-d, although they wish to keep their Jewish identity and remain a part of the Jewish community.

The nature of G-d

The Jewish Scriptures describe how Abraham came from a city in which many gods were worshipped before he became convinced that there was only one G-d who had 'spoken' to him. This is the moment at which the Jewish faith was born.

Jews believe that G-d:

- is One – Jews are strict monotheists;
- is the Creator of the universe. No one created G-d, He has always existed;
- is eternal, beyond time and space;
- knows all things (omniscient) and is to be found everywhere (omnipresent);
- is all-powerful (omnipotent);
- is the source of all life in the universe, including human and animal life;
- actively intervenes in the lives of human beings;
- makes heavy moral and spiritual demands on those who belong to the Jewish faith.

The covenant

In the Jewish Scriptures, we are told how this all-powerful G-d made a **covenant** (agreement) with one family – that of Abraham, who is called the 'Friend of G-d'. In this covenant, G-d promised that He would remain faithful to the descendants of Abraham, the Jewish people, and would treat them as His special people. They were different from the other nations, not because they were 'better', but because they were 'chosen' by G-d. In turn, the Jews were expected by G-d to remember Him at all times, serve Him and keep all of His laws. The most important of these laws were the **Ten Commandments**.

3. The authority of the Torah and the Talmud

The Tenakh

The Jewish holy Scriptures, the **Tenakh**, were completed and put together by the Synod of Jamnia in 96 CE. The comments of the Jewish scholars on the books of the Tenakh were later collected together in the **Talmud** and the Mishnah.

▲ *Jews believe that Moses received the Ten Commandments from G-d on Mount Sinai.*

There are three parts to the Tenakh.

The Torah

The **Torah** ('teaching' or 'guidance') is the most important part of the Tenakh and contains five books – Genesis, Exodus, Leviticus, Numbers and Deuteronomy – which are at the beginning of the Jewish Scriptures. Jewish tradition teaches that these books were given to Moses by G-d on Mount Sinai and that he wrote them down directly.

The Torah contains the laws (**mitzvot** or commandments) that were given to Moses. The most well-known of these laws are the Ten Commandments but these ten laws are in amongst 613 mitzvot altogether. The mitzvot cover all matters ranging from the law and the rights of the people to personal and family hygiene. Strict Jews try to keep as many of the mitzvot as possible but many Jews believe that they have to be reinterpreted as times change.

Jews treat the Torah with the greatest possible respect. It is handwritten by specially trained scribes on animal skin and then wound around large rollers. These scrolls are decorated with covers and a bell is hung from them. These decorated scrolls are placed in the **ark** in the **synagogue** from which they are taken when they are read in a service. When they are read, it is important that they are not touched by human hands and so a metal hand pointer (a **yad**) is used so that the reader can follow the Hebrew text.

The Prophets

This is the second most important part of the Tenakh. It is made up of two kinds of book:

▼ The metal hand that is used to follow the Hebrew text when it is being read in the synagogue.

1. Books that cover the history of the Jews from the time of Joshua onwards. During this time, holy men, called prophets, told the Jews about G-d and tried to guide them in their worship. They told the people that if they wanted G-d to accept their worship, then they must live G-d-fearing lives.

2. Books that contain the prophecies of such people as Isaiah, Jeremiah and Ezekiel. These were important prophets whose message was, in the main, rejected by the people.

The Writings

These books are considered to be less valuable than the Torah and the Prophets. The Writings, however, do contain the book of Psalms, which is used regularly in synagogue worship. The Psalms were originally written for use in **Temple** worship. Other readings from the Writings also take place – usually on festival days.

The Talmud

The Talmud is a collection of the teachings of the **rabbis** compiled between the final destruction of the Temple in Jerusalem in 70 CE and the end of the fifth century. After the five books of the Torah, the Talmud is the highest legal authority in Judaism. It provides legal rulings covering such topics as agriculture, the Temple and its sacrifices, cleanliness and impurity, criminal and civil law. The rabbis were attempting to 'search out' meanings in the Torah which were not immediately obvious.

TASK 1

1. What is the Shema?
2. What is the Tenakh?
3. Write a summary of what most Jews believe about G-d.
4. What are two obligations of the covenant that G-d made with Abraham and the Jewish people?
5. Look up Exodus 20.1–14 to find the Ten Commandments and then summarise them.

✳ TO TALK ABOUT

The Talmud is still used for study in Jewish academies and schools. Do you think that judgements made around 2000 years ago can still be useful today?

4. The activity of G-d in the world

Through miracles

There are many examples of G-d performing miracles in the Jewish Scriptures. Here are four of them:

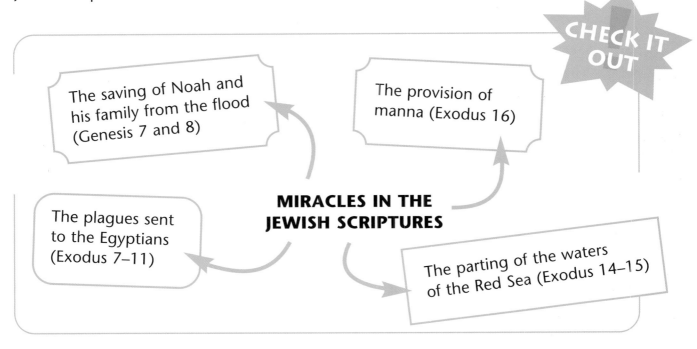

CHECK IT OUT

The saving of Noah and his family from the flood (Genesis 7 and 8)

The provision of manna (Exodus 16)

MIRACLES IN THE JEWISH SCRIPTURES

The plagues sent to the Egyptians (Exodus 7–11)

The parting of the waters of the Red Sea (Exodus 14–15)

Most of these miracles in the Jewish Scriptures are connected with the greatest event in Jewish history – the **Exodus**. This event brought freedom for the Jews after 400 years of Egyptian slavery. For the Jews, the Exodus was the greatest miracle of all.

Through the prophets

Prophets were men and women sent by G-d to the Jews to deliver His message. The prophets warned the Jews of what would happen if they continued to ignore G-d's demands. The three most important prophets were Isaiah, Ezekiel and Jeremiah, although there were many others.

EXAM HELP

Make sure that you know about:

CHRISTIANITY

- The five reasons why Christians believe in God. A personal experience of God and the influence of upbringing and environment are the most important.
- What Christians believe about God. God is omnipotent, omniscient, perfect, eternal, the Father and the Judge. The meaning of the Christian belief in the Trinity – God the Father, God the Son and God the Holy Spirit.
- The authority of the Bible for Christians. The Old and New Testaments. The different approaches that Christians have towards the Bible.
  - * Important definitions to learn: agnosticism, atheism, Bible, Christmas, Gospel, Holy Spirit, Incarnation, Lent, monotheism, New Testament, Old Testament, parable, resurrection, Trinity, Virgin Mary.

HINDUISM

- The three reasons why Hindus believe in God. The main reason is that Hindus are brought up to believe and worship.
- The beliefs that Hindus hold about God. The Trimurti – Brahma, Vishnu and Shiva. Ganesha and Krishna – the most popular Hindu deities. Avatars are very important.
- The holy books of Hinduism. The difference between smriti and shruti. The Vedas, the Upanishads and the Bhagavad Gita. The importance of oral transmission (passing on stories by word of mouth).
  - * Important definitions to learn: avatar, Bhagavad Gita, Brahma, brahmin, Ganesha, guru, Krishna, murti, puja, Sacred Thread, Shiva, shruti, smriti, Upanishads, Vedas, Vishnu.

ISLAM

- The reasons why Muslims believe in Allah. The main reason is that Muslims are brought up in a Muslim home to believe.
- The Muslim beliefs about Allah. The Tawhid and the Shahadah are the most important.
- The 99 different names of Allah express the two sides of His character revealed in the Qur'an.
- The authority of the Qur'an. The revelations to Muhammad ☙, collecting the surahs, the contents of the holy book and the Day of Judgement.
  - ✳ Important definitions to learn: Al-Fatihah, Allah, Muhammad ☙, prophet, Qur'an, Shahadah, Tawhid.

JUDAISM

- The reasons why Jews believe in G-d. Almost all Jews believe because they have a Jewish mother. The expression of this belief is in the Shema – a central prayer and a statement of faith in G-d.
- The Jewish beliefs about G-d. Oneness, Creator, Eternal, Omniscient, All-powerful, the source of all life, active in the world and demanding of His followers. The covenant between G-d and the Jewish people is central.
- The Jewish holy books. The authority of the Torah and the Talmud. The Torah – what it is and how it is treated. The Prophets and the Writings.
  - ✳ Important definitions to learn: ark, Covenant, Exodus, rabbi, Shema, synagogue, Talmud, Tenakh, Ten Commandments, Torah.

EXAM HELP

IN THE EXAMINATION

Here are sample questions for you to try:

CHRISTIANITY

(a) Describe the reasons Christians might give in support of their belief in God. (8 marks)

(b) Explain how believing that the Bible is the word of God might affect the lives of Christians. (7 marks)

(c) 'There is no way of knowing what God might be like.'

Do you agree? Give reasons to support your answer and show that you have thought about different points of view. You must refer to Christianity in your answer. (5 marks)

HINDUISM

(a) Describe the reasons Hindus might give in support of their belief in God. (8 marks)

(b) Explain how believing that the Vedas are holy books might affect the everyday lives of Hindus. (7 marks)

(c) 'There is no way of knowing what God might be like.'

Do you agree? Give reasons to support your answer and show that you have thought about different points of view. You must refer to Hinduism in your answer. (5 marks)

ISLAM

(a) Describe the reasons that Muslims might give in support of their belief in Allah. (8 marks)

(b) Explain how believing that the Qur'an is a holy book might affect the lives of Muslims. (7 marks)

(c) 'There is no way of knowing what Allah might be like.'

Do you agree? Give reasons to support your answer and show that you have thought about different points of view. You must refer to Islam in your answer. (5 marks)

JUDAISM

(a) Describe the reasons that a Jew might give for their belief in G-d. (8 marks)

(b) Explain how believing that the Torah is a holy book might affect the lives of Jews. (7 marks)

(c) 'There is no way of knowing what G-d is like.'

Do you agree? Give reasons to support your answer and show that you have thought about different points of view. You must refer to Judaism in your answer. (5 marks)

Exam hints:

These hints apply to each of the religions:

(a) In this question, you are being asked to describe the religious beliefs of the religion that you have studied. You are not being asked for any personal opinions. Make sure that your answer is confined to your chosen religion. Try to use the correct technical words and language in your answer. This will gain you extra marks. So, for instance, if you are answering the question on Christianity, then you should mention the word Trinity, while an answer on any of the four religions which mentions the word 'monotheism' and explains what it means would gain marks.

(b) In this question, it is your understanding of the material that is being tested. To obtain good marks, you need to think of as many ways as you can to show how religious believers value and make use of their holy books. For instance, a Jewish child goes to religion school in the synagogue to learn about the Torah so that they can use it in their prayers, find out what it has to say about G-d and discover its teachings, which tell them how they should live day by day.

(c) Use the time that remains to answer this question. It asks you to show that you understand that people hold different opinions about the statement. These people may belong to a different religion or not hold a religious outlook at all. Someone might insist, for example, that they do not find the holy books any help at all in knowing about God. The Christian, Jew, Muslim and Hindu, however, would say that they can know a little about God from what the holy books teach them.

CHRISTIANITY

What you will learn about in this section:

1. Private and public Christian worship
2. Christian prayer and contemplation
3. The importance of food and fasting in Christianity
4. The architecture of church buildings
5. The use of music and art in Christian worship
6. The use of Christian symbols

1. Private and public Christian worship

The word 'worship' means 'worthiness'. Christians believe that in their worship, they are offering something that is worthy and precious to God – because He is worth it. Worship is important to Christians because God, the almighty Creator of the universe, should be praised. It is also important because it gives each worshipper the opportunity to say and show how much God means to them. God is loving and so Christians should respond by loving Him in return – and also by loving their neighbours to express their love for God.

Private worship

Many Christians set aside a time each day when they read their Bible and pray quietly. Some Christians refer to this as their 'Quiet Time'. They will use this time to pray for:

▲ This person is taking a few minutes out of a busy life to pray quietly on their own.

- anything in the world that concerns them. It might be something that they have read about in the newspaper or seen on television;
- the needs of their family and friends. Someone might be facing a decision about their future, be worried about their health or about to retire;
- themselves and their own needs. Jesus encouraged people to pray for themselves but only after they had prayed for others.

Christians feel that this time of private worship gives them a solid foundation on which to base their lives day by day.

Public worship

Most Christians belong to a local church and attend services in their place of worship on **Sundays**. Church services mostly fall into one of two categories:

Liturgical worship: liturgical worship follows a written pattern set down in a prayer book. While the Bible readings and the hymns vary from service to service to suit the theme of the worship, the basic structure of the service remains the same from week to week. Many people enjoy this kind of service because it means that the service is familiar to them and they feel comfortable with it. They are also using a form of words that has remained largely unaltered for centuries and this gives them a link with the past. It also gives worshippers a sense of belonging to a worldwide Church since similar services are being held around the world. Services in **Anglican**, **Roman Catholic** and **Orthodox** churches mainly follow a set liturgy.

Non-liturgical worship: this is worship that does not follow a set order of service or liturgy. It is not set down in a written form and worshippers do not have the words to follow in front of them. While the services may have a general structure, the form that it takes varies from week to week. Non-liturgical worship is likely to be Bible-centred, with an emphasis on modern rather than traditional hymns. There is a stronger feeling of freedom and emotion in the service, as worshippers feel free to express their feelings openly by dancing and waving their arms in the air. The emphasis is very much upon the participation of the worshippers. Anyone may lead the congregation in spontaneous prayer during the service or give a message to the people from God (called 'prophecy').

▲ Roman Catholic services follow a liturgy that is laid out in the **missal**, the Roman Catholic prayer book.

Non-liturgical services, however, are not all the same. Far from it! Many different **Pentecostal** groups, for example, participate in highly emotion-filled services while the **Quakers**, an older group going back to the seventeenth century, spend their time worshipping in almost unbroken silence. **Baptist** and **Methodist** churches do have a regular structure to their services but they are non-liturgical since their services do not follow a prayer book.

▶ The Methodist Church was founded in the eighteenth century and its chapels are to be found all over the world.

CHECK IT OUT

Hymns – hymns are poetry set to music. By singing them together, worshippers are expressing their spiritual unity and fellowship with each other.

Bible readings – this is the part of the service where a passage from the Bible is read aloud, often by a member of the congregation. In many services, there is more than one reading from the Bible and these follow a pattern throughout the year.

WHAT YOU FIND IN MOST CHURCH SERVICES

Prayers – prayers play a very important part in all Christian public worship. The worshippers add 'Amen' ('So be it' or 'Lord') at the end of the prayer. Sometimes though, the people speak the words of a prayer together, such as the Lord's Prayer.

Sermon – the sermon, sometimes called the 'homily', is a talk given by the vicar, **minister** or a member of the congregation. It explains the meaning of a passage from the Bible and tells the people how they might apply it to their own lives.

The **Lord's Prayer** (called the 'Our Father' in the Catholic Church) is the most important of all Christian prayers. This is because it is the only one that Jesus actually taught his own disciples to use.

> " *Our Father in heaven,*
> *hallowed be your name,*
> *thy kingdom come,*
> *thy will be done,*
> *on earth as it is in heaven.*
> *Give us today our daily bread.*
> *Forgive us our debts as we also have forgiven our debtors.*
> *And lead us not into temptation.*
> *But deliver us from the evil one.* "
>
> *(Matthew 6.9–13)*

Church services

There are many different kinds of church service. For the majority of churches, the most important service is that of **Holy Communion** – a service which is also called the **Eucharist** (Anglican Church), the **Mass** (Roman Catholic Church) and the **Lord's Supper** or the **Breaking of Bread** (**Nonconformist** Church). This is the service at which worshippers share the symbols of bread and wine to help them share spiritually in the death of Jesus. By taking part in Holy Communion, worshippers are re-enacting the Last Supper – the last meal that Jesus shared with his disciples before he was crucified. The only two major Christian churches that do not celebrate Holy Communion are the **Salvation Army** and the Quakers.

▲ *A service of infant baptism in an Anglican church. For many, this is the beginning of their Christian life.*

In some churches, services of **baptism** are very important. This can take one of two different forms:

Infant baptism: infant baptism involves sprinkling holy water over the head of a young baby to indicate that he or she is being welcomed into the fellowship of the Christian Church. It is Roman Catholic, Anglican and Orthodox churches that baptise babies.

Believer's baptism: Baptists and a few other Nonconformist churches baptise adults who have come to believe in Jesus Christ as their Saviour. Those baptised are fully immersed beneath the water. This is why the service is often called 'baptism by immersion'.

▲ *A service of Believer's baptism. To some Christians, this is a major milestone on their Christian journey.*

TASK 1

1. Use the Internet to visit one Pentecostal, Quaker, Baptist and Methodist website. What can you discover from each website about the different ways in which each Church worships?

2. What is the main difference between liturgical and non-liturgical forms of Christian worship?

3. What four elements would you find in almost all acts of Christian worship?

▲ *For most Christians, the service of Holy Communion is the most important act of worship.*

2. Christian prayer and contemplation

For Christians, prayer is the basic way in which they communicate with God. This means that they speak to God when they pray and listen to Him in return. In any family, it is important that children speak openly to their parents as Christians are part of God's family – He is their Father and they are His children. Christians pray to God when they are on their own and also when they are with other believers. They believe that God loves them and wishes to look after and support them, just as human parents take responsibility for their children. Christians strongly believe that God answers their prayers and this shows how much He cares for them.

When they pray, Christians are following the example of Jesus in the Gospels. From them, we learn that Jesus often prayed to his Father in heaven, sometimes spending the whole night doing so before he had an important decision to make – such as choosing his twelve disciples. Because of the importance that he attached to prayer in his own life, Jesus also encouraged his followers to pray. Christians feel that, as they pray, they are entering into God's presence where they receive the divine strength and guidance that they need to serve God in their daily lives.

Asking for God's help is part of prayer but true prayer is much more than this. Jesus taught his disciples that they should love God and love their neighbours as much as they love themselves (Mark 12.28–31).

Adoration – praising God for his greatness.

Thanksgiving – thanking God for all his good gifts. Christians believe that everything comes directly, or indirectly, from God.

CHRISTIAN PRAYER INCLUDES

Confession – Christians believe that they are sinners who need to ask for God's forgiveness before they pray.

Intercession – praying for other people who are in need.

Petition – praying for their own needs.

✳ TO TALK ABOUT

What are the ways that Christians might try to bring up their children to believe as they do? Do you think it is right for them to try to do this?

▲ *Christians believe that it is very important that their children are taught to pray.*

Meditation and contemplation

Meditation is an important spiritual activity in many religions. When some Christians meditate, they try to focus their thoughts quietly on God. They may do this by trying to imagine scenes and events in the Bible and using this to think about their meaning. They may simply sit still and listen to a piece of music or sit in front of a religious painting (called an **icon**) to meditate, as many Orthodox Christians do. They may just sit still in an empty church or be in their favourite place in nature and know that they are in the presence of God. After all, two people who are in love do not always need to talk to each other – it is often enough just to be with the loved one and enjoy their presence. This is just what Christians who try to meditate do in the presence of God.

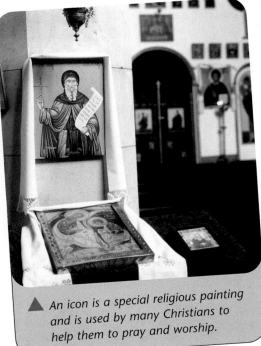

▲ An icon is a special religious painting and is used by many Christians to help them to pray and worship.

Contemplation is a slightly different form of this in which believers find themselves taken up with God. This is a form of prayer that some Christian saints did in the past.

The Jesus Prayer

As well as using icons in their spiritual devotions, Christians from the Orthodox tradition also make use of the 'Jesus Prayer'. This prayer can take several different forms but it basically says:

'Lord Jesus Christ, Son of God, have mercy on me.'

More than just a prayer, this is really a cry for help. Many Christians use it as an 'arrow' prayer, one that they use when they do not have time for anything longer. The Jesus Prayer recognises two things:

- who Jesus is – the Son of God. This means that Jesus has the power to help because he is divine – God Himself;

- we are all sinners and so need God's help – we cannot enter God's presence unless we have His forgiveness.

Many Christians use this prayer as the basis for their spiritual meditation, thinking deeply on the depth of meaning to be found in each word. They say the prayer in rhythm with their own breathing so that it is uttered many times a day – almost without the person being aware of saying it.

Ask and it will be given to you

Christians believe that Jesus is God's own Son and very close to Him. The favourite name that Jesus applied to God was that of 'Father' and he encouraged his followers to think of God in the same way. He told his disciples:

> 66 *Ask and it will be given to you; seek and you will find; knock and the door will be opened to you. For everyone who asks receives; he who seeks finds; and to him who knocks the door will be opened.* 99
>
> (Matthew 7.7–8)

Jesus is not telling his disciples that all of their prayers will be answered in the way that they want or expect. That clearly does not happen. Christians, like followers of other religions, have to struggle with the problem of unanswered prayer. Every good parent knows that he or she has to say 'no' to their children sometimes. Christians believe that God will answer their own prayers in His own way and in His own good time.

TASK 2

1. Explain what meditation is.
2. What do Christians mean when they speak about meditation?
3. What is the Jesus Prayer and how might Christians use it?
4. Explain why a Christian's prayers might sometimes go unanswered?
5. This notice is often seen outside a church:

   SEVEN PRAYERLESS DAYS MAKE ONE WEAK

   What do you think the notice is trying to say?

3. The importance of food and fasting in Christianity

Food and Christianity

Unlike many other religions, there are no rules in Christianity about what a believer can and cannot eat. Probably, like other Jews, Jesus did eat meat but we have no reason to think that he did not keep the Jewish rules about only eating **kosher** meat. We read in the New Testament about Jesus feeding a large crowd of people with just a small number of loaves and fish (Mark 8.1–13) while on another occasion, he told his disciples, who were professional fishermen, where to find a good catch (Luke 5.4–6). He also encouraged his followers to use the symbols of bread and wine to remember, and celebrate, his death on the cross (1 Corinthians 11.23–25).

Some Christians are vegetarians but there is nothing in the life or teaching of Jesus to encourage them to believe that they should not eat meat. One incident in the life of the apostle **Peter** – Acts 10.9–16 – suggests that Christians have been given permission by God to eat all kinds of meat because all animals have been given by God for them to enjoy. The clear teaching of this incident is that there is no such thing as 'clean' and 'unclean' animals as some religions teach.

Fasting

In many religions, fasting – going without food and sometimes liquid – is an important religious discipline. Many people believe that fasting is important because it is a form of self-denial and self-discipline. It leads the worshipper to realise that some things, such as the worship of God, are much more important than the physical needs of their body, such as food. Fasting is not, however, an important or widespread discipline for the vast majority of Christians today. A few people may give up some luxury during the season of **Lent**, leading up to **Easter**, but this is not real fasting.

▼ *Bread and wine eaten at Holy Communion are two of the most important Christian symbols because they are a regular reminder of the death and resurrection of Jesus.*

1. Explain what is meant by 'fasting'.
2. How important is fasting for most Christians today? Is this true for all Christians? How could you find out?

4. The architecture of church buildings

Christians have been building churches in which to worship God since the third century CE. Until then, they had worshipped in each other's homes but there were now too many of them to continue doing this. From the very beginning, the designs of the buildings and the furniture that was in them were designed to suggest certain 'truths' about God and so help the people to worship God.

Two types of church building

There are two different types of church building:

- Churches that are dominated by the **altar**. The oldest churches still standing in England go back to about the twelfth century and these are either Roman Catholic or Anglican. Most of these churches were built in the shape of a cross with the altar at the far end of the building. This was to make God seem distant from the worshipper – remote and holy – since the altar was the place where God met with worshippers during the Eucharist. A rail was placed around the altar and only the **priest** was allowed inside the rail. In an Orthodox church, the same idea of God's holiness is conveyed by a screen, called the **iconostasis**, which is covered with icons and which hides the altar from the gaze of ordinary worshippers. The service of Holy Communion, conducted at the altar, is at the centre of all Catholic, Anglican and Orthodox worship. In these churches, worshippers are expected to celebrate this **sacrament** regularly.

▲ *The iconostasis in an Orthodox church is a constant reminder of the distance between God and the worshippers.*

Churches built in more recent times, however, are likely to be very different. Instead of placing the altar as far away as possible, it is often situated in the middle of the congregation. Seats are then gathered around the altar in a circle or semi-circle. The priest stands in the middle of the people as he or she conducts the service, instead of being separate from them behind a distant altar. This indicates that God is in the middle of the people rather than being separate from them. People who worship in modern buildings, such as Clifton Cathedral in Bristol, say that the shape and design of the church helps them to feel that God is close to them.

- Churches dominated by the **pulpit** – a raised platform from which the sermon is given during the service. Nonconformist church buildings, such as Methodist and Baptist churches, tend to be very simple and centred around the pulpit, since the preaching of God's Word, the Bible, is at the heart of their worship. Sermons are preached in other church services but it is not considered to be so important. Most Nonconformist churches are called 'chapels' although members of the Salvation Army call their places of worship **citadels**.

▲ *Pulpits were built in chapels so that the message of the minister in his sermon could be seen to have more authority.*

TASK 4

1. What is the altar in a church?
2. What important service is conducted at the altar?
3. Why were altars put at the far end of older churches?
4. What is a pulpit?
5. What does the important position given to pulpits in many churches indicate?

5. The use of music and art in Christian worship

Music

Music has always played a very important part in most acts of Christian worship. Vocal music going back to the fifteenth century, and sung by a choir, plays an important part in the services of larger churches and cathedrals today. Christian

hymns have long been one of the most important forms of music in the Western world and they still play a part in most acts of Christian worship. Traditionally, hymns sung in church have been accompanied by an organ but they are now more likely to be accompanied by guitars, drums and a piano. In recent years, thousands of new hymns and choruses have been written.

▲ Some of the most beautiful music ever written was composed to be part of Christian worship. The organ, as a musical instrument, was thought to give it the dignity that it deserved.

Art

Many Christian churches are richly decorated with art in various forms – including stained-glass windows, statues, banners and icons. These are used to illustrate stories from the Bible and the many different symbols that Christians find to be useful in their worship. Although stained-glass windows are still being created, they are very expensive and have been largely replaced by banners. These can be hung up and then replaced very easily. Statues of saints, particularly the Virgin Mary, are found in most Roman Catholic churches. Icons are a characteristic of Orthodox churches and they form an important part of the worship of many believers. They usually depict a particular saint, the Holy Family (Joseph, Mary and Jesus) or Jesus on his own.

▶ Many churches have stained-glass windows, often showing events from the Bible or from the lives of the saints. At a time when many people could not read, these windows were an important teaching aid.

6. The use of Christian symbols

Religion deals with spiritual and abstract realities. It is usually very difficult, therefore, to speak directly of these things. The language that is available for us to use is often inadequate. For this reason, Christians and other religious believers have always had to make use of symbols as the main way of conveying spiritual truth. Over the centuries, many Christian symbols have been widely used and many of them can still be found in places of worship today. Here are four of the most important Christian symbols:

CHECK IT OUT

The cross – this is the most well-known and important Christian symbol. It reminds worshippers of the death of Jesus on the cross. Christians believe that the death of Jesus brought them God's forgiveness of their sins and everlasting life.

The Chi-Rho – this is an old Christian symbol taken from two Greek letters, the first two letters of the word 'Christ'.

FOUR IMPORTANT CHRISTIAN SYMBOLS

The fish – in the earliest days of Christianity in the Roman Empire, Christians were persecuted and killed. The fish was used as a sacred sign so that Christians would know that other believers were around. The word 'fish' in Greek was used to mean 'Jesus Christ, Son of God, Saviour'.

Alpha and Omega – alpha and omega are the first and last letters of the Greek alphabet. They were used to speak of God at the beginning and end of time.

Choose any one of the four main Christian symbols. How is it used in Christianity – or by Christians – around the world today?

▶ *The cross is the most important, and the most familiar, of the Christian symbols.*

The Nature of Belief

HINDUISM

What you will learn about in this section:

1. Private and public Hindu worship

2. Hindu prayer and meditation

3. The use of food and fasting by some Hindus as a response to God

4. The architecture of the mandir

5. The use of music and art in Hinduism

6. The use of Hindu symbols

1. Private and public Hindu worship

Most Hindu worship takes place in the home rather than in the mandir (the temple). This is because Hindu society is firmly based on the family unit, which has the responsibility of safeguarding society's religious traditions and customs. The traditional Hindu family is an extended one in which several generations live together and it is this that gives Hindus their strong sense of solidarity and identity. It is also in their family that Hindu children learn the customs of their religion and the obligations that stem from the **caste system**.

Hindu children are brought up to observe five daily duties:

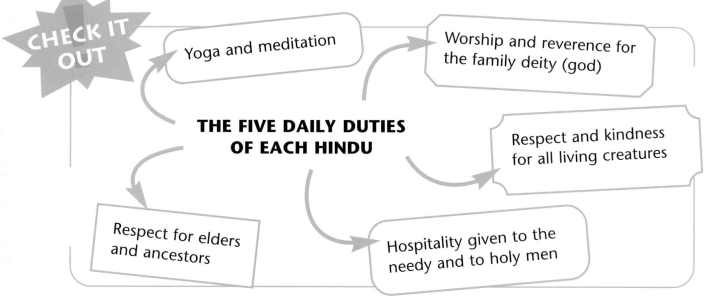

CHECK IT OUT

Yoga and meditation

Worship and reverence for the family deity (god)

THE FIVE DAILY DUTIES OF EACH HINDU

Respect and kindness for all living creatures

Respect for elders and ancestors

Hospitality given to the needy and to holy men

Hindu worship at home

Puja is an act of religious worship that is most likely to take place in front of a shrine in a Hindu home. This involves presenting offerings to the deity in the shrine room and chanting special holy words called **mantras**. Every Hindu home has its own shrine and this is treated as a very special place. Sometimes it is little more than a shelf on a wall, which is dedicated to the family's god. An image of the god, called a murti, is surrounded by offerings of fruit, flowers and incense which are renewed every day.

Women play the central role in the religious ceremonies that take place daily in the home. These begin early in the morning when the god is 'woken up' by a lighted candle placed in front of it. The murti is then washed and wiped all over with ghee (melted butter) as a sign of great respect. The family sometimes chants a mantra, although they can meditate in silence. The day then begins for most Hindu families with an act of worship in front of the home shrine.

The Gyatri Mantra

Of all the prayers offered by a Hindu, the most popular is the Gyatri Mantra. **Brahmins** repeat this prayer three times each day – at dawn, at midday and at sunset. It is used in public worship and on ceremonial occasions, such as births, marriages and the opening of a public building. The Gyatri Mantra contains these words:

▲ A Hindu home shrine, the place where Hindus feel most comfortable praying to their god.

> 66 O God, the giver of life, the remover of pains and sorrows, bestower of happiness, and creator of the universe, thou art most luminous, pure and adorable. We meditate on thee. May thou inspire and guide our intellect in the right direction. 99
>
> (Rig Veda 10.16.3)

FROM THE SCRIPTURES

The role of women

Women in Hindu homes have the main responsibility for:

- making sure that the appropriate worship traditions are followed by all members of her family;
- ensuring that the major religious festivals are kept faithfully by all members of her family;
- encouraging her children to learn the great legends and stories of their culture and religion.

It is largely up to Hindu women to make sure that the traditions and customs of the faith are passed on unbroken from one generation to the next. People know that this alone will guarantee that the religion of Hinduism survives into the future.

Hindu worship in the mandir

Most Hindu temples have at least one priest, or brahmin. He carries the important responsibility of looking after the murti of the god and of helping the people to worship God in an appropriate way. The people do not worship the murti. They worship the one God, Brahman, of whom the murti is believed to be an appropriate symbol. This means that Hinduism, like Christianity, Judaism and Islam, is a monotheistic religion, whose worshippers believe in one God.

To worship in the mandir, worshippers usually arrive early in the morning and ring a bell-rope to announce their arrival. They also take their shoes off as a mark of respect. The worshippers present their gifts to the brahmin who takes them to the throne room to lay them before the murti. In the larger Hindu temples, the priest then offers prayers in front of the people.

▲ By running their hands over the flame of the fire, the people hope to receive God's power.

He waves a small tray containing five lights in front of the deity. It is then taken round to the people who run their hands over the flame before wiping them over their head. Hindus believe that when they do this, they are receiving God's power. This act of worship is called the **arti**.

Brahmins (priests) form the highest caste in Hindu society. Only people from this caste can officiate in the temple.

1. Why do many important Hindu religious ceremonies take place in the home rather than in the mandir?

2. Write down three things that each worshipper does as he or she arrives at the temple to worship.

3. Making suitable offerings is a very important part of Hindu worship. What makes an offering acceptable to God?

2. Hindu prayer and meditation

Hindus believe that there are four paths to salvation or liberation. Through using one of them, a person may eventually find release from the seemingly unending cycle of birth, marriage, death and rebirth, through which we all pass countless times. Two of these paths are particularly important here:

The path of bhakti

This is the path of loving devotion to the family deity, which most Hindus attempt to follow. As we have seen, a daily act of devotion to the deity before the day begins is offered in the home of every Hindu at the family shrine. This worship consists of:

- hymn singing;
- telling and learning the legendary stories of the gods which are told in the many Hindu holy books;
- celebrating the many Hindu religious festivals.

These are all part of the bhakti tradition. Apart from daily worship at the home shrine and serving others in the name of the family god, worshippers also try to follow the bhakti tradition by trying to remember their god at all times. Devotion to God is expected to affect the everyday life of each believer.

Learning the stories of the gods from the holy books is part of the path of bhakti.

The path of yoga (meditation)

Yoga is a series of physical and mental exercises that are designed to give a person control over their mind and body. For Hindus, yoga is a strict spiritual discipline that has been used for thousands of years. It can, however, also be used by worshippers of other religions and also by those who have no religious faith.

To master and use yoga successfully, people must learn certain important physical positions, in particular, the 'lotus' position, in which a person sits cross-legged with their feet resting on their thighs. Breathing exercises also aid concentration, as does focusing the mind on an image of the god. In this way, an awareness of a person's oneness with the Supreme Spirit, Brahman, can grow.

This person, in the lotus position, is trying to make himself aware of his oneness with God.

TASK 2

Explain how a Hindu might use the paths of devotion to God and meditation (yoga) to move closer to liberation or salvation.

3. The use of food and fasting by some Hindus as a response to God

Although there are few hard and fast rules in Hinduism about diet and fasting, there are two beliefs which do have a considerable effect on what Hindus eat. They are:

1. Vegetarianism

Most Hindus are vegetarians. This is because they believe that all life is sacred and so they are committed to the principle of non-violence (ahimsa) towards animals, insects and all fellow human beings. All Hindus believe that it is wrong to kill animals for food and many believe that it is wrong to eat eggs as well.

▼ *The cow is venerated by Hindus and never killed for food.*

2. The sacred cow

Hindus do not eat beef. Although for Hindus all life is sacred, the cow is held in special regard. The cow is looked upon as a symbol of the earth, which gives its

riches freely to all human beings to enjoy and asks for little in return. The free gifts of the cow that human beings receive are milk and milk products – butter, ghee, cheese and yoghurt – which are so essential to the Indian diet. To harm a cow or eat beef would result in bad **karma** – bad effects brought over from bad actions in previous lives.

Explain:
a. What a vegetarian is.
b. Why many Hindus are vegetarians.
c. Why Hindus avoid eating beef.

TASK 3

Fasting

As in many other religions, fasting is a very important spiritual discipline in Hinduism. Many Hindus fast on certain religious holidays and at other times as well. Some devout Hindus fast for one day a week or even more. Others have a partial fast during which they only take liquids and certain grains. The purpose of this fasting is to concentrate the mind of the worshipper on God and to prevent him or her from becoming too attached to such earthly pleasures as sex, food or wine. It helps each worshipper to realise that the search for ultimate truth, God, is much more important than any passing pleasure to be had from life.

✳ TO TALK ABOUT

Do you think that it is wrong to eat animals for food? Are there some animals that you feel comfortable eating but not others? Are you inclined to follow a vegetarian way of life? Produce as many reasons as you can for your answers – whatever they are.

4. The architecture of the mandir

Most mandirs are surrounded by a wall which separates the holy space of the temple from the world outside. Inside the wall are several small shrines as well, containing murtis of the various gods and goddesses and these lead to the heart of the temple. The main murti is usually at the back of the temple in a small chamber lit with oil lamps – an area known as the garbha-griha. Worshippers show their deep respect for the gods by walking around the murtis. There is often a tower or a dome built above the garbha-griha.

5. The use of music and art in Hinduism

Music

Music is a very important part of most Hindu worship. Sacred songs are sometimes accompanied by instruments such as drums and small finger cymbals. Dance, accompanied by music, is a popular way in the Hindu tradition of telling religious stories to children and people who cannot read or write. There are travelling groups of musicians and dancers who take their performances into the villages and towns of India. This tradition, going back thousands of years, makes use of elaborate costumes combined with hand and eye movements.

Art

Art has always played a very important part in Hindu culture and religion. Sculptures and carvings representing the different Hindu gods cover the outside of many temples while religious paintings and icons are to be found in many Hindu homes. The murtis, such as those shown in the photo, are usually beautifully carved and made out of a variety of materials.

▼ Hindu temples are very often beautiful works of art.

Images of the gods, called murtis, are to be found throughout India, both indoors and also by the roadside.

6. The use of Hindu symbols

Each murti is a symbol of the Supreme Spirit, Brahman. Apart from these symbols, however, there are two other important Hindu symbols:

The AUM symbol

The most important Hindu symbol is that of the sacred sound, **AUM**, which is to be found everywhere in India – in temples and homes as well as on books and birthday cards. The sacred sound is made up of three separate sounds – A, U and M – and when it is chanted, it can be taken to represent:

- the three great Hindu gods – Brahma, Shiva and Vishnu. Together, these three gods are called the Trimurti;

- the cycle of birth, death and rebirth;

- the three 'worlds' of the earth, the atmosphere and heaven;

- three very important Hindu texts – the Sama Veda, the Yajur Veda and the Rig Veda.

The AUM sound is believed to be eternal and to go to the very heart of reality. When believers chant the sacred sound, they believe it takes them closer to God.

The AUM symbol – the most important of the Hindu symbols and one that is believed to take the Hindu to the heart of reality.

The swastika

During the Second World War, the swastika was taken to be the symbol of the Nazi party in Germany. As the Nazi party stood for all that was evil, so the swastika became much less popular as a Hindu symbol for prosperity and good luck. The symbol is still used, however, at times of Hindu celebration, such as weddings and the **Divali** festival.

Write two sentences about each of the following symbols and what they mean in Hinduism:

a. The AUM.

b. The swastika.

TASK 4

ISLAM

What you will learn about in this section:

1. Muslim worship
2. The mosque and its architecture

1. Muslim worship

The Five Pillars of Islam

As a religion, Islam is much more than just a system of beliefs. It is a way of life, thought, word and deed. To the Muslim believer, faith without action is meaningless. Faith must lead to action and action brings faith into the outside world where it can grow and deepen. Islam is based on the **Five Pillars** of the faith. They are called pillars because they are the foundations on which the whole faith of Islam is built. They act as a daily guide to every Muslim who is trying to follow the will of Allah for his or her life.

Pillar One – the Shahadah

The Shahadah is the Muslim declaration of faith in the one God, Allah. Islam is very firmly a monotheistic religious faith. The Shahadah says:

> ❝ *ilaha illi'Allah, Muhammad*⊛ *rasul Allah.* ❞
>
> *(There is no god except Allah, Muhammad*⊛ *is His messenger.)*

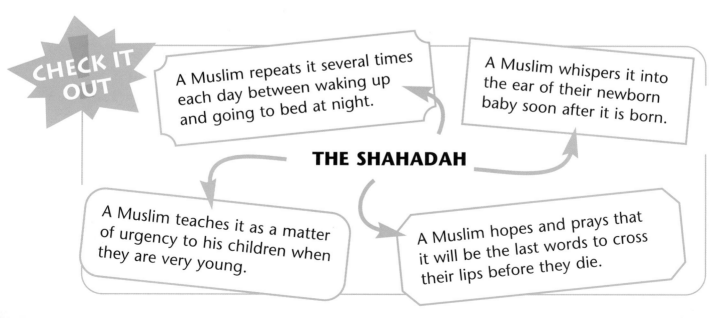

CHECK IT OUT

A Muslim repeats it several times each day between waking up and going to bed at night.

A Muslim whispers it into the ear of their newborn baby soon after it is born.

THE SHAHADAH

A Muslim teaches it as a matter of urgency to his children when they are very young.

A Muslim hopes and prays that it will be the last words to cross their lips before they die.

Pillar Two – Salah (prayer)

After the profession of faith, the next most important duty for every Muslim is that of prayer (**salah**). There are five times for prayer in each day:

- at dawn
- at noon
- mid-afternoon
- after sunset
- before going to bed.

Before praying, each Muslim must cleanse their body with clean, running water and they do this by performing **wudu**. They wash their hands, mouth, nose, face, arms, head, ears and feet three times in a certain order. Running water is provided in the courtyard of the **mosque**. If running water is not available, then sand is a suitable substitute. Once wudu has been performed, the worshipper is ready to say the set prayers which are all quotations from the Qur'an. One complete sequence of prayers is called a **rak'ah**. A different number of rak'ahs have to be performed at different times during the day.

▲ *Wudu is the important washing ritual that always precedes prayer for a Muslim.*

Pillar Three – Zakah (giving alms)

From his early experiences as an orphan, Muhammad ﷺ knew that life could be very hard and this experience greatly influenced his subsequent teaching. He had a deep compassion and concern for all those in need – especially the orphans, the widows and the sick. At the end of each year, all Muslims must give at least 2.5% of their income as **zakah** (alms) for the welfare and upkeep of the poor. In Muslim countries, this is collected as a tax but in non-Muslim countries, it is collected in the mosque. The teaching of the Qur'an is that everything that a person has comes from Allah in the first place and so it is only right that a small amount should be given back to Him each year. Zakah is not the same as charity. It is the right of every poor person to receive the money.

◀ *Zakah is the main way that a Muslim gives to the poor, although they can make a voluntary gift over and above this compulsory offering.*

Pillar Four – sawm (fasting)

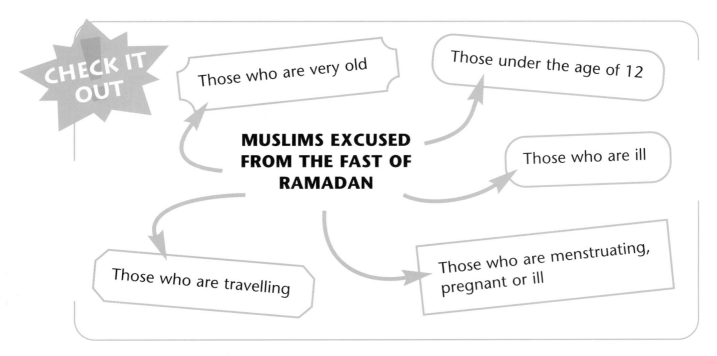

CHECK IT OUT

MUSLIMS EXCUSED FROM THE FAST OF RAMADAN

Those who are very old

Those under the age of 12

Those who are ill

Those who are travelling

Those who are menstruating, pregnant or ill

Apart from the young, the sick and the elderly, those who miss the fast should make it up as soon as they can. Each day of the fast lasts from sunrise to sunset. As the Qur'an says:

> 66 *And eat and drink, until the white thread of dawn appear to you distinct from its black thread; then complete your fast till the night appears...* 99
> (Surah 2.187)

The rules of the fast forbid the eating of food, the drinking of liquids, smoking and any form of sexual contact. Anyone who breaks the fast without a good reason is expected to provide a meal for 60 people or continue the fast for another 60 days!

Pillar Five – the hajj (pilgrimage to Makkah)

The **hajj** is the annual pilgrimage that Muslims make to the holy city of **Makkah**.

Each able-bodied Muslim is expected to undertake this pilgrimage, or holy journey, at least once during their lifetime. If, for some reason, they are unable to make the journey, then they can pay for someone else to go in their place. A Muslim man who has made the journey can call himself a 'Hajji' and a woman, a 'Hajjah'. The pilgrimage always takes place each year during the twelfth month of the Muslim year.

During the pilgrimage, Muslims visit several sites in and around Makkah. Many also travel on to the second most holy city in Islam – **Madinah**.

1. Explain what you think this saying of the Prophet Muhammad ﷺ has to tell us about prayer:

    ❝ *Worship Allah as if you see Him; if you do not see Him, know that He sees you.* ❞

2. On more than one occasion, Prophet Muhammad ﷺ is said to have likened praying to washing in a stream as it flows past the door. Why do you think that he chose this particular image for prayer?

3. Make a list of those groups who are excused from the fast of Ramadan. Do you think that any of the exceptions are surprising?

2. The mosque and its architecture

Inside a mosque

Muslims pray together in a mosque – a 'house of prayer'. The building is not, however, just the focal point for Muslim worship, but a meeting place for the whole Muslim community. The building is not essential for prayer and Muslims do not have to go to the mosque to pray. Muhammad ﷺ taught his followers that prayer can, and should, be offered to Allah in any available place.

❝ *Wherever the hour of prayer overtakes you, you shall perform it. That place is a mosque.* ❞

He also taught his followers that anyone who builds a mosque dedicated to Allah would enter directly into paradise, since their act of love would be so pleasing to Allah. Although a mosque in Britain is most likely to be a converted house or church, one that has been purpose-built will include:

-   a main hall in which prayers are conducted. There is no furniture in a mosque and the worshippers stand or kneel on the carpeted floor to pray. One wall must face the holy city of Makkah and this contains a thin arched alcove or opening which indicates the direction of the holy city. This shows the Muslim which way they should face to pray – this is called the **mihrab**;
-   facilities (taps) for washing. This is where wudu is performed;
-   a place set aside for study and teaching children;
-   a room in which the dead are prepared for burial.

When Muslims enter a mosque, they must remove their shoes as a sign of respect for Allah. There are no seats inside a mosque since no one would think of sitting down in Allah's presence. On entering the prayer hall, many Muslims spread their prayer mat on the floor – the decoration on the mat includes an arch that is placed to point towards the holy city of Makkah. No pictures or statues are allowed inside the mosque, although the walls and pillars can be decorated with traditional Muslim patterns, verses from the Qur'an or the names of Allah or Muhammad ﷺ, the Prophet of Allah.

Because figurative art is forbidden in Islam, calligraphy is very highly valued. The art of writing calligraphy is an almost holy activity for Muslims and highly respected. You can see an example of calligraphy in the photograph below. Arabic calligraphy, mainly of verses from the Qur'an, is to be found in almost every mosque and also in many beautiful hand-written copies of the holy book.

▲ *All Muslim worshippers face the mihrab in the mosque as they pray so that they know that they are facing the holy city of Makkah.*

The main service in the mosque is Friday prayers which all male Muslims are expected to attend unless they are unwell or travelling. At this service, the imam leads the congregation through their prayers and delivers his sermon from a raised platform of three steps called the **minbar**.

► *The prayer room of a mosque.*

The outside of a mosque

The outside of a mosque has two distinguishing features:

- The dome. The dome is onion-shaped and represents the universe over which Allah is Lord and has total control.

- The **minaret** – from which the Call to Prayer (the **Adhan**) is given by the **muezzin** five times a day. A minaret symbolises the light and truth of Islam, which shines out from every mosque into a dark world.

Tawhid and **shirk** are two very important Muslim beliefs and they are closely linked to each other.

Tawhid

Tawhid is at the heart of Islam. It simply states that Allah is One. By this, the Muslim means that Allah is totally beyond all human understanding; beyond space and time, the Truth before all other truths. Allah is the First and the Last, the One and only Creator of the material world. Alongside Allah, there are no other supernatural and divine beings. Allah is supremely one and alone.

▲ From this photograph, you can see the dome of the mosque.

Shirk

Shirk is the most serious sin that a Muslim can commit. It is the sin of believing that anything, or anyone, can be as great as Allah. To make any kind of image of Allah or even of a living person or creature is shirk.

TASK 2

1. Explain, in your own words, the meaning of:
   a. Tawhid.
   b. Shirk.
2. Describe two features that you would find on the outside of a mosque and explain their importance.

JUDAISM

What you will learn about in this section:

1. Jewish worship in the synagogue and home
2. Jewish prayer
3. The importance of food and fasting in Judaism

1. Jewish worship in the synagogue and home

The architecture of the synagogue

The Temple that had stood in Jerusalem for centuries was finally destroyed in 70 CE. The Jews were dispersed throughout the known world as a result. This dispersion is known as the **diaspora**. The Jews began to build places for study and worship in the towns and villages where they settled. These buildings, called synagogues (meaning 'gathering together') became important community centres for the Jewish community.

In Orthodox synagogues, only men sit in the worship area. At one end of this area is the ark, a cupboard covered by a curtain, where the scrolls of the Torah are stored. On the front of each scroll is a breastplate, which is a reminder of the one worn by the High Priest in the Temple of old. No statues or photographs are allowed in the synagogue. There is a platform in front of the ark, the **bimah**, where the scroll of the Torah is placed when it is being read. In Reform synagogues, however, men and women sit together to worship. Jewish people are expected to follow the will of G-d as is found in the Ten Commandments. These laws are so important that they are displayed in an abbreviated form in Hebrew on the wall in every synagogue. You can find out what the Ten Commandments are by reading Exodus 20.1–14.

The Shema is the most important statement of faith in the Jewish Scriptures. It begins with the words:

> *Hear, O Israel: The LORD is our G-d, the LORD is the One and Only. You shall love the LORD, your G-d, with all your heart, with all your soul, and with all your resources…*
>
> (Deuteronomy 6.4-5)

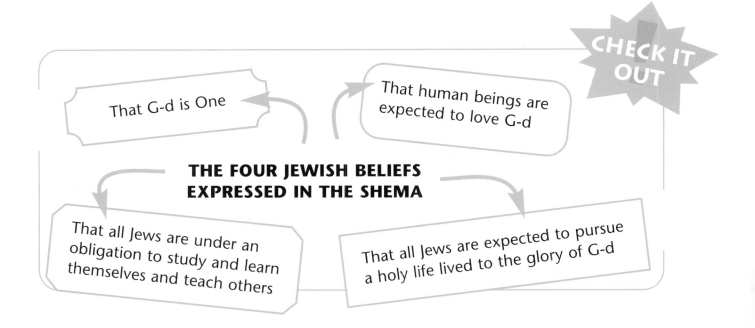

That G-d is One

That human beings are expected to love G-d

THE FOUR JEWISH BELIEFS EXPRESSED IN THE SHEMA

That all Jews are under an obligation to study and learn themselves and teach others

That all Jews are expected to pursue a holy life lived to the glory of G-d

Apart from believing that G-d is One, Jews also believe that G-d is all-powerful (omnipotent), to be found everywhere in the world (omnipresent) and knows everything (omniscient). These beliefs are constantly repeated and emphasised throughout the Jewish Scriptures and in the Jewish prayer called the **Kaddish**. The beliefs form the basis for the 613 mitzvot or commandments which are found in the Torah and which each **Orthodox** Jew tries to follow in his or her everyday life. 90% of Jews in the world today are Orthodox.

What are the four main things that Jews believe about G-d?

TASK 1

Worshipping in the home and in the synagogue

While services are held in the synagogue each day of the week, the most important time for Jews is **Shabbat** (the Sabbath Day), the day on which they rest from all work. While most Jews worship in the synagogue on this day, the most important activities take place at home. The custom of setting aside one day of the week for complete rest – the word 'shabbat' or 'sabbath' actually means 'ceasing' – is an ancient one and marked out the Israelites from the beginning from all the nations around them who expected their slaves and servants to work without rest each day. Celebrating the Sabbath day is the oldest religious tradition that Jews actively follow today.

In the Jewish Scriptures, observing Sabbath is linked with the two most important biblical events in Jewish history and these events are recalled each time the holy day is celebrated:

- The creation of the world. As the Jewish Scriptures say:

> **For in six days the Lord made the heavens and the earth, the sea and all that is in them, and He rested on the seventh day. Therefore the Lord blessed the Sabbath Day and sanctified it.**
>
> (Exodus 20.11)

Put quite simply – if G-d needed to rest after creating the world in six days, then his followers certainly need to rest after six days of work.

- The journey of the Israelites out of slavery in Egypt about 4000 years ago – an event known to all Jews as the Exodus. As the Order of Service for the Sabbath day says:

> **The Sabbath Day is a sabbath of the Lord your G-d ... and you shall remember that you were a slave in the land of Egypt...**

This event is the most important in Jewish history and is remembered by all Jews at the annual **Passover** festival.

The Sabbath day starts at sunset on Friday evening and finishes at nightfall on Saturday. All of the food for the family is prepared before the day begins and the table is laid at home for a special meal. Then, at sunset, the woman of the house lights two special candles to welcome in the Sabbath day. As she does so, she says a special blessing and then the whole family gathers for a special ceremony, called the Kiddush, at which:

- wine (the symbol of joy) is blessed and drunk;
- the Sabbath day is blessed;
- the wife and children are blessed by the father. The blessing of the father has special significance in a Jewish family.

The Sabbath meal begins with the breaking of bread. There are always two loaves on the Sabbath table and these are twisted or plaited in a distinctive way. Songs are sung and the meal ends with a prayer of thanksgiving.

▲ Jews drink a glass of wine at the beginning of Sabbath because the day ahead is one of joy, happiness and celebration.

The service held in the synagogue on the Sabbath morning is an important act of worship. As people arrive, they wish each other 'Shabbat shalom' (a peaceful Sabbath). During the service, the Torah is taken ceremonially out of the ark and placed on the bimah, from which it is read.

Just as the Sabbath day begins in the home, so it ends there. The special ceremony that ends the holy day at sunset on Saturday is called **Havdalah** (meaning 'separation'). Its name comes from the fact that it 'separates' the Sabbath day from the six days of work that follow it. For this beautiful ceremony, a special candle with several wicks is lit and a spice box opened up to wish everyone a sweet week ahead. The parting wish is 'shavua tov' (a 'good week') and wine is poured over the candle to extinguish it.

TASK 2

1. What is the most important day of the week for Jews and what does its name mean?

2. Which two very important events in Jewish history are Jews celebrating on the Sabbath day each week?

▶ *The Havdalah ceremony. Its name comes from the way that it is used to 'separate' the holy Sabbath day from the other six days of the week.*

2. Jewish prayer

Although a Jew is expected to be constantly aware of G-d's presence in his or her life, there are three times a day when it is particularly important to pray – in the morning, at noon and in the evening. In addition, there are prayers to be said at meal times, on holy days, to the Torah and in special months of the year. One of the most important Jewish prayers is the **Amidah**, part of which says:

❝ *O Lord, our G-d, hear our cry!*
Have compassion on us and pity us;
Accept our prayer with loving favour...
For you mercifully heed Your people's supplication.
Praised are you, O Lord, who is attentive to prayer. ❞

Jewish prayer is accompanied by several external symbols. According to Jewish tradition, prayers offered together by a congregation are more meaningful than those said by a worshipper on his or her own. This is because it is the congregation that upholds and sustains the individual.

CHECK IT OUT

The **tallit** – in the Jewish Orthodox communities and some other communities, the tallit, a shawl with fringes on each corner, is worn by male worshippers during morning prayer and sometimes evening prayer.

▲ The tallit is worn on the eve of the **Day of Atonement**.

THE THREE VISIBLE SYMBOLS OF JEWISH PRAYER

The **tefillin** – the tefillin are leather boxes worn by men when praying and are strapped to the left arm and the forehead.

The **yarmulke** – the yarmulke is a skullcap which most male Jews wear at all times in the synagogue, including prayer times.

◄ The tefillin are strapped to the left arm and forehead.

► Many Jews wear the yarmulke at times of prayer.

3. The importance of food and fasting in Judaism

Forbidden food

It was while the Jews were travelling across the desert during the Exodus that they were given rules about which animals they could, and could not, eat. You can find these rules in Leviticus 11.1–23; 41–42. There is a list of birds that live off carrion, most insects and reptiles that Jews are not allowed to eat. Jews are also forbidden to mix meat with dairy products and were not allowed to cook them in the same pot. They were not allowed to eat any product from the pig or any other forbidden animal.

Most Jews still continue these traditional food restrictions today. The food that Jews are allowed to eat is called kosher (permitted) while food that is forbidden is called treifah (forbidden). All kosher meat must be slaughtered by a method called **shechita** during which a blessing is said over the animal before it is killed instantaneously by a single stroke of a very sharp knife across its throat. It is then hung upside down until all of its blood has drained out.

TASK 3

1. What are the main food laws by which many Jews live?
2. Why do you think they choose to live by these laws? How might these laws help Jews in strengthening their faith?

Fasting

The ten days of celebration for the Jewish New Year, **Rosh Hashanah**, end with the most solemn day in the Jewish year, **Yom Kippur** (the Day of Atonement). This 'day' is marked by 25 hours of prayer and fasting, following the example of G-d's angels who do not, according to Jewish tradition, eat or drink, but spend all of their time praising G-d. On this one day of the year, Jews attempt to serve G-d as if they are angels. To do this, they follow the teaching of the Talmud, which forbids eating, drinking, washing, sexual intercourse, anointing with oil and wearing sandals or leather shoes on Yom Kippur.

According to Jewish tradition, **Satan** is allowed by G-d to tempt the Jewish people on every day of the year except Yom Kippur. On that day, G-d declares to Satan, 'You have no power over them today, nevertheless go and see what they are doing.' Satan finds all Jews fasting and dressed in white clothes. He returns to G-d embarrassed. He says, 'They are like angels and I have no power over them.' At this confession, G-d binds Satan in chains for a year and declares to His people, 'I have forgiven you all.'

To Jewish people, Yom Kippur is, above everything else, a day of forgiveness. As they seek forgiveness from all relatives, friends and neighbours they have wronged, so G-d extends His forgiveness to them.

TOPIC 2   The Nature of Belief

EXAM HELP

IN THE EXAMINATION

Here are sample questions for you to try:

CHRISTIANITY

(a) Describe how a Christian might worship God at home. (8 marks)

(b) Explain how praying every day might help Christians in their daily lives. (7 marks)

(c) 'Religious pictures help people to worship God.'

Do you agree? Give reasons to support your answer and show that you have thought about different points of view. You must refer to Christianity in your answer. (5 marks)

HINDUISM

(a) Describe how a Hindu might worship God at home. (8 marks)

(b) Explain how praying every day might help Hindus in their daily lives. (7 marks)

(c) 'Religious pictures help people to worship God.'

Do you agree? Give reasons to support your answer and show that you have thought about different points of view. You must refer to Hinduism in your answer. (5 marks)

ISLAM

(a) Describe how a Muslim might worship God at home. (8 marks)

(b) Explain how praying every day might help a Muslim in their daily lives. (7 marks)

(c) 'Religious pictures help people to worship God.'

Do you agree? Give reasons to support your answer and show that you have thought about different points of view. You must refer to Islam in your answer. (5 marks)

JUDAISM

(a) Describe how a Jew might worship G-d at home. (8 marks)

(b) Explain how praying each day might help a Jew in their daily lives. (7 marks)

(c) 'Religious pictures help people to worship G-d.'

Do you agree? Give reasons to support your answer and show that you have thought about different points of view. You must refer to Judaism in your answer. (5 marks)

Exam hints:

These hints apply to each of the religions:

(a) In this question, you are being asked to think of as many pieces of information as you can to show how the follower of your chosen religion worships God at home. You are not being asked to pass any personal opinion. Make sure that your answer is confined to your chosen religion. Try to use the correct technical words and language in your answer. This will gain you extra marks. Worshipping God in the home is more important in some religions than in others. It matters very much, for example, in Hinduism and Judaism. It is the place where most Muslim women worship but it is less important in Christianity.

(b) In this question, it is your understanding that is being tested. To gain a good mark, you need to think of as many ways as you can to show how praying affects the daily life of a worshipper in the religion that you have studied. Through prayer, religious worshippers learn how God wants them to behave and it draws them closer to other believers.

(c) Christianity and Hinduism make extensive use of pictures in their religious worship. Christians, for example, have used stained-glass windows, statues and icons for centuries in some of their denominations. Hindu temples are full of carvings of the gods. Islam and Judaism, however, strongly condemn the use of such pictures and carvings, believing that they lead to idolatry. Some people find them helpful in worshipping God.

INTRODUCTION

Since the holy texts of the different religions were written, scientists have told us a great deal about the origins of the universe and life on earth. This knowledge has totally transformed the way that we look at life – and our place, as insignificant human beings – in the vast universe. Obviously, this raises many questions about the accounts of creation that we find in the different holy books.

The Copernican revolution

A great change took place in the sixteenth century, associated with the name of Nicolaus Copernicus (1473–1543). Copernicus, a Christian priest, was also an astronomer. Until his time, people thought that the Earth was at the centre of the universe – with the Sun, Moon and stars acting as lights in the heavens to light up the Earth. The whole universe was believed to revolve around the Earth. This was thought to be important for religious reasons, as man was believed to be at the centre of God's creation.

Copernicus upset many people when he said that the Earth was just one of billions of planets in millions of solar systems. Our solar system, just one of millions in the universe, travels around the sun and not vice versa. In terms of the whole universe, the Earth is a very small and insignificant part. This made human beings even less important.

The origins of the universe

In the seventeenth century, James Ussher, the Archbishop of Armagh, used the Bible to date the creation of the universe by God to 4004 BCE. He did this by working his way backwards through the many genealogies in the Bible to the opening chapter of the book of Genesis. We now know, of course, that the universe is much older than that. It is thought by scientists to be between 18 and 20 billion years old!

Most scientists believe that everything started with a Big Bang, an explosion that led to plasma flying through the universe at terrifying speed. This explosion eventually led to the formation of galaxies and these are still moving away at great speed from the centre of the explosion. As these galaxies travel through the universe, they cool and slow down. The universe is still expanding but at a much slower rate. The cooling of the gases led to the formation of stars and planets, including Earth.

▲ *The Big Bang – the way that scientists believe the universe began about 20 million years ago.*

The origin of life on earth

The theory of evolution was the most important scientific theory to emerge in the nineteenth century. This was a far greater challenge to religious understanding than the work of Copernicus. The theory is associated with the name of Charles Darwin who spent some years on the Galapagos Islands studying plant and animal life. His work convinced him that all life developed (evolved) over a very long period of time. As life grew, it adapted itself to surrounding conditions (called 'natural selection'). Those species of life that did not do this died out. The strongest survive while the weakest die (called 'the survival of the fittest'). Darwin actually described nature as being 'red in tooth and claw' in this fight to survive.

Many people at the time were very worried that this was in conflict with the teachings of the Christian religion. They were far more worried, however, when Darwin said that this was not only true of plants and animals – but of human beings as well. Church leaders and others had always thought that human beings were unique – now they were being told that humans were only animals and subject to the same laws as the rest of the animal kingdom.

1. What is meant by the 'Copernican Revolution'?
2. What do scientists mean by the 'Big Bang'?
3. Explain what is meant by evolution.

Science and religion

Religion is, of course, much older than science. Many holy books contain myths or stories to explain how the world and human beings were created. It is natural that many people think that science and religion would always be on a collision course with little agreement between them. There are, however, two interesting thoughts that might challenge this conclusion.

1. Science and religion deal with two different aspects of experience. Science deals with facts and how they should be understood. These facts have to be discovered first and then investigated. To investigate them, we use our five senses – seeing, hearing, touching, tasting and smelling. Religion also claims to deal with facts but these facts are different. These 'facts' are discovered and understood spiritually. To appreciate life fully, we need both a scientific and a religious understanding of things.

2. Most world religions claim that the world was created by God and based on laws that He put in place. Science believes that its task is to discover those laws and then begin to understand them. Science and religion could be the two sides of the one coin. This is why many scientists are also religious believers. Science and religion do not necessarily conflict with each other.

✳ TO TALK ABOUT

In 1999, the *Today* programme on BBC Radio 4 invited listeners to name 'the most significant British figure of the second millennium'. Almost everyone mentioned Shakespeare and Churchill but there was barely a mention of any scientist. Do you think this is surprising?

CHRISTIANITY

What you will learn about in this section:

1. The origin of the world and human life

2. Human beings and animals

3. Christian ideas about stewardship

4. Christian responses to environmental issues

1. The origin of the world and human life

The creation of the world

A 'Creed' is a statement of religious belief. One of the oldest and most important Christian statements of belief is the Nicene Creed, which goes back to the fourth century CE. It opens with the words:

> **I believe in one God ... Maker of heaven and earth, and all things visible and invisible...**

This is the point at which the Bible also begins. The first section of the Bible, which Christians call the Old Testament, is shared between Christians and Jews. This means that they share the same creation story. The first chapters of the Bible (the book of Genesis) tell the story of the creation of the universe, the creation of the world and the creation of the first human beings.

There are, in fact, two accounts of creation in the Bible:

● The first story takes us through the six 'days' of creation during which light and dark; seas and the dry land; plants and trees; the sun and the moon; birds, sea creatures and land animals; and the first man and woman were all created.

Having completed the work of creation to his own satisfaction ('God saw what He had made and was pleased...'), God then rested on the seventh day. Jews believe that this provided the pattern for the seven-day week, with the most important day, the Sabbath day (the day of rest), drawing each week to a close. A close examination of this creation story suggests that there is a real conflict with the picture of the beginning of things that is painted by science. In Genesis, everything appears on earth fully formed, although we are not told how this happened. Science, on the other hand, teaches that plants, animals and human beings have only reached their present state after a very long period of growth and evolution. This life is still evolving today.

● The second story concentrates on the creation of the first man, Adam, and the first woman, Eve. This account tells us that it was God's will to make human beings male and female so that they could support one another and begin the task of populating the earth. This story is called a 'myth' to underline that it is not a literal description of what happened. It does not tell us how the world and human beings were actually created. Instead, it is a myth (a story with a spiritual message) that is designed to teach its readers some important lessons about God and His purpose for the world. If this is true, then scientists and Christians are not necessarily in conflict with each other. Some Christians, called 'creationists', disagree with this way of understanding the story. They maintain that the story explains what actually happened and that the world is only a few thousand years old, since it was created by God. This viewpoint, however, wins very little support from scientists.

TASK 1

1. What is the main difference between the two creation stories that are found in the book of Genesis?

2. Why should there be no conflict between scientists and Christians over creation?

Creation out of nothing

The Bible teaches that God created the world. There is no clear indication, however, as to how this creation took place. It is often assumed that the Bible teaches that God created the world 'out of nothing' (creatio ex nihilo), but this is not necessarily the case. Most Christians accept the scientific explanation of how the world and human beings began without too much trouble.

There are many religious creation myths but the one in the Bible is special. It introduces God at the very beginning of the Bible story and this is the same God who showed Himself later in the Bible to be the Ruler of the universe, the Lawgiver, the Judge, the Living Father, the Lord of History and the Creator. The universe, the world and human beings are not divine – as God is. They are created; God is the Creator. That is the real message behind the two creation stories in Genesis.

2. Human beings and animals

The Fall

The story of creation makes a very important point. The birds, animals and the land creatures were all created on day five, but human beings were created on their own a 'day' later. The creation story makes it clear that there is something special about human beings which makes them very different from animals – they were made in the 'image of God'.

To understand this, we need to take the story a step further. When the first man and woman were created, they were perfect. God placed them in a perfect garden where they had everything that they needed. They didn't even need to work for their food. Everything was provided by God for them to enjoy. God told them that they could eat anything in the garden except the fruit from the tree of knowledge of good and evil, which stood in the centre. It was Satan, disguised as a snake, who tempted them to eat this fruit and, as a punishment for their disobedience, God banished them both from the perfect garden for ever.

As if this were not enough, they were also punished further:

- The man had to work hard in future to tame the earth before any food would grow to feed himself and his family.
- The woman would have to undergo the pain of childbirth.

Yet, despite sin, the image of God in human beings remains. According to the Bible, human beings alone can worship God. This is what makes them different from the animal world and is another difference of opinion between Christianity and science. Science looks upon humans as animals, although their greater intellectual power places them much further up the evolutionary ladder. Christianity teaches that there is a basic difference between human beings and animals. Only human beings bear a spiritual likeness to God.

In the story of creation, we are told that:

> **And God created man in His image, in the image of God He created him, male and female He created them.**
> (Genesis 1.27)

FROM THE SCRIPTURES

Being made in God's image means that human beings share something of His nature. Christians refer to this as their 'spirit' or 'soul'. It is this that worships God. After death, the spirit or soul lives on since it is immortal (eternal).

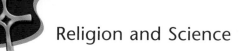

✳ TO TALK ABOUT

Talk with others in your group about those things that make human beings different from animals. In particular, decide what is the biggest difference between human beings and animals.

3. Christian ideas about stewardship

We have seen that the story of the creation of the universe and all forms of life, both animal and human, is told in the opening chapters of the book of Genesis. The description there speaks of the essential goodness of God's creation:

> 66 *God looked at everything he had made and he was very pleased.* 99
> *(Genesis 1.31)*

The creation was perfect and God was totally satisfied with all that He had made.

Christians as stewards

The poem of creation speaks of humanity's God-given responsibility for looking after the earth. The human race is to 'rule over' the earth. It is told:

> 66 *Be fertile and increase, fill the earth and master it;*
> *and rule the fish of the sea, the birds of the sky and all*
> *the living things that creep on the earth.* 99
> *(Genesis 1.28)*

These words have always caused problems to Christian believers – what does it mean to 'rule' and subdue the earth? In the past, people have thought that it gave them the freedom to do as they liked with the earth. Christians no longer think like this. They now know how fragile the world is. Science has taught them this very clearly.

Instead, Christians today believe that human beings have been called by God to be 'stewards' of the world that He has created. This simply means that each generation is responsible for passing on God's good gifts to the next generation in a good shape. A steward is someone who looks after the possessions of their master. The steward is expected to be faithful in carrying out their duties and responsibilities.

The earth does not belong to us. It belongs to God. As stewards, Christians are expected to hand it on to their children and their grandchildren in good condition. That is the responsibility that God has given to each successive generation. In practice, this means that the current generation of Christians must take steps to deal with pollution and the depletion of natural resources now, before the damage to the planet becomes irreparable. They must fight to combat the extinction of vulnerable species. They must struggle to maintain the purity of the oceans, the rivers and the atmosphere.

▶ Christians believe that it is both the grandeur and also the detail of creation that show the handiwork of God.

> **❝** *The earth is the Lord's and everything in it,*
> *the world, and all who live in it;*
> *for he founded it upon the seas*
> *and established it on the waters.* **❞**
> *(Psalms 24.1–2)*

FROM THE SCRIPTURES

4. Christian responses to environmental issues

Christians have not always been as concerned about environmental issues as they should have been. We have already seen that the teaching of the early chapters of Genesis has led many to believe that they could do as they liked with the earth and exploit its resources. Now, though, Christians are showing a much greater awareness of the planet and its many needs. Along with people of other religions, they now know that the destruction of the rainforests, the depletion of invaluable resources, the pollution of rivers, seas and land, and the loss of so many species of animals and plants present the greatest possible threat to the future health and happiness of the human race. They even threaten its very existence. To leave the world a better place means that Christians must not only try to reduce pollution and preserve resources, but also try to improve the standard of living of the less fortunate in the world. Christian stewardship means a fairer sharing out of the world's resources for everyone to enjoy. This is the clear teaching of the **Sermon on the Mount**, in which the teachings of Jesus about a whole range of social issues are brought together.

▲ *Christians try to put the teachings of Jesus into practice in a world that is becoming ever more complicated.*

The teachings of Jesus mean that:

1. Christians have a duty to support and share in the work of groups that try to reduce pollution and conserve resources. There are many such groups in modern society, such as Greenpeace, Friends of the Earth, the National Trust and so on.

2. Christians should be judging what they are doing in their own lives by the standards of Christian stewardship. They have a personal duty to take better care of the planet. Christians should encourage the recycling of resources and make sure that they conserve energy in their everyday lives.

▲ Although recycling facilities are available to everyone in this country, less than 25% of suitable material is recycled.

✳ TO TALK ABOUT

With other people in your group, make a list of as many different ways as possible in which Christians, and others, might work to save the planet.

1. What do Christians mean when they speak of human beings being made 'in the image of God'?

2. Should Christians be particularly concerned about the future health of the planet? Why?

TASK 2

HINDUISM

What you will learn about in this section:

1. The origin of the world and human life
2. Human beings and animals
3. Hindu responses to environmental issues

1. The origin of the world and human life

FROM THE SCRIPTURES

This quotation comes from one of the Hindu holy books:

> *Then neither Being nor Not-being was, Nor atmosphere, nor firmament, nor what is beyond. What did it encompass? Where? In whose protection? What was water, the deep, unfathomable?*
> (Rig Veda, X, CXXIX)

There is no single creation story in Hinduism. There are enough references, however, in the different holy books to suggest that the world was originally made out of nothing. The holy books suggest that a contemplation of the world will leave the observer lost in wonder and amazement. If that happens, then it does not matter too much if we don't know just how the world came into being. Buddhism, which has a very close link with Hinduism, also teaches much the same thing.

One particularly important Hindu myth about creation, however, has had a great influence on the Indian way of life for centuries. The Purusha Sukta talks about a 'cosmic man' who was sacrificed so that the world could be created. This is the first sacrifice, an event that provides a pattern for all later sacrifices that play such an important part in Hindu worship. The myth goes on to show how different parts of the universe were created from the different parts of the body of the cosmic man, called Purusha.

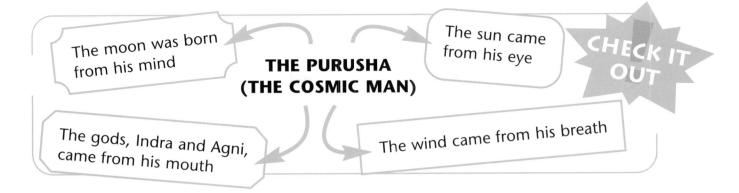

The moon was born from his mind

THE PURUSHA (THE COSMIC MAN)

The sun came from his eye

CHECK IT OUT

The gods, Indra and Agni, came from his mouth

The wind came from his breath

The varnas

The Purusha Sukta states that there were different social groups, or **varnas**, in society that were part of the original creation formed from the body of Purusha. For centuries, these social divisions were a crucial part of the Indian way of life and, although they are now illegal in India, they still greatly affect the way of life of millions in the rural parts of the country.

A cyclical view of history

Christianity, Islam and Judaism teach a 'linear' view of history. This means that history is viewed as having a beginning, a middle and an end. At some time in the future, the whole of history will end. Hinduism, however, has a 'cyclical' view, with history going round in a cycle until it has gone full circle and then the cycle begins again. There have been many such cycles since the beginning of time.

Hindus believe that there is a oneness in the universe and in nature, which was created by God and in which God is present. There is an eternal law of nature and the human soul should seek some form of union with this to find peace with God. After many reincarnations, the Hindu hopes to be absorbed into God and the world. In this cycle, things continually come into existence, grow, change, fade away and die. They are replaced by other things that go through the same cycle. As you can imagine, this idea fits in well with the theory of evolution. There is no real conflict between the teachings of science and those of Hinduism.

1. How does the view of history held by Christians, Muslims and Jews differ from that held by Hindus?

2. What does the Purusha Sukta teach about the creation of the world?

3. What are the varnas?

TASK 1

2. Human beings and animals

Hindus respect animal life more highly than any other major religion. In his avatars (visits to earth), Vishnu appeared on earth disguised as a fish, a tortoise, a boar and a lion. Krishna, one of the avatars, was a cowherd. Many Hindus believe that they have been animals in previous reincarnations and may well reappear as one in a future rebirth. Hindus believe that all forms of life are related to one another because all forms come, in the beginning, from God. Animals are also closely associated with many of the Hindu gods. The very popular elephant-headed god, Ganesha, for instance, is linked with the tortoise.

▲ The cow is a symbol in India for that which gives everything to human beings and asks for almost nothing in return.

Most Hindus express their reverence for all forms of life by following a vegetarian way of life. They cannot kill animals because of the danger of killing someone who, in a previous life, was a human being. Hinduism is committed to the doctrine of ahimsa, which teaches a life of non-violence to all living things. Almost all Hindus believe that the cow is sacred because of its links with the god Krishna. This is one reason why the cow is not slaughtered for food and there are said to be more cows in India than human beings!

TASK 2

Write down three reasons why Hindus have such a high regard for animals and how this is shown.

3. Hindu responses to environmental issues

The forest

The environment is very precious to Hindus and this is especially true of forested areas. The fourth ashrama (stage in life), after that of the student and the householder, is the forest dweller. Hindus believe that forests are pure nature, untouched by humans, and it is by living there that people can find union with God. According to Hindu legends, Krishna spent much of his time in the forest and this also makes it very special for Hindus. Certain trees are also thought to be very special, such as the banyan tree. It was while sitting under this tree that the Buddha was 'enlightened'.

The Chipko Movement

Some 300 years ago, the followers of a Hindu sect, led by a woman, decided to protect trees from woodcutters by embracing the trees so that the workmen would harm them rather than the trees. In 1974, a group of village women hugged the trees that were about to be cut down by a sports goods company, as they knew that this would ruin their lives. Some people recalled a teacher in the fifteenth century who had taught that human beings would be destroyed because they had destroyed nature. So the Chipko (hug-a-tree) Movement began. This Movement, mainly made up of women, was determined that the rapid industrialisation that was taking place in India should not be allowed to destroy the environment. The Movement continues today.

Hinduism and the environment

Hindus have two strong reasons for being deeply concerned about the condition of the world in which they live:

1. Hindus believe in reincarnation and the prospect of returning to the earth many times. It is important, therefore, that the world is preserved. The Hindu teaching is that life will always exist on earth – as long as human beings continue to look after it.

2. Hindus believe that human beings need to work closely with the earth to produce crops. Their faith teaches them that if farmers work with the earth, then the earth will continue to provide the food that they need.

Not all Hindus, however, feel this way. Some Hindus believe that as human beings are the most advanced life form, they can use the earth as they see fit. There is real conflict in India today between those who want industrial progress, whatever the cost, to lift the living standards of the poorest and those who think that the environment must be protected and not exploited.

What are the two reasons why most Hindus are very concerned that the environment should be preserved?

TASK 3

JUDAISM

What you will learn about in this section:

1. The origin of the world and human life
2. Jewish beliefs about the place of human beings in the world
3. Jewish beliefs about the place of animals in the world
4. Jewish responses to environmental issues

1. The origin of the world and human life

Looking after the land

The Jewish holy books, especially the Torah, emphasise the importance of looking after the world that G-d has made. Both Jews and Christians share the same creation story in Genesis, chapters 1 and 2. The emphasis of this story is that it was G-d alone who made the world and that G-d was very pleased with his handiwork.

The Jewish Scriptures emphasise the overwhelming need for the people to look after the land that G-d had provided. The Jews were an agrarian people for whom the land provided all that they needed – as long as it was cared for. They were also a nomadic people who left the land in a good state before they moved on. This is why the Torah stipulated that the agricultural land of Israel must be allowed to lie fallow for one year in every seven – to allow it time to recover. This was linked with the Jewish celebration of the Sabbath day on which human beings were expected to rest just as G-d had rested after six days of creation.

There were other laws in Israel that also set out to safeguard the land on which the nation depended. Fruit could not be taken from a tree, for instance, which was less than two years old, while the owner could not profit from a tree in its third year. It was only in the fourth year after it was planted that a tree could be sold. Today, trees are planted in Israel by Jews from all over the world to celebrate such events as weddings and **bar mitzvahs**.

▲ *Great attempts have been made in recent years to 'green' the country of Israel.*
To help with this, Jews from all over the world have arranged for a tree to be
planted whenever a special event is being celebrated.

G-d's creation is good

Kibbutzim are voluntary collective communities in Israel that started in 1910
and were particularly popular in the 1960s and the 1970s. Some of them grew
their produce in trays that were suspended above the ground during one year in
seven. This gave the earth a rest.

Rabbis have always highlighted that the Genesis account of creation continually
notes that G-d's work is 'good'. The only part of creation that is not described in
this way is the creation of human beings. In his activities, 'man' is told to think
about the effect of what he is doing on the environment. Jews are instructed, in
particular, on the importance of looking after the land when a battle is being
fought. The Torah states that great care must be taken of the trees that grow
around a city that is being besieged. Even if a siege lasts for a long time, the
fruit trees around the city are not to be cut down. The soldiers are told to eat
the fruit but not to destroy the trees. Why?

> **66** *...do not destroy its trees by swinging an axe against them...* **99**
> *(Deuteronomy 20.19)*

✱ TO TALK ABOUT

> **Do you think it would be practical today for farmers to leave every**
> **field fallow for one year in seven so that it could recover from the**
> **previous six years?**

1. Why were the Jews instructed to let every field lie fallow in one year out of seven?

2. How were Jews told to take care of the trees?

2. Jewish beliefs about the place of human beings in the world

Human beings

The first Jewish story of creation makes it clear that the universe and the world were created, followed by the plants, trees and creatures. On the last 'day' of G-d's creative work, He made the first man and woman. The second story, however, is only concerned with the creation of the male and the female and their placement in the perfect Garden of Eden. Without question, they were looked upon as the pinnacle of G-d's creative work. Just how true this is is spelled out in one of the most beautiful passages in the Jewish Scriptures, Psalms 8.2–10. You should read this passage for yourself. As you do so, you will notice two things:

1. The heavens, the moon and stars all declare the glory of G-d. The heavens are described as the work of G-d's fingers! G-d is the Lord of the universe.

2. In comparison with the greatness of G-d's creation, human beings are very insignificant. The writer is simply amazed that G-d should be interested in human beings in comparison with His great creation:

'What is man that you are mindful of him, the son of man that you care for him?'

Yet it is the very frailty of human beings that makes them great. To G-d, they are only a little lower than the angels. In such an exalted position, human beings are:

● 'crowned with glory and honour';

● 'ruler over the works of your hands';

● lord over everything which is placed below their feet – flocks and herds; the beasts of the field; the birds of the air; the fish of the sea and 'all that swim the paths of the seas'.

Human beings are called on by G-d to play a unique part in creation.

3. Jewish beliefs about the place of animals in the world

In the first creation story in Genesis (1.26–28), man was given the authority to 'rule' over 'the fish of the sea, the birds of the air and every living creature that moves on the ground.' In the second creation story (2.19–20), G-d brought all living creatures to the first man and told him to name them. In ancient times, this was significant because naming something was an expression of control over it. Possessing their own animals was very important to every Jew because it was their work in the fields that largely provided the food that kept every family alive. For this reason, it was essential that animals were looked after properly. Jews were told not to muzzle their oxen when they were threshing because it is a cruel thing to do (Deuteronomy 25.4). The writer of the Proverbs makes it clear just how the people were expected to treat their animals.

> **" *The righteous one knows [the needs of] his animal's soul, but the mercies of the wicked are cruel.* "**
> *(Proverbs 12.10)*

FROM THE SCRIPTURES

Perhaps the most important indication of the way that G-d expected all Jews to treat their animals comes in the Ten Commandments, and especially the directive about keeping the Sabbath Day. The Commandments recognised that all human beings needed one day each week on which all work would stop. To mark the Jews out from all the other nations around, however, the prohibition about work on the Sabbath Day also included all slaves – and animals (Deuteronomy 5.12–14). Oxen and donkeys are mentioned, in particular.

At the same time, this Jewish respect for animals did not make them sentimental about them. There is no Jewish tradition of vegetarianism. Animals were also killed as sacrifices in the Jewish Temple, when the blood of animals was believed to cover the sins of the people. Strict rules, however, were laid down to make the act of killing an animal as painless and humane as possible. This was a very important part of Jewish religion until the Temple was destroyed by the Romans in 70 CE. Sacrifices were never reinstated and after this the local synagogue became the centre of the Jewish community instead of the Temple in Jerusalem.

This lack of sentimentality is also apparent in the Jewish attitude towards using animals in medical experiments. Jews cannot support anything that results in unnecessary cruelty to animals. At the same time, they recognise that such experiments are sometimes necessary if advances in medicine are going to be made. In the world that G-d has created, human beings are much more important than animals.

4. Jewish responses to environmental issues

Judaism teaches that the earth belongs to G-d and that human beings have been entrusted with the task of looking after it carefully for Him. Jews believe that the responsibility given to humanity in Genesis 2 means that human beings are expected to use the resources of the earth wisely without any unnecessary waste. They have a 'green' approach to life. The emphasis is on conserving the environment and recycling things rather than just dumping them.

Tu B'Shevat and Sukkot

Religious festivals are a very important part of the Jewish way of life. Two, in particular, teach them about the importance of the environment:

Tu B'Shevat: the special Jewish festival of Tu B'Shevat shows the respect that Jews have for the land and its trees. The beginning of the agricultural year in Israel is marked by the planting of trees in areas where they are most needed. Jews accept that trees need to be cut down for building projects but insist that they are always replaced. This festival has been particularly important since the formation of the State of Israel in 1948, since when, attempts have been made to turn desert areas in the country into useful land.

Sukkot: this festival comes in the autumn months and many Jews build a sukkah (booth) in their garden or outside the synagogue. During the festival, families eat and sometimes sleep in the booth. The roof is made from leafy branches through which it is possible to see the sky. Staying in their booth reminds Jews that they are dependent on G-d and His creation.

Migrash

In building towns and cities, Jews have to follow a principle laid down in their Scriptures called 'migrash'. This principle states that there must be an area of open land around every town that cannot be used in any way – not even for growing crops. This then provides an opportunity for everyone to live in a pleasant environment with space for relaxation. The Talmud goes a stage further, teaching that migrash should be surrounded by a circle of fruit trees. This is intended to keep the environment of the people as pleasant as possible.

The Jewish National Fund

Many Jewish homes and shops show their support for the environment by putting charity money into their blue Jewish National Fund charity collecting box. These familiar boxes were first used in 1904 and, since then, the money collected has bought about 13% of all the land in Israel. To begin with, a large part of the funds was used to develop the land by planting trees. In recent years, however, more attention has been directed to the importance of providing water for drinking and irrigation purposes.

TASK 2

1. Which two teachings are underlined in Psalm 8?

2. Why was it very important for the Jews in ancient Israel to look after their animals very carefully?

3. What can we learn from the Jewish Scriptures about the way that G-d expected Jews to look after their animals?

4. Explain what 'migrash' is and why it was a very important principle in ancient Israel.

5. What is the Jewish National Fund? Research some of its recent activities.

▲ Jewish people try to spend some time in the sukkah, the temporary shelter, during the festival of Sukkot.

EXAM HELP

Make sure that you know about:

CHRISTIANITY

- The Christian beliefs about the creation of the world. Christians and Jews share the same creation story although there are two versions. There are many differences between the two versions of the creation story, which are found in the book of Genesis. The nature of myth. The creationists. The idea of creation 'out of nothing'.

- The relationship between animals and human beings. Humans made 'in the image of God'.

- The fall of human beings from a state of perfection when Adam and Eve sinned in the Garden of Eden. Satan. The punishment of human beings as a result of the Fall – work to subdue nature (male) and the pain of childbirth (female).

- The idea of stewardship. Human beings told by God to 'rule' over the rest of creation. The misuse of creation by human beings through the centuries. Human beings as God's stewards – those who faithfully look after their master's possessions.

- The response of Christians to environmental concerns. The duty to look after the environment.

- Concern for the environment expressed in daily life – recycling etc.

  * Important definitions to learn: Satan, Sermon on the Mount.

HINDUISM

- The varnas. Purusha – the Cosmic Man. The difference between a linear (Christian, Jewish and Muslim) and a cyclical (Hindu) view of history.

- The relationship between animals and human beings. The avatars. Close links between animals and the gods. Ahimsa – non-violence.

- The Hindu response to environmental concerns. The importance of forests – link with Krishna. Chipko Movement. The link between concern for the environment and reincarnation. The belief that God and the environment are one.

  * Important definition to learn: ashrama.

ISLAM

- The Muslim belief that Allah is the Creator of all. Human beings are God's agents and are entrusted with the care of creation.
- The relationship between human beings and animals. Human beings must maintain balance in nature. Loving care must be extended to all animals.
- Muslims and environmental concerns. The Day of Judgement.
  * Important definition to learn: Hadith.

JUDAISM

- The Jewish responsibility to look after the land that G-d has provided – shown by leaving land fallow for one year in seven. Kibbutzim. G-d's creation is good.
- The place of human beings in the world. The greatness of the universe and the place of humans within it.
- The place of animals in the world. Essential care given to animals. Sabbath laws.
- Jews and environmental issues. Festival of Tu B'Shevat. Sukkot – reminder of Exodus.
  * Important definition to learn: bar mitzvah.

EXAM HELP

IN THE EXAMINATION

Here are sample questions for you to try:

CHRISTIANITY

(a) Describe Christian beliefs about how the world began. (8 marks)

(b) Explain how and why a Christian might show concern for the environment. (7 marks)

(c) 'Scientific ideas about how the universe began prove that Christianity is wrong.'

Do you agree? Give reasons to support your answer and show that you have thought about different points of view. You must refer to Christianity in your answer. (5 marks)

HINDUISM

(a) Describe Hindu beliefs about how the world began. (8 marks)

(b) Explain how and why a Hindu might show concern for the environment. (7 marks)

(c) 'Scientific ideas about how the universe began prove that Hinduism is wrong.'

Do you agree? Give reasons to support your answer and show that you have thought about different points of view. You must refer to Hinduism in your answer. (5 marks)

ISLAM

(a) Describe Muslim beliefs about how the world began. (8 marks)

(b) Explain how and why Muslims might show concern for the environment. (7 marks)

(c) 'Scientific ideas about how the universe began prove that Islam is wrong.'

Do you agree? Give reasons to support your answer and show that you have thought about different points of view. You must refer to Islam in your answer. (5 marks)

JUDAISM

(a) Describe Jewish beliefs about how the world began. (8 marks)

(b) Explain how and why Jews might show concern for the environment. (7 marks)

(c) 'Scientific ideas about how the universe began prove that Judaism is wrong.'

Do you agree? Give reasons to support your answer and show that you have thought about different points of view. You must refer to Judaism in your answer. (5 marks)

Exam hints:

These hints apply to each of the religions:

(a) Do not forget that in this question you are being asked to provide facts and not your own opinions. Make sure that your answer is confined to the religion you have studied. Always try to use the correct technical words and language in your answer. You answers must be accurate. You might have a quotation from the holy books that you can use in your answers. It is important to remember that not all members of the same religion believe exactly the same thing.

(b) This part asks you to work out the links between a person's religious beliefs and their attitude towards looking after the environment. The question you have to answer is 'What is the link between a person's religious beliefs and the environment of which they are a part?' You also need to say something about how they put those beliefs into practice – do they, for instance, belong to an organisation that is concerned with looking after the planet?

(c) This section asks you to think carefully about the areas in which scientific information and religious beliefs seem to be in conflict. It asks you to consider more than one point of view. How, for instance, might a Muslim or a Jew explain the apparent conflict between their own beliefs and the scientific evidence? You also need to explain your own opinion and why you hold it.

CHRISTIANITY

What you will learn about in this section:

1. The Christian understanding of body and soul
2. Christians and the afterlife
3. God, the Judge
4. Christian funerals

1. The Christian understanding of body and soul

All of the major religions teach that human beings are more than just a physical body. They also have a spiritual nature that is referred to as their 'spirit' or 'soul'. Although the body and its five senses are involved in religious worship to some extent, religious worship involves the spiritual nature far more.

The Christian belief that everyone is a body and a soul is rooted in the story of creation in the book of Genesis. It says that human beings were created in the 'image of God'. This seems to indicate that something of the nature of God has been built into human beings. Christians have always believed that it is their soul that makes human beings different from the rest of creation. Human beings are a body and a soul. Animals are only a body.

FROM THE SCRIPTURES

This is how the Bible describes the spiritual nature of human beings:

> 66 *...the Lord God formed the man from the dust of the ground and breathed into his nostrils the breath of life, and the man became a living being.* 99
> (Genesis 2.7)

The early Christians

The early Christians were almost all Jews. When they became Christian believers, they still retained their Jewish belief that the body disintegrates after death – but the soul lives on. The soul is immortal and so cannot die. The most prominent of the early believers was Paul and he largely shaped the beliefs of the early

Christians through his preaching and writing. In his letters, Paul wrote of them experiencing a conflict within themselves between their physical desires (the body or the flesh) and their spiritual nature (the soul or the spirit).

▶ *Christians believe that the Resurrection of Jesus guarantees the resurrection of their own bodies and souls in the future.*

In his letter to the Romans, he made this observation about this conflict:

> 66 *Those who live according to the sinful nature have their minds set on what that nature desires; but those who live in accordance with the Spirit have their minds set on what the Spirit desires...* 99
> *(Romans 8.5)*

For Paul, the most important event in history was the Resurrection of Jesus. This was brought about by the power of God, who raised Jesus from the dead shortly after he had been crucified. Christians believe that their own resurrection from the dead is guaranteed by the resurrection of Jesus.

What do Christians believe about the origin of the 'soul'?

TASK 1

2. Christians and the afterlife

In the Gospels, we are told that the body of Jesus was brought back to life by God after he had been crucified. His new body, though, was not the same as it was before he died. People could still recognise him but he could pass through doors and disappear and reappear at will.

Paul believed that the resurrection of Jesus guaranteed that all believers would be raised from the dead. This Christian view of life after death involves two separate beliefs:

1. The resurrection of the body. Christianity teaches that the body of each believer stays in the grave until the end of the world, when everyone is brought back to life. In some way, the actual body of each Christian is resurrected.
2. The immortality of the soul. This is the belief that when a person dies, their soul continues to survive because it is immortal. It is important to realise that Christians do not believe in reincarnation or rebirth.

Heaven

Christians differ in their views about life after death. They all believe, however, that this present life has a meaning and a purpose that is sacred and should not be destroyed by anyone. There are two broad Christian points of view about death and the afterlife:

1. *The Protestant viewpoint:* when people die, they stay in the grave until the end of the world, when God will raise everyone. This will be followed by God's judgement. Everyone, Christian and otherwise, will have to face this judgement. Good Christians will be rewarded by going to heaven while evil people will be punished by being sent to hell.

They believe this because:
- it is what St Paul said in 1 Corinthians 15, where he is writing about resurrection;
- it was the body of Jesus that rose from the dead.

Other Protestants believe that when people die, their soul goes straight to heaven.

They believe this because:
- Jesus said this to one of the thieves who died with him on the cross – 'Today you will be with me in paradise...';
- the soul seems to be separate from the body.

2. *The Roman Catholic viewpoint:* Roman Catholic Christians believe that when people die, the souls of very good Christians are rewarded by going directly to heaven, while other Christians are punished by being sent to **purgatory** to pay for their sins. Very few people are good enough to go directly to heaven. For the vast majority, a time of cleansing and purification is needed. The Catholic Church believes that if those left on earth pray for the people in purgatory, then their time there can be shortened. Intercessions (prayers) can be made through **indulgences** and **penance**. Then, at the end of the world, everyone will be raised from the dead and Christians will go to heaven, while others go to hell. Those who have been in purgatory will be cleansed enough to reach heaven. In the Church calendar, the month of November is set aside to pray for those in purgatory.

They believe this because:

- it is the teaching of the Roman Catholic Church;
- it seems to fit in with the teaching of Jesus and Paul, although neither of them mention purgatory.

In
Memory Of
A Devoted Husband and Wife
MARK AND ANN MAGGS
A Very Dear Dad and Mum
SADLY TAKEN FROM US
IN JANUARY 1994
AGED 80 AND 73 YEARS
Time passes but love and
memories still remain
God bless you both
until we meet again
X X X

Gravestones in Christian cemeteries often express clear beliefs about life after death.

✻ TO TALK ABOUT

There are two Christian creeds that are widely used in worship. Both of them have something to say about life after death:

- **The Nicene Creed: 'I look for the resurrection of the dead and the life of the world to come.'**
- **The Apostles' Creed: 'I believe in ... the resurrection of the body and the life everlasting.'**

Make a list of three things about life after death that these two creeds say.

TASK 2

Explain, in your own words, the differences between the Protestant and the Roman Catholic beliefs in life after death.

Hell

Along with other Jews at the time, Jesus certainly believed in and thought about hell. In one of his most well known parables, Jesus spoke of the time when he would return to the earth and all human beings would be gathered in front of him. He would then divide them into sheep (those destined for heaven) and goats (those destined for hell). You can read this parable for yourself in Matthew 25.31–46.

Christians, through the Middle Ages and beyond, believed strongly in hell as a place of torment and punishment for non-believers. This is reflected in many paintings from the period. Few Christians today, however, believe this because it seems to be in conflict with their belief in a loving and merciful God.

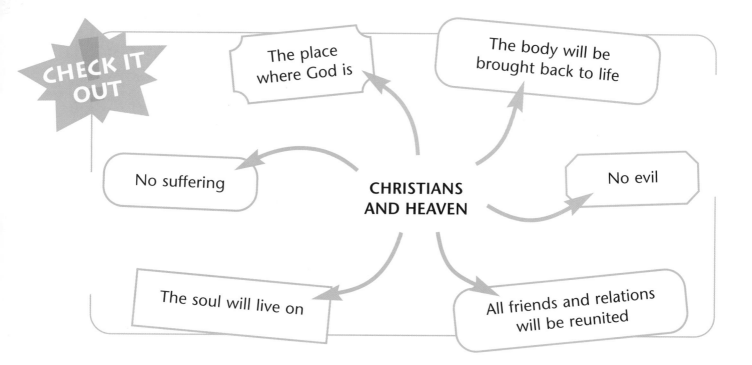

CHECK IT OUT

The place where God is

The body will be brought back to life

No suffering

CHRISTIANS AND HEAVEN

No evil

The soul will live on

All friends and relations will be reunited

Although most Christians accept either burial or cremation these days, some are happier with burial because of their belief in the resurrection of the body at the end of time.

TASK 3

✱ TO TALK ABOUT

Talk with others in your group about the beliefs that you hold about
life after death. In particular:

1. Do you believe in some form of survival after death?
2. If so, what form do you think this survival takes?
3. Do you believe in a form of heaven or hell?
4. Do you believe in resurrection as Christians, Jews and Muslims do
   or in reincarnation as Hindus and others believe?

Write two sentences about the Christian belief in:
a. Heaven **b.** Hell **c.** Purgatory

3. God, the Judge

Christians believe that God created all human beings. Throughout their time on
earth, Christians experience God as love, merciful and gracious. After death,
however, they will stand before God as their Judge. We have already referred to
the parable of the sheep and goats, a story that Jesus told (Matthew 25.31–46)
to teach his followers that they would, one day, have to account for their
actions on earth. Look at the questions that they will be asked by God
according to the parable:

Have they fed the hungry?

Have they given water to the thirsty?

Have they invited the stranger into their house?

CHECK IT OUT

THE SHEEP AND THE GOATS

Have they clothed the naked?

Have they looked after the sick?

Have they visited the prisoner in his prison cell?

Christians believe that God loves and has provided a way for them to be forgiven
when they stand before Him as their Judge. This is their faith in Christ who died
and rose again so that their sins could be forgiven. As John's Gospel tells us:

> **For God so loved the world that he gave his one and only Son, that whoever believes in him shall not perish but have eternal life... Whoever believes in him is not condemned.**
> *(John 3.16–18)*

4. Christian funerals

As we have seen, Christianity strongly teaches that death is not the end and that the soul lives on forever. Christians believe that at the end of time, the body of each believer will be resurrected to share in Christ's own victory over death – this belief is at the heart of every Christian funeral service.

An Orthodox funeral

At a funeral in an Orthodox church:

- As soon as a person has died, their body is washed, dressed in new clothes and placed in an open coffin at the front of a church. The coffin remains open during the whole service to remind everyone that death is God's punishment for sin.

- The tragedy of death is accompanied by the hope of resurrection. This hope is symbolised by the candles that are burning throughout the service and the incense that is sprayed over the coffin.

- Readings from the Bible emphasise the resurrection of the dead and the hope that is shared by all believers in God that death is not the end.

FROM THE SCRIPTURES

The Kontakion is an Orthodox funeral prayer. It contains these words:

> **Give rest, O Christ, to all thy servants with thy saints. Where sorrow and pain are no more, neither sighing but life everlasting. Thou only art immortal, the creator and maker of man, And we are mortal born of earth and unto earth will we return, all we go down to the dust.**

A Roman Catholic funeral

At a funeral in a Roman Catholic church:

- The coffin is taken into the church the night before the funeral so that prayers for the soul of the dead person can be offered. Roman Catholics believe in praying for the dead because their soul will be in purgatory. This is not a belief that is shared by Protestant Christians.

- The priest wears white robes for the funeral – the colour that is traditionally associated with life after death and the resurrection of the body.

- The priest meets the coffin at the door, sprinkles it with holy water and says:

  ❝ *I am the resurrection and the life. Those who believe in me will live; and all those who live and believe in me will never die.* **❞**
  (John 11.25)

The service then takes the form of a **Requiem Mass**, during which the prayer is offered:

❝ *Eternal rest grant unto them, O Lord, and let light perpetual rest on them.* **❞**

A Nonconformist funeral

At a funeral service in a Nonconformist church:

- There will be hymns, prayers, Bible readings and a short eulogy (hymn of praise) about the dead person.
- A short service will be held in church that is likely to be followed by another service, called the 'committal', which is held in the crematorium or at the graveside. In this, the body of the dead person is either committed to the ground or to the flames of the fire – and in either case, to God's safe keeping.

▲ *Christians believe strongly that death is not the end, but the beginning of everlasting life.*

FROM THE SCRIPTURES

These words are taken from a funeral service conducted in the United Reformed Church, but similar words are used in other Protestant services:

❝ *For as much as it hath pleased Almighty God of His great mercy to take unto Himself the soul of our dear brother/sister departed, we therefore commit his/her body to the ground: earth to earth, ashes to ashes, dust to dust; in sure and certain hope of resurrection to everlasting life through our Lord Jesus Christ.* **❞**

✳ TO TALK ABOUT

What beliefs do Christians hold about life after death and how are these reflected in the different funeral services?

The purpose of each life is to perfect one's wisdom and purity of mind. This allows the Atman to escape and reach the final goal of existence, which is called moksha. This is rather like trying to make gold from impure metals – it takes many attempts but, if you persist, you will finally make the most precious metal of all. Hindus believe that karma is the reason why humans and all living beings are continually reborn.

✳ TO TALK ABOUT

Many people criticise the Hindu doctrine of karma – especially when it is used to explain why people are suffering in the present life. They may, for example, be very poor or disabled. How would a Hindu explain their disability? Do you think this is fair?

Karma

'Karma' means 'action' and the law of karma, which Hindus believe covers all of life, is the law of cause and effect. Your present life is unlikely to be your first. The karma from your previous life/lives is carried over into your present existence and beyond. Any evil or selfish actions that you have committed lead to suffering of some kind for you. Unselfish and generous actions, on the other hand, will lead to a happy life.

If you believe in the law of karma, then nothing happens to you by accident. Everything that happens in your present life has taken place because of something you have done in a past life. This, of course, should make you want to live a good life. You can do nothing about the past, but you can influence your future. For traditional Hindus, the caste system can be justified by the law of karma (see 'From the Scriptures'). If you belong to a low caste, or are even an outcaste, you only have yourself to blame.

FROM THE SCRIPTURES

❝ *Those whose conduct on earth has given pleasure, can hope to enter a pleasant womb, that is the womb of a Brāhman, or a woman of princely class, or a woman of the peasant class; but those whose conduct on earth has been foul can expect a foul and stinking womb, that is, the womb of a bitch or a pig or an outcaste.* ❞
(Chandogya Upanishad V X verse 7)

Moksha

Hindus believe that moksha is the state of perfect peace and happiness. This state is described in other religions as heaven or paradise. In Hinduism, it is the bliss of union with God. It is a state in which neither good nor bad things can happen. It is the time when perfect peace and tranquillity fill the soul. Deep knowledge and wisdom beyond all human understanding are experienced. It can be experienced but it cannot be described. You can find some very well known words from one of the Hindu holy books, which attempt to describe moksha.

TASK 1

1. Write down two things that Hindus believe about the body.
2. Write down two things that a Hindu believes about the Atman or soul.
3. What do Hindus believe happens to the Atman when a person dies?
4. What is:
   a. Samsara?   **b.** The law of karma?   **c.** Moksha?

3. Rebirth and moral behaviour

Hindus believe that everything that a person does affects their next rebirth. As we have seen, this is called 'the law of karma' and is one of the most important beliefs in Hinduism. The person who does good deeds in this life will be rewarded when he or she returns in the next life. They may return in a better situation, enjoying the things that were denied to them in this life. The good person will be rewarded in the next life. The person who lives an evil life will be punished in the next life. They may be born into poverty or as a disabled person. The evil person will be punished in the next life. This means that many Hindus try their best to build up good karma during their lifetime.

4. Hindu funeral rites

Before cremation

In Hindu families, the dead body is usually cremated. The only exceptions to this are a child under the age of puberty, a holy man or a pregnant woman. The cremation usually takes place on the same day the person has died because of the hot climate. Soon after death, the body is washed and dressed in special clothes, often a red cloth, by members of the family. It is then carried to the cremation ground on a stretcher. If there is a river nearby, then the cremation ground will be close to it. By tradition, it is the eldest son of the family who leads the funeral party to the cremation ground and the youngest son who leads the party home afterwards.

The funeral rites

If possible, a Hindu hopes to die within reach of the River Ganges. Mourners do not weep for their dead relative since death is seen as a release from this world and the opportunity to come back to a better life. The dead body is sprinkled with sandalwood oil and covered in garlands of flowers. It is dipped once in the river and then placed on a pyre of wood for cremation. The eldest son walks anti-clockwise around the fire – in death everything is reversed – before setting light to it. When the corpse is almost consumed, the son cracks the skull with a long stick to release the Atman. Then he puts the fire out by throwing a pail of water over his left shoulder, before walking away.

▼ *A body is cremated on one of the steps, a ghat, on the banks of the River Ganges.*

In the next day or two, the bones and ashes of the deceased are collected together, placed in a cloth and lowered into a river, preferably the Ganges. If the river is the Ganges, then any further reincarnation is prevented and the person is reunited immediately with God, Brahman. It is almost as good if the ashes are scattered on the waters of another river, since all the waters of the earth eventually join up with each other. That is why Hindus living in Britain are content to have the ashes of a dead relative scattered on the sea.

Helping the mourners

Daily ceremonies (called **shraddha**) are carried out for 11 days after cremation so that the naked soul can find another body in which to enter its next reincarnation. Balls of cooked rice and milk are presented as offerings for the welfare of the dead person's spirit. If this is not done, then the soul will remain as a ghost, haunting and upsetting relatives. Only sons can perform these ceremonies. On the fourth day after the death, friends visit the dead person's house and comfort the relatives, give presents and say prayers for the soul of the dead person. A final sympathy meeting, on the twelfth day, marks the time when the soul is free to pass on to a new life.

✳ TO TALK ABOUT

1. Why do you think that Hindus readily accept death and how does this affect the way that they treat it?

2. Can you imagine a situation in your life or that of a close family member in which death might be almost 'welcome'? If so, describe what it might be.

1. Describe the process of events at a Hindu funeral.

2. How does Hinduism encourage the bereaved to mourn?

TASK 2

ISLAM

What you will learn about in this section:

1. **Muslim beliefs in heaven and hell**
2. **Moral behaviour and life after death**
3. **Muslim funeral rites**

1. Muslim beliefs in heaven and hell

The Day of Judgement

The Day of Judgement, on which all men and women will be called to account by Allah for the way they have lived, is a very important Muslim belief. It is clearly taught in the Qur'an. The shattering events of this day will take place at a time known only to Allah. On that day, life as we know it will end and a new order will begin.

On the Day of Judgement:

1. All of the graves will be opened.
2. All of the dead will be brought back to life.
3. All of the people will stand before Allah, their Judge.
4. Those who have died for Allah in battle will pass directly into heaven (paradise).
5. The deeds of everyone else will be weighed in the balance. Allah's judgement will be shown by the presentation of a book to every person:
   - if the book is placed in their right hand, they can be counted as blessed and will pass directly into heaven;
   - if the book is placed in their left hand, they can be counted among the damned and will pass directly into hell.

Heaven

After judgement, both the righteous and the damned pass over the very narrow Assirat Bridge. Three groups of people will find themselves in heaven:

- those who have lived charitable and faithful lives;
- those who have been persecuted for Allah's sake;
- those who have fought for Allah's sake.

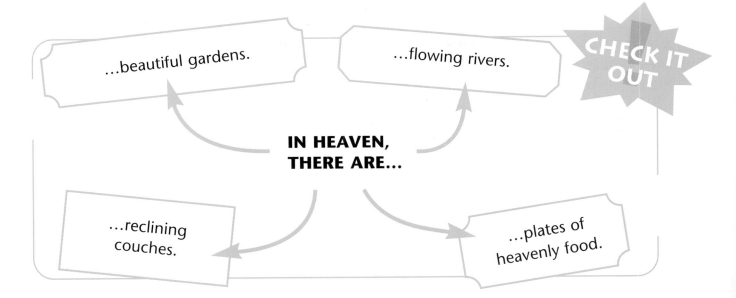

CHECK IT OUT

The imagery of heaven with its rivers, plants and trees is much appreciated by those who have spent their lives living in desert areas. The real joy of heaven, however, is to experience the continual presence of Allah. This is what all true Muslims long for and it will last forever.

> 66 *And he will be in a life of Bliss,*
> *In a Garden on high,*
> *The Fruits whereof (will hang in bunches) low and near.*
> *'Eat ye and drink ye, with full satisfaction; because of the (good) that*
> *ye sent before you, in the days that are gone!'* 99
>
> *(Surah 69.21–24)*

FROM THE SCRIPTURES

Hell

The wicked (those who are damned) will fall off the Assirat Bridge and go down to hell. The suffering of those in hell is eternal and without any respite. The Qur'an describes what happens to them:

> 66 *These two antagonists dispute with each other about their Lord: but*
> *those who deny (their Lord) – for them will be cut out a garment of*
> *Fire: over their heads will be poured out boiling water. With it will be*
> *scalded what is within their bodies, as well as (their) skins.* 99
>
> *(Surah 22.19–20)*

According to Muslim tradition, heaven and hell are both actual and symbolic places. Besides suffering physically in hell, those who are sent there also have 'fire in their bellies'. The last act by Allah is to abolish death so locking the damned into hell forever.

TASK 1

1. What do we know about the Day of Judgement?

2. Write down three things that the Qur'an says about heaven and hell.

2. Moral behaviour and life after death

We have seen that every man and woman will stand before Allah on the Day of Judgement. Each person only has one life and they will be judged on how they have lived it. They will be judged on how well they have followed:

1. The teaching of the Five Pillars (the Shahadah, prayer, fasting, giving alms and the pilgrimage to Makkah) and the rest of the Qur'an. Above everything else, the Five Pillars are a great test of their faithfulness to Allah.

2. The example provided by the life of the Prophet Muhammad ﷺ.

These two guides should have given each Muslim a clear idea of how they should live their lives as Allah intended. They help Muslims to make the right decisions about their own lives and, particularly, the difficult moral choices that they have to make. When they come to stand before Allah on the Day of Judgement, therefore, they can have no excuse.

There is one other consideration that is taken into account on the Day of Judgement. When Allah comes to decide a person's fate, He will not only take into account what they have done, but also what they intended to do. The following quotation from the Hadith makes this very clear.

TASK 2

1. Read the extract from the Hadith in 'From the Scriptures' carefully.

2. Put it into your own words to show that you understand what it is saying.

> **❝** *If a person intends to do something wrong and does not do it, this is a good deed.*
> *If a person intends to do something wrong and does it, this is a bad deed.*
> *If a person intends to do a good deed but cannot manage to carry it out, this is a good deed.*
> *If a person intends to do a good deed and carries it out, this is equal to ten good deeds.* **❞**
>
> *(Hadith)*

3. Muslim funeral rites

As a Muslim approaches death, he or she tries to follow the example of the Prophet Muhammad ﷺ who prayed that Allah would help him through the trial that was fast approaching. Muslims believe strongly in the resurrection of the body and life after death so they approach death with hope. They also hope that they can recite the Shahadah before they die so that their sins will be forgiven. The confidence of each Muslim on their deathbed is in Allah.

Death

Every mosque has a room where dead bodies are prepared for burial. Immediately after death, the body is washed three times in the mosque, wrapped in three white sheets and carried on a stretcher to the place of burial.

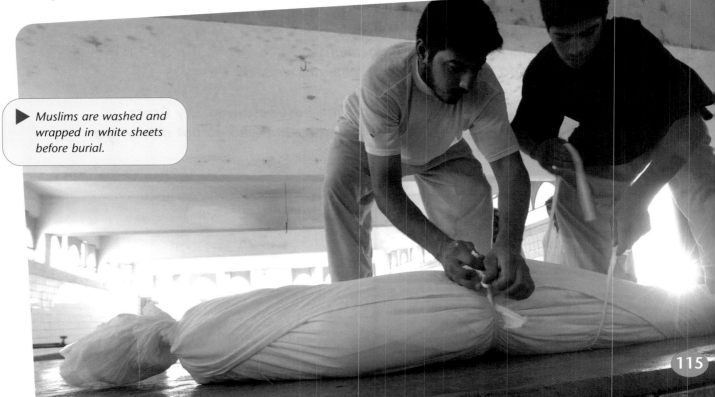

▶ Muslims are washed and wrapped in white sheets before burial.

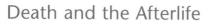

It was centuries later that one of the most important prophets of Israel wrote:

> **Behold, all souls are Mine; like the soul of the father, so the soul of the son, they are Mine. The soul that sins – it shall die.**
> (Ezekiel 18.4)

G-d's judgement

Jews believe that people will be judged by G-d for the lives that they have lived. Everyone is accountable to G-d for their own actions. If they have lived good lives and followed the commandments that G-d has given them, then they will go to heaven. If they have rejected G-d and His commandments, then they will end up in Gehenna, or hell. For Jews, the important thing about life is the way that it is lived here on earth. As a Midrash says:

> **The righteous bask in the ray of G-d's sunshine.**

Jews do not believe in hell as a place of eternal torment. They believe that nothing can be so evil as to deserve eternal torment. The Jewish hell is like a kind of laundry, a process by which the soul is eventually cleansed of its sins so that it can enter G-d's presence.

FROM THE SCRIPTURES

The Talmud tells the story of Elisha ben Abuya, a righteous man who lost his faith and began to commit sins. After he died, the heavenly court was unsure whether he should be rewarded for his righteousness or punished for his sins. Rabbi Meir, his disciple, declared that it would be best for him to be cleansed in hell so that he could draw close to G-d.

Jews also believe in the resurrection of the dead, when souls and bodies are reunited once more. However, the Jewish holy books say little about this. They are much more concerned with the practicalities of serving G-d in the present world.

TASK 2

Describe how Jews are expected to live in this life to prepare themselves for life after death.

4. Jewish funeral rites

The Psalmist leads all Jews to believe that they can hope to live for seventy years (Psalms 90.10) and this is the hope of every believer. Moses, though, lived until he was 120 years old and Jewish people often wish each other 'until 120' on their birthday. For Jews, life is a gift from G-d to be cherished and valued. Death is a tragic, although inevitable, event.

Dealing with death

Each synagogue has its own **Chevra Kadishah** ('holy fellowship') – a group of men and women who are noted for the holiness of their lives. They stay with a dying person and take care of the body once he or she has died. Belonging to this group is considered to be a great honour. The voluntary act of love that its members show to the dead is a true mitzvah (act of kindness) since it is carried out without any thought of reward.

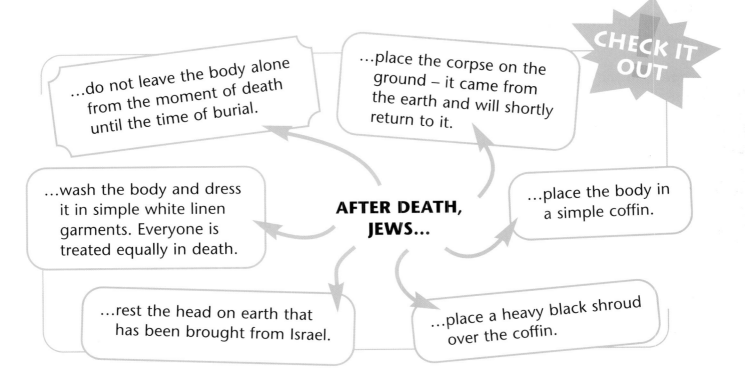

...do not leave the body alone from the moment of death until the time of burial.

...place the corpse on the ground – it came from the earth and will shortly return to it.

CHECK IT OUT

...wash the body and dress it in simple white linen garments. Everyone is treated equally in death.

AFTER DEATH, JEWS...

...place the body in a simple coffin.

...rest the head on earth that has been brought from Israel.

...place a heavy black shroud over the coffin.

The funeral

Jewish funerals take place as soon as possible after death, usually within 24 hours. Orthodox Jews are always buried, but cremation is allowed by Reform synagogues. A Jewish funeral is always very simple. The rabbi delivers an eulogy in praise of the dead person. Psalms from the Scriptures are chanted and the Kaddish prayer is recited.

EXAM HELP

Make sure that you know about:

CHRISTIANITY

- The nature of the soul – the difference between human beings and animals. The conflict between the soul and the body. Body and soul reunited after death.
- Christians and the afterlife. The resurrection of the body and the immortality of the soul. The differences between Protestants and Roman Catholics in their understanding of heaven – purgatory. Christian views about hell.
- God, the Judge. Judgement by God after death.
- Christian funerals. Similarities and differences between funerals in the Orthodox, Roman Catholic and Anglican (Protestant) traditions.
   * Important definitions to learn: purgatory, Requiem Mass.

HINDUISM

- The difference between the body and the Atman (soul). The immortal soul and the fragile body. Reincarnation.
- Samsara. The wandering of the soul from one body to another. Moksha – the end of the cycle of birth, life and death.
- Hindu funeral rites. The importance of cremation and the rites carried out by the eldest son – the value of spreading ashes on running water, the river Ganges if possible. Mourning is carefully structured.
   * Important definitions to learn: moksha, samsara, shraddha.

ISLAM

- Muslim beliefs about heaven and hell. The Day of Judgement. The groups admitted into heaven. Hell.
- Muslim behaviour and life after death. The standards by which people are judged – the Five Pillars and the example of the Prophet Muhammad ﷺ.
- Funeral rites. Muslim hopes before and after death. Mourning.

JUDAISM

- Jewish beliefs about life after death. Lack of clarity in Jewish beliefs. Link between sin and death. Children held responsible for sins of parents. G-d's judgement – responsibility for own actions.
- Jewish funeral rites. The role of the Chevra Kadishah – taking care of death, a true Mitzvah (act of loving kindness). Simplicity of a funeral. The four stages of mourning.
  * Important definitions to learn: Chevra Kadishah, Messiah.

TOPIC 5   Good and Evil

CHRISTIANITY

What you will learn about in this section:

1. Different beliefs about God and Satan

2. Christian responses to the problem of evil and the suffering of Christ

3. Discovering the right way to behave

4. Following a moral code

1. Different beliefs about God and Satan

What is evil?

Suffering and evil present a serious problem for every Christian. The question they have to ask is: 'How can a God, who is all-powerful and loving, allow suffering and evil to exist?' If God is all-powerful, He must be able to do something about suffering. If God is all-loving, He must want to do something about suffering. Suffering, however, continues to exist.

Christians believe that there are two kinds of evil leading to suffering in the world. They are:

1. Moral evil

Moral evil is evil that a person brings upon themselves, or on others, by their own behaviour, ignorance or selfishness. It can be because they are cruel or dishonest. It is the kind of evil that people choose to bring on themselves or on other people. This moral evil takes place because God has given all human beings free will. God has shown all human beings how they should live. It is up to them whether they do what God tells them or not. If they do not live as God intends, then they bring suffering on themselves.

2. Natural evil

Natural evil is very different from moral evil. This is the evil that shows itself through natural disasters, such as earthquakes, hurricanes, floods and disease. This does not appear to be anyone's fault. The problem with natural evil is not so much that it happens, but the unfairness of it all. It strikes people living in certain areas frequently, while other people avoid natural disasters altogether. What's more, those who are affected most are usually the poorest people who are least able to withstand the disaster. Such disasters strike good as well as evil people. The evil people in the world do not seem to suffer any more than the good people. Is that fair?

Famine and poverty are brought about by the selfishness of human beings.

Good and Evil

The aftermath of the 2004 tsunami. Due to global warming, natural disasters are becoming more common but it is usually the poor who suffer most.

Satan

Some Christians believe that there is evil in the world because of Satan. 'Satan' is an ancient Middle Eastern word meaning 'the accuser'. In Christian belief, Satan, or the Devil, was once one of God's chief angels but he rebelled against God by challenging His authority. As a punishment, God expelled Satan from heaven and he made his home in hell. From that moment, he set himself up in opposition to God and set himself the task of trying to lead everyone astray.

There are three places in the Bible where Satan plays an important part in events:

- Genesis 3. This is the story of the first man and woman who, having been created by God, are placed in the perfect Garden of Eden. The woman is then tempted by a snake to eat fruit from the one tree in the garden that God has forbidden them to touch. Traditionally, Christians have understood the snake to be Satan in disguise. Throughout the Bible, he becomes the 'tempter' who tries to persuade human beings to disobey God.

- In the story of Job in the Old Testament, Satan, the Devil, causes a man of outstanding goodness to lose his health, his ten children and his own wealth. Inspite of this, Job refused to take his wife's advice and curse God. He also refused to believe three friends who told him that everything was his own fault. Job eventually found healing and had his fortune restored to him.

- Matthew 4. This is the story of the temptation of Jesus by Satan at the start of his earthly ministry. There were three separate temptations:
    1. To turn stones into bread after Jesus had fasted for 40 days.
    2. To throw himself off the pinnacle of the Temple because, as God's Son, he would be kept safe.
    3. To be given all the kingdoms of the world by Satan if he bowed down to worship him.

According to the record, Jesus resisted all three temptations by quoting from the Jewish Scriptures on each occasion. Then:

> 66 *The Devil left him and the angels came and attended him.* 99
> (Matthew 4.11)

Most Christians today do not believe in an actual Devil. They believe that he is a symbol for all that is bad and evil in human nature.

2. Christian responses to the problem of evil

There are six different Christian responses to the problem of evil and suffering. They are:

Response 1 Suffering is a necessary part of life. You cannot have life as we know it without some kind of suffering. The Christian writer, C S Lewis, lost his wife to cancer less than two years after he married her. After this very sad experience, Lewis wrote: 'Try to exclude the possibility of suffering which the order of nature and the existence of free will involve and you will have excluded life itself.'

He said this because he believed that suffering presents a challenge to human beings to search for inner strength. In a world without suffering, people would have nothing to fight against or to strive for. It is largely this that makes us the people we are. While people are undergoing suffering, or when they come out of the experience, they are much stronger.

Response 2 After death, all the suffering and evil in the world will be forgotten in the joy of a new risen life. The Apostle Paul wrote:

> 66 *I consider that our present sufferings are not worth comparing with the glory that will be revealed in us.* 99
> (Romans 8.18)

Those people who suffer most in this life have most to look forward to after death. This was the theme of the old Negro Spirituals that were sung by people who suffered greatly because they were slaves. They had very little to look forward to in this life – all their hopes were in the life to come.

Response 3 The sufferings of Jesus Christ. Jesus Christ, the Son of God, was put to death by his enemies. This is the supreme example for all Christians who are suffering. Yet Christians believe that God brought him back from the dead. Light and hope came out of his suffering and death. The same will happen to us. The resurrection of Jesus is the strongest guarantee that we will be raised from the dead as well.

Response 4 Suffering is caused by sin. Sin is part of human nature and affects us all. Sin is not just doing wrong, but a whole attitude of heart and mind that leads us away from God and suffering is the result. Much of the suffering that we experience can be traced directly to foolish and sinful actions – either by ourselves or by someone else.

Response 5 Human beings have free will – they are free to choose between good and evil. If people were to become more aware of themselves and others around them, the world would be a much better place. The world could be free of such things as war, disease, violence, cruelty and oppression. Human beings could prevent so much of the suffering that is in the world – if they changed the way that they behave.

Response 6 God suffers alongside his people in the tragedies of the world. God is not outside looking in, but is part of the struggle that involves us all. Christians who believe this say that God actually suffers when other people suffer. They say that God suffered when He saw His Son, Jesus, dying on the cross.

Christians do not believe that there is a single answer to the problem of evil and suffering. They do, however, believe that everything in the end will be made clear – including the reason for suffering. In the meantime, they have to accept that God's will is always done. Suffering has to be accepted. They can reach this acceptance through prayer. Prayer will help them to bring their lives more and more into line with the will of God.

3. Discovering the right way to behave

Christians believe that they are expected by God to live holy and God-fearing lives. This means making the right choices throughout their life and following God's will. There are three ways in which they can know what God expects of them:

Through the Bible

Most Christians believe that the Bible reveals God and His will to them in some way. To find out what this will might be for them, they need to study the Bible and its teachings carefully. To do this, they study the Bible on their own and pray that God, through the Holy Spirit, will help them to understand what it is saying to them. They will probably also meet with other Christians to study the Bible together. They often meet together in the weeks leading up to the Christian festival of Easter, during Lent, to study the Bible's teaching on the death of Jesus. Easter is the most important festival in the Christian year and an opportunity for Christian believers to learn more about their faith.

▲ *Meeting together to study the Bible in a group is an important activity for many Christian believers.*

The idea of meeting with other Christians to study the Bible is so that more experienced Christians can help those who are new to the faith. It is not always easy to translate the teachings of the Bible into the present time. The books of the Bible were written for a very different time and age. Sometimes the teachings of the Bible are simply not relevant to the modern world.

There are, however, universal rules in the Bible that seem to apply to all times and circumstances. Many people, for instance, find the Ten Commandments to be a very good guide for everyday life. The Sermon on the Mount (Matthew 5–7) includes the famous golden rule (Matthew 7.12), which sums up for many the whole teaching of Jesus.

Good and Evil

The golden rule, in almost the same form, is found in both Christianity and Judaism. It says:

> **In everything, do to others what you would have them do to you...**

From the example of Jesus

Most Christians find the example of Jesus, from what we know about him in the Gospels, to be their supreme guide. They believe him to be the Son of God who came to set up the Kingdom of God on earth. He taught people about God and told them how to enter God's kingdom. In the last few days of his life, he showed his followers how to accept God's will, even if that involved intense suffering. He left behind many parables, or stories, which taught others how they might follow his example in their everyday lives.

From their conscience

Everyone has a conscience, although it seems to be stronger in some people than in others. Our conscience comes from a combination of factors, including the influence of our upbringing, our parents, our teachers, our friends and our religious faith. Almost always, our conscience tells us the difference between right and wrong. Our conscience cannot, however, compel us to make the right choice. We can always go against our conscience. That is, of course, when people begin to feel guilty about what they have done.

▲ *Jesus left behind many parables to help others.*

TASK 1

1. What do people mean when they speak of their conscience?
2. Do you think that people should always try to do what their conscience tells them?
3. How can Christians hope to know what God's will is for their lives?

4. Following a moral code

Christians believe that God has a plan for their lives. They also believe that they have been called to live a moral and holy life. Although the Bible is far from being a simple guidebook to living such a life, it does provide Christians with much guidance and help. It is helpful to look at the Bible in this respect in two parts:

The Old Testament The first part of the Bible is the same as the Jewish Scriptures, although the books are in a different order. Although Christians do not follow most of the laws and rules in the Old Testament, which mean so much to Jewish believers, they do find devotional help in its pages. For example, the 150 Psalms are almost as precious to Christians as they are to Jews.

The New Testament There are two important sections in the New Testament and they are very different from each other.

1. The four Gospels record all that we know about the teachings of Jesus. Just as the example of Jesus inspires Christians, so his teachings tell them what is needed to enter the Kingdom of God. Much of this teaching came in the many parables of Jesus. In his Gospel, Matthew brought together the teachings of Jesus on a wide variety of subjects in the Sermon on the Mount (chapters 5–7). At the heart of this is a series of statements about the person who is 'blessed' and these are called the **Beatitudes** (Matthew 5.3–11). This is the clearest statement by Jesus of the kind of people that he expected his followers to be. The Sermon also contains the teaching of Jesus on such subjects as murder, **adultery**, divorce, revenge and loving one's enemies.

2. There are also many letters in the New Testament and most of these were written by Paul. These letters lay down many rules about the problems that early Christians found living in the Roman Empire. Paul gave guidance about some of the issues that Jesus mentioned – adultery, marriage and divorce, anger and so on – but made no reference to the teachings of Jesus. Many Christians today find that the letters of Paul, and others, are very helpful guides to living the Christian life.

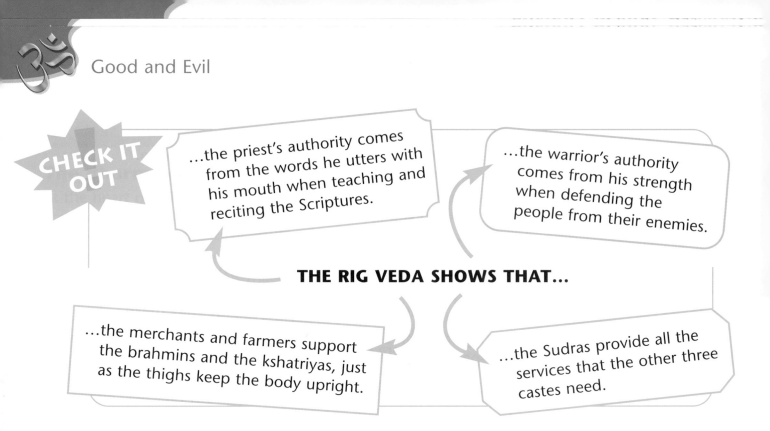

CHECK IT OUT

...the priest's authority comes from the words he utters with his mouth when teaching and reciting the Scriptures.

...the warrior's authority comes from his strength when defending the people from their enemies.

THE RIG VEDA SHOWS THAT...

...the merchants and farmers support the brahmins and the kshatriyas, just as the thighs keep the body upright.

...the Sudras provide all the services that the other three castes need.

The Mahabharata and other holy books

The battle between right and wrong is often the theme of Hindu holy books. The classic example of this is found in the Mahabharata, the world's longest poem. It tells the story of the struggle between two royal families representing good (the Pandavas) and evil (the Kauravas). The conflict between the two families arose over the right to the throne. The Kauravas planned to burn the Pandava brothers alive but they escaped to the forest where they lived in disguise. The greatest warrior among the Pandavas was a skilled archer called Arjuna.

When the Kauravas heard that their father, the blind king, had given 50% of his kingdom to the Pandava brothers, they tricked them into a gambling match. The Pandavas lost their share of the kingdom and were banished to the forest for a further 13 years. When they returned, an enormous battle raged for 18 years, at the end of which, the Kauravas and their army were completely destroyed.

A scene from the holy Hindu book of Ramayana.

The victory of the Pandavas shows that good finally triumphs over evil. This is the theme of many stories in the Hindu holy books. The Pandavas finally retired from worldly activities to the mountains of the Himalayas. There they prepared themselves for the final liberation of their soul and union with God. Traditionally, this is what Hinduism expected old men to do at the end of their lives.

The same theme of good triumphing over evil occurs in other holy books as well. In the Ramayana, it is presented through the story of Rama and Sita, a story which is recited each year at the festival of Divali. The Puranas tell the stories of the miraculous exploits of the god Krishna when he visited the earth as an avatar of Vishnu. They tell how Krishna performed miraculous feats to protect villagers from the disasters of floods. Wherever his influence was felt, there was peace, harmony, goodness and happiness.

4. Following a moral code

Hindus believe that what they do in the present life will affect their state in the next. If they live a good life, then they can hope to return at a higher level – to enjoy a comfortable life without much suffering. If, however, they live a bad and evil life, then this will be reflected in the condition in which they return – they may be poor, disabled and without a large family to support them. The holy books make it clear that living a good life is the only way to be sure of pleasing the gods. Beyond the law of karma, the person who has a good and comfortable life does so for one good reason – he or she has pleased the gods by the life they have lived previously.

TASK 2

1. What is dharma?
2. What is the caste system and what are the four main varnas?
3. Describe one story from the Hindu holy books that shows that good triumphs over evil in the end.

✳ TO TALK ABOUT

Find out from your group how many are inclined to believe in reincarnation. What reasons do other members of the group have for trying to live a good life?

People who respond to Iblis and listen to his lies are like a cancer in Islam. They destroy the faith of many believers. It is for this that they will be brought to account on the Day of Judgement. There is only one real protection against the lies and deceptions of Iblis. Those who wish to remain faithful to Allah must keep Him and the words of the Qur'an constantly in the front of their minds. They must attempt to learn the Qur'an off by heart, pray constantly and give freely to those in need.

2. Muslim responses to evil

The Qur'an seems to suggest that life is a series of tests. Allah has given human beings the great gift of free will. This means that they are free to choose their own path through life. Suffering will happen at some time or other, but those who hang on to their faith in Allah will be blessed in the end.

FROM THE SCRIPTURES

❝ Be sure we shall test you with something of fear and hunger, some loss in goods or lives or the fruits (of your toil), but give glad tidings to those who patiently persevere – Who say, when afflicted with calamity: 'To Allah we belong, and to Him is our return.' – They are those on whom (descend) blessings from their Lord, and Mercy, and they are the ones that receive guidance. ❞

(Surah 2.155–157)

Muslims believe that there is a life after this one that is far more important. In this present life, human beings are on earth to serve Allah, to help others and to comfort them in their suffering.

FROM THE SCRIPTURES

❝ What is the life of this world but amusement and play? But verily the Home in the Hereafter – that is life indeed, if they but knew. ❞
(Surah 29.64)

3. Muslim responses to suffering

Islamic law is based on the principle of justice for all. Justice should always be administered with compassion. Suffering comes about through injustice and a lack of compassion. The Prophet Muhammad ﷺ clearly taught that it is the duty of every Muslim to:

- do good;
- live by the law of Allah;
- oppose injustice;
- relieve suffering.

One of the Five Pillars of Islam is zakah, the obligation of every Muslim to give 1/40 (2.5%) of their income to relieve suffering. Muslims fast during the month of Ramadan, both as a spiritual discipline and also to help them to share in the sufferings of those who are less fortunate. By sharing in this experience, they know what suffering is like and they also do something to relieve it. A Muslim should never be prepared to simply accept suffering in any part of life. Yet in the end, suffering has to be accepted as the will of Allah. Every Muslim must accept this even if he cannot understand it. Allah always knows best. Through prayer, the believer will come to know the will of Allah better and be able to accept it.

The Muslim must make sure that he or she does not add to the amount of suffering in the world. They must give other people what they owe them, weigh their goods with even and fair scales, not cheat them of anything that rightly belongs to them and not corrupt the land with evil. Suffering in any form is against the will of Allah and must be resisted.

4. Discovering the right way to behave

The word 'Islam' means 'submission' to the will of Allah and, to Muslims, this means living by the Five Pillars, the teachings of the Qur'an and following the example of the Prophet Muhammad ﷺ. The Five Pillars stand at the centre of a Muslim's life.

The Five Pillars

Pillar One – the Shahadah (the profession of faith)

No religion carries a shorter statement of faith than Islam – 'There is no god except Allah and Muhammad ﷺ is the Messenger of Allah'. This statement is:

- whispered in the ear of every newborn baby before he or she can hear anything else;
- one of the first sentences that a young child is taught to say;

- repeated several times each day by Muslim worshippers between getting up in the morning and going to bed at night;
- hoped to be the very last utterance that crosses the lips of a dying Muslim.

Six conditions have to be met before saying the Shahadah makes a person a true Muslim. It must be:

1. said aloud;
2. understood perfectly;
3. believed in the heart;
4. professed until the person dies;
5. recited correctly;
6. declared without any hesitation.

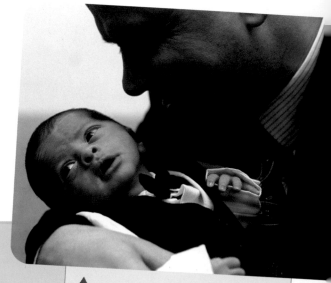

TASK 1

1. Why do you think that belief in Allah comes before the other Pillars of the faith?

2. When would a Muslim be likely to recite the Shahadah?

▲ One of the most important duties of a Muslim father is to whisper the Shahadah into the ear of his newborn baby.

✳ TO TALK ABOUT

Why do you think that Muslims try to ensure that the Shahadah is the first and the last words that each Muslim hears?

Pillar Two – Salah (prayer)

After keeping the Shahadah, the most important religious duty for every Muslim is that of prayer. The Qur'an specifies that prayer must be performed three times a day but Muslim tradition indicates five times – at dawn, noon, mid-afternoon, evening and at night. These prayers may be said anywhere as long as it is a 'clean place', although many Muslim men prefer to pray in a mosque under the direction of the imam.

Prayers must be preceded by washing – called wudu. This washing of the body begins with 'the declaration of intent', in which the worshipper openly declares that he will worship Allah with a pure heart. Then the hands, the mouth, the face, the arms as far as the elbows, the top of the head, the ears, the back of the neck and the feet as far as the ankles are washed three times.

Every male Muslim is expected to be in the mosque for Friday prayers, when the imam delivers his sermon. Otherwise wudu and salah can be performed in the mosque or in any clean place. Prayer for a Muslim involves a sequence of inner and outer actions. Each sequence is called a rak'ah and the number to be performed varies from two to four, depending on the time of day. Each action is accompanied by the recitation of appropriate verses from the Qur'an.

Muslim men often pray in the mosque, but women are much more likely to pray at home.

The performance of the wudu shows that the worshipper is physically clean before he comes to be made spiritually clean by Allah.

Pillar Three – Zakah

From his early experiences as an orphan who had lost both of his parents by the age of six, Muhammad ﷺ knew what it was like to be poor. This meant that he had a special concern for widows and orphans throughout his ministry. He encouraged his followers to give money to the poor as a sign of their devotion to Allah. There are two kinds of almsgiving:

1. The legal requirement – zakah – which amounts to giving 2.5% of personal wealth each year to charity.

2. A voluntary donation that can be given at any time, preferably in secret.

These donations stop people from becoming too greedy or concentrating their mind on simply making money. They also remind them that all wealth is a gift from Allah.

Pillar Four – sawm (fasting)

This specifies that a Muslim must fast during the daylight hours of the month of Ramadan each year. This was the time that the Prophet Muhammad ﷺ received his first revelation from Allah through the Angel Jibril. Those who keep this fast in a spirit of sincere repentance, thought to be 30 times more powerful than fasting at any other time, are assured that their sins will be forgiven.

FROM THE SCRIPTURES

> **"** *O ye who believe! Fasting is prescribed to you as it was prescribed to those before you, that ye may (learn) self-restraint – (Fasting) for a fixed number of days; but if any of you is ill, or on a journey, the prescribed number (should be made up) from days later.* **"**
> (Surah 2.183–184)

▲ Reading the Qur'an is an important accompaniment to fasting during the month of Ramadan.

Fasting is the activity that links together Muslims throughout the world. It is a reminder to those who have never known what it is like to be hungry and poor. It is also an opportunity to concentrate the mind and heart on Allah by praying more and by reading the Qur'an.

Pillar Five – the hajj (pilgrimage to Makkah)

The final duty of all Muslims is to make a pilgrimage to the holy shrine of the **Ka'bah** in Makkah. It is an obligation that has to be met by every fit Muslim at least once in his or her lifetime. The pilgrimage can only be performed between the eighth and thirteenth days of the last month, Dhul-Hijjah, in the Islamic year. Every pilgrim must be able to provide for the needs of their family while they are away and meet the full cost of the journey.

Hajj, meaning 'setting out with a definite purpose', is designed to purify all pilgrims from their pride. It is to make them realise that everyone, rich and poor, will be equal before Allah on the Day of Judgement. It is hoped that the spirit of oneness that all pilgrims experience will remain with them when they return home. Most Muslims find a visit to places closely associated with the Prophet Muhammad ◉ to be a deeply moving spiritual experience.

Muslims want to live according to the will of Allah. The teachings of the Qur'an and the example of the Prophet Muhammad ◉ show that Allah wants them to follow the Five Pillars. These help them to distinguish between what is 'right' and 'wrong'.

FROM THE SCRIPTURES

> 66 *For hajj are the months well-known. If any one undertakes that duty therein, let there be no obscenity, nor wickedness, nor wrangling in the hajj. And whatever good ye do, (be sure) Allah knoweth it. And take a provision (with you) for the journey, but the best of provisions is right conduct.* 99
> (Surah 2.197)

TASK 2

1. Explain each of the following:
   a. Salah
   b. Wudu
2. Why is fasting an important Muslim duty?
3. Why is undertaking a pilgrimage to the holy city of Makkah an important Muslim duty?

✳ TO TALK ABOUT

Why do you think that all pilgrims on the hajj, rich and poor, dress identically? What spiritual lesson do you think this is designed to teach them?

5. Following a moral code

Muslims are helped to follow a moral code by putting the teachings of the Qur'an into practice and following the example of the Prophet Muhammad ﷺ. They gain from these a very clear idea of how Allah expects them to live. They also guide each Muslim to know the difference between 'right' and 'wrong'. The most important thing is for a Muslim to live in submission to Allah. By doing this, each Muslim shows respect for Allah and finds the key to true happiness.

TOPIC 5   Good and Evil

JUDAISM

What you will learn about in this section:

1. The goodness of G-d and the nature of Satan
2. Jewish responses to evil
3. Coping with suffering through acceptance and prayer
4. Following a moral code

1. The goodness of G-d and the nature of Satan

Judaism teaches that those who love G-d and keep His commandments will enjoy His love and mercy. G-d is good and will always care for the universe He has created and the human beings He has made. G-d has shown His goodness by choosing the Jews to be His special people. He gave them the Torah, especially the Ten Commandments, so that they could know the will and purpose of G-d. This is why the Torah is often described as 'G-d's greatest gift' to the Jews.

One theme that runs throughout the Jewish Scriptures is the suffering of the Jewish people. This was believed to be because the Jews failed to live up to the very high standards that G-d expected of them.

Satan

When Satan first appeared in the Jewish Scriptures, it was in the form of a snake – the tempter in the Garden of Eden. There are two further occasions on which Satan appeared:

1. He tempted Israel's much-loved king, David. On this occasion, he tempted him to carry out a census of the number of people in Israel. The temptation behind this was for the king to rely on the weight of numbers in his army instead of relying on G-d for victory in battle (1 Chronicles 21).

2. The story of Job. Job is described in the Jewish Scriptures as a man who:

> **❝** *...was wholesome and upright, he feared G-d and shunned evil.* **❞**
> (Job 1.1)

Satan is described in the book of Job as the Adversary, a supernatural being who had access to the presence of G-d. He challenged G-d to see whether Job continued to believe in Him if he lost everything – his wealth, his property and lands, his family and his health. G-d gave Satan permission to take everything away from Job. He did so. Three friends gave Job advice – based on the assumption that G-d had deserted him. Job, though, remained faithful and eventually everything was restored to him.

2. Jewish responses to evil

When the kingdom of Israel fell in 721 BCE and then the kingdom of Judah collapsed in 586 BCE, the Jews were taken into exile. Many of them were scattered among the other nations. Later, in 70 CE, the Romans suppressed a revolt by the Jews and destroyed the Temple in Jerusalem. This time, the Jews were scattered far and near among the surrounding nations. They were not able to return to Jerusalem for centuries and the Temple was never rebuilt.

Most of the early Christians were Jews and these Christians began to hold the Jews responsible for the death of Jesus. Later, Jews were accused of killing Christian babies and using their blood to make the unleavened bread they used during the festival of Passover.

This false claim, known as the 'blood libel', was the cause of many Christian mobs killing large numbers of Jews in the twelfth and thirteenth centuries. During the Black Death, in the fourteenth and fifteenth centuries, Jews were accused of poisoning wells and spreading the plague. This hatred of the Jews became known as **anti-Semitism**. It continued across Europe in the centuries that followed. It was not until the middle of the twentieth century, however, that it received its most frightening expression, when the Nazi Party was elected to power in Germany.

▲ *For centuries after the crucifixion of Jesus, Christians held Jews responsible for his death.*

The Holocaust

When the Nazis in Germany began to put their plan into practice to eliminate all Jews in the 1930s, many Christians supported them – at least in the beginning.

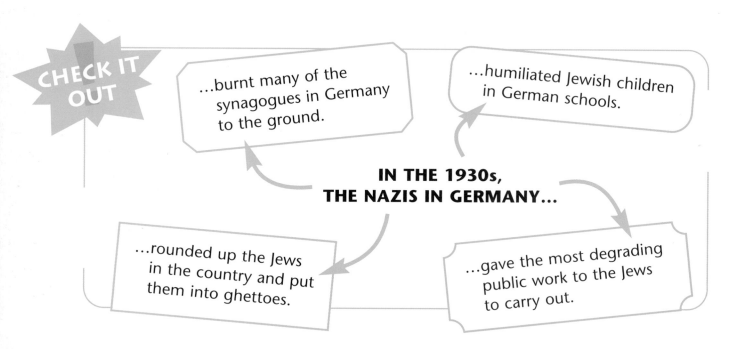

CHECK IT OUT

...burnt many of the synagogues in Germany to the ground.

...humiliated Jewish children in German schools.

IN THE 1930s, THE NAZIS IN GERMANY...

...rounded up the Jews in the country and put them into ghettoes.

...gave the most degrading public work to the Jews to carry out.

During the Second World War (1939–45), over 6 000 000 Jews were murdered by the Nazis. The world describes this event as the **Holocaust** (a burnt-offering). Jews prefer to call it 'Shoah', meaning 'catastrophe'. In this period, 30% of all the Jews in the world died in concentration camps and death camps throughout Europe. In two of these, Auschwitz and Treblinka, over 5000 Jews a day were put to death. The Nazi intention was to wipe out all the Jews in Germany and then, by winning the war in Europe, to eliminate them worldwide. This is called **genocide**.

When the world learned the awful truth in 1945 of what had happened, there were two responses:

1. The non-Jews in the world were determined that no one should be allowed to forget what had happened – and to make sure that it could not happen again. Days of memorial and remembrance were held. Many concentration camps were opened to the public.

2. Many Jews were horrified. They felt that G-d had let them down and should have intervened directly to save them. Some lost their faith in G-d completely. Others, though, believed that the Jewish faith must continue at all costs – to do otherwise would be to hand a victory to Hitler. Despite everything that had happened, however, some Jews believed that G-d had been alongside them in the concentration camps, suffering with His people.

This is the Yad Veshem memorial in Israel, which is a reminder of the millions of Jews who died in the Shoah.

What is meant by:
a. Anti-Semitism?   **b.** The Holocaust?   **c.** The Shoah?

TASK 1

3. Coping with suffering through acceptance and prayer

As we have seen, the Jews have suffered many times throughout their history. Most Jews have been able to accept that this suffering is part of G-d's overall plan for His people. The story of Job in the Jewish Scriptures is an example of this. Although Job suffered greatly, he still did not lose his faith in G-d.

The Day of Atonement, Yom Kippur, is the most serious day in the Jewish year. It is the day which Jews set aside to spend mostly in the synagogue to seek the forgiveness of G-d and other Jews for the sins that they have committed against others in the past year.

▶ *Many synagogues have their own private reminders of the suffering of the Jews.*

4. Following a moral code

Jews believe that they are the descendants of their ancestors Abraham, Jacob and Isaac. Just as those ancestors had a special relationship with G-d, so Jews today believe that they enjoy a similar relationship with the Almighty. This relationship, called a 'covenant', was first made with Abraham and had two parts to it:

- It stated what G-d promised to do for the Jews. He promised to provide them with a homeland of their own.

- It outlined what G-d expected from the Jews in return. He expected them to remain faithful to Him and keep His laws. G-d spelled this out when He gave to them the 613 mitzvot (laws) and, in particular, the Ten Commandments. These mitzvot were written down, and recorded, in the five books of the Torah. These books are the most precious part of the Jewish Scriptures.

For centuries afterwards, Jewish teachers, or rabbis, explained to the people what the mitzvot in the Torah meant. These comments were handed down from generation to generation – which is why they are called the 'oral Torah'. In the second and third centuries CE, the work of collecting them together began. This was finally published as the Talmud. It is used to settle any legal disputes between Jews. It also helps Jews to decide how they should live their lives day by day. Jews can also consult their rabbi if they are unsure about how they should behave or find guidance through following their own conscience.

▶ *There is a strong Jewish tradition that Jewish men should study their Scriptures together.*

EXAM HELP

Make sure that you know about:

CHRISTIANITY

- The basic problem that suffering presents to the Christian. Moral and natural evil. The three instances where Satan appears in the Bible.
- Christian responses to the problem of evil. The six different Christian responses.
- Christians and the will of God for their lives. The importance of reading and studying the Bible, the example of Jesus and following one's own conscience.

  * Important definition to learn: Beatitudes.

HINDUISM

- Good and evil. Everything, including good and evil, are found in God. Future rebirth is dependent on present good and evil actions.
- The response of Hindus to good and evil. Karma – explains the wide differences in the fortunes of people. The duty to help others.
- Discovering the right way to behave. Dharma. Ahimsa. The four social groups. The conflict between the Pandavas and the Kauravas. Good triumphing over evil in the holy books.
- The importance of following a moral code. The link between what a person does in this life and the way that they come back in the next.

  * Important definition to learn: dharma.

ISLAM

- The goodness of Allah and the evil deeds of Iblis. The Bismillah.
  The 99 names of Allah.
- The eight characteristics of Allah. The argument between Allah and Iblis – the character of Iblis.
- The Muslim responses to suffering. The duties of every Muslim – to do good, live by the laws of Allah and relieve suffering. Zakah. Suffering is God's will.
  * Important definitions to learn: Iblis, Kab'ah, rak'ah, salah, sawm, zakah.

JUDAISM

- The goodness of G-d and the nature of Satan. The Jews as G-d's chosen people – expected to love G-d and keep His commandments. The Torah expresses the will of G-d.
- The suffering of the Jews throughout history.
- Jewish responses to evil. Frequent experience of exile. Anti-Semitism.
  The Holocaust. World responses to the Holocaust.
- Making moral decisions. The Covenant and its importance to all Jews.
  The Torah as G-d's most important gift to the Jews.
  * Important definitions to learn: anti-Semitism, genocide, Holocaust.

EXAM HELP

IN THE EXAMINATION

Here are sample questions for you to try:

CHRISTIANITY

(a) Describe Christian beliefs about the reasons for there being evil in the world. (8 marks)

(b) Explain how a Christian might find out the right way for him or her to behave. (7 marks)

(c) 'People should try to be happy, there is no point in them trying to be good.'

Do you agree? Give reasons to support your answer and show that you have thought about different points of view. You must refer to Christianity in your answer. (5 marks)

HINDUISM

(a) Describe Hindu beliefs about the reasons for there being evil in the world. (8 marks)

(b) Explain how a Hindu might find the right way for him or her to behave. (7 marks)

(c) 'People should try to be happy, there is no point in them trying to be good.'

Do you agree? Give reasons to support your answer and show that you have thought about different points of view. You must refer to Hinduism in your answer. (5 marks)

ISLAM

(a) Describe Muslim beliefs about the reasons for there being evil in the world. (8 marks)

(b) Explain how a Muslim might find the right way for him or her to behave. (7 marks)

(c) 'People should try to be happy, there is no point in them trying to be good.'

Do you agree? Give reasons to support your answer and show that you have thought about different points of view. You must refer to Islam in your answer. (5 marks)

JUDAISM

(a) Describe Jewish beliefs about the reasons for there being evil in the world. (8 marks)

(b) Explain how a Jew might find the right way for him or her to behave. (7 marks)

(c) 'People should try to be happy, there is no point in them trying to be good.'

Do you agree? Give reasons to support your answer and show that you have thought about different points of view. You must refer to Judaism in your answer. (5 marks)

Exam hints:

These hints apply to each of the religions:

(a) This part is asking you to give information about the religion you have studied and not your personal opinions. Everyone accepts that there is evil and suffering in the world but how does your chosen religion explain this? Is it put mainly down to the existence of an evil force – such as Satan (Christianity and Judaism) or Iblis (Islam)?

(b) There are two main ways in which different religions teach that people can discover the right way for them to behave. The first is by studying their holy books. Religious people believe that this is the main way that God speaks to them. The second is through their own conscience if they are prepared to listen to it.

(c) Here you are being asked to give your own personal opinion but you are also asked to refer to your chosen religion and its teachings as well. This is not a sentiment that a religious person would express. All of the religions, in their own ways, believe that human beings are expected to try to live good lives – although they accept that people will often fail in this quest.

CHRISTIANITY

What you will learn about in this section:

1. The roles of men and women within a Christian family
2. The Christian marriage ceremony
3. Christian beliefs about divorce
4. Christian beliefs about sexual relationships
5. Christian beliefs about contraception

1. The roles of men and women within a Christian family

There are different attitudes in Christianity to the role of men and women in the modern family. We can separate these out into:

The traditional viewpoint: many Christians believe that men and women have separate and different roles to play within marriage and the family. They believe that:

1. It is the role of the woman to have children, to bring them up and to run a Christian home for the family. It is believed that women must submit to their husbands in the home, accepting his overall authority.

2. It is the role of men to provide for the physical needs of their families by bringing in a regular wage. They should lead the family in religious matters, including worship in the home. Men should love their wives as much as they love themselves and take the lead in church life.

This teaching is based upon the writings of Paul in the New Testament about women not being allowed to teach or speak in church. It is based on the account of creation in Genesis 2, where the man was created by God first. It was only after he was given the task of naming the animals and returned to tell God that he could not find a close friend from among them that God created the woman. God created Eve to be Adam's 'helpmate'. This attitude also comes from the teaching of Peter (1 Peter 3.1–7) where he encourages husbands to be considerate to their wives and to treat them with respect 'as the weaker partner'.

Only a few Christians in Western countries today accept this teaching at its face value, although it is more widely accepted in some African countries.

a. 　**" *Wives, submit to your husbands as to the Lord. For the husband is head of the wife as Christ is the head of the Church ... Husbands, love your wives just as Christ loved the church ... In the same way, husbands ought to love their wives as their own bodies. He who loves his wife loves himself ... each one of you must love his wife as he loves himself and the wife must respect her husband. "***
(Colossians 3.18–19 and Ephesians 5.25.28)

b. 　**" *A woman should learn in quietness and full submission. I do not permit a woman to teach or have authority over a man; she must be silent. For Adam was formed first and then Eve. And Adam was not the one deceived; it was the woman who was deceived and became a sinner. "***
(1 Timothy 2.11–14)

The modern viewpoint: most Christian Churches now accept that men and women are equal – and they have female vicars, ministers and priests. Among these Churches are the Anglican Church, the Baptist Church and the Methodist Church. Also, within family life, most Christian couples accept that this is the best way to organise their lives in the twenty-first century.

They accept this as coming from the ministry of Jesus who:
● treated men and women as equals;
● preached in the Court of the Women in the Jerusalem Temple (Matthew 21.23–22.14);
● treated a Samaritan woman as his equal (John 4);
● had women followers who stayed with him at the cross (Matthew 27.55) and ministered to him. Although there were no women among the 12 disciples of Jesus, there were many women who travelled with him and supported him in many ways;
● first appeared to women after his resurrection before appearing to his male disciples.

This is the teaching that is followed by the vast majority of Christians in Western countries.

2. The Christian marriage ceremony

The Order of Service

The Order of Service outlined on p163 comes from the Church of England. Most denominations follow a similar pattern. To begin with, the couple are reminded that their marriage is taking place 'in the sight of God'. Although there must be a minimum of two witnesses at a wedding, the most important witness to a Christian wedding is God. The couple are then reminded of the three purposes of marriage:

1. To provide each other with mutual help and support in both the good and the bad times together.

2. To have sexual intercourse in a secure environment where both man and woman can feel equally loved.

3. To have children and bring them up in a Christian home.

Christian marriage is intended to be a lifelong commitment between two people – broken only by the death of one of the partners. This is why, in all services, the couple promise that they will be faithful to each other 'until death us do part'. The vows that the couple take cover the whole range of human experience through which they are likely to pass – health and sickness, poverty and plenty. Through all of life's experiences, the couple promise 'to love and cherish' one another until the end of their days. Rings are exchanged as a visible sign of the vows that they have taken. The ring, a perfect and unending circle, symbolises that love which, it is hoped, will last and grow through life into eternity.

▼ Rings are exchanged as a visible sign of the vows that a couple have taken.

✳ TO TALK ABOUT

Here are two comments for you to discuss in a small group before reporting back to your class:

1. 'Before embarking on marriage, it is a good idea for a couple to live together for a year or so. At least they would then know if they wanted the arrangement to be permanent.'

2. 'Sex before marriage is acceptable for both Christian and non-Christian young people.'

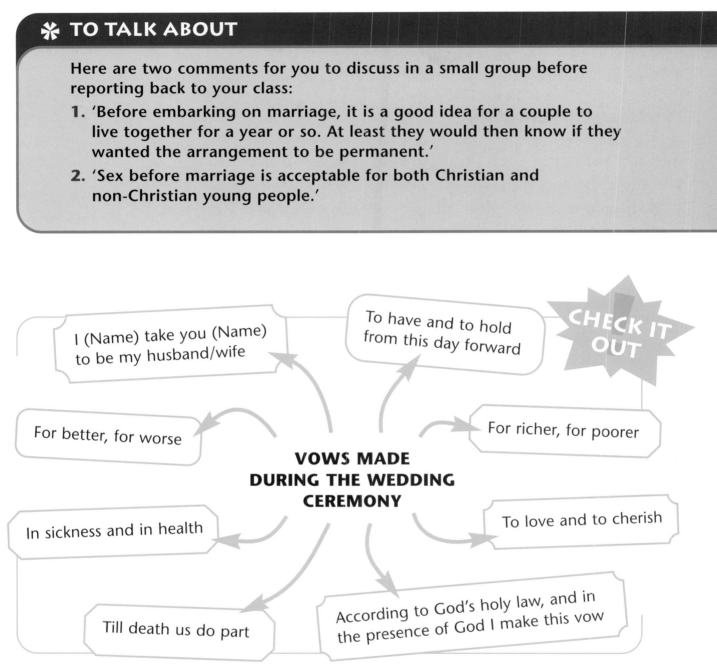

I (Name) take you (Name) to be my husband/wife

To have and to hold from this day forward

CHECK IT OUT

For better, for worse

For richer, for poorer

VOWS MADE DURING THE WEDDING CEREMONY

In sickness and in health

To love and to cherish

Till death us do part

According to God's holy law, and in the presence of God I make this vow

(Taken from *The Anglican Book of Common Worship*, 2000)

Variations

There are two important denominational variations in the wedding service:

1. Roman Catholics and many other Christians believe that marriage is a 'sacrament'. A sacrament is a Christian service that is a special way in which God passes on his blessing to the couple. It is an outward sign of an inward blessing from God. Catholics believe that, in marriage, each partner becomes a channel of God's blessing to the other. This is why a wedding service involving two Roman Catholics ends with a **Nuptial Mass**.

2. In the Orthodox Church, the service is called the 'crowning', during which crowns are placed on the heads of the man and woman. In this way, the two of them receive the power of the Holy Spirit to love each other and any children that they may have. The crowns indicate both joy and self-sacrifice.

Christian teaching about marriage

As you would expect, the wedding service reflects, and underlines, the most important beliefs that Christians hold about marriage.

1. In the beginning, marriage was designed and created by God.

2. Marriage is a solemn agreement between two people that is made in the presence of God.

3. Marriage is the only suitable relationship in which sexual intercourse can take place.

4. Marriage is the ideal relationship in which to have and bring up children.

5. Marriage is intended to be a permanent relationship.

6. Within marriage, the couple are intended by God to be sexually faithful to each other.

TASK 1

1. There are two broad approaches within the Christian community to the roles expected of men and women within family life. Describe both of them, showing that you understand the main differences between them.

2. What are the three purposes of marriage that are underlined in a Christian wedding service?

3. Describe the main features of a Christian wedding ceremony.

4. Outline the Christian teaching about marriage.

3. Christian beliefs about divorce

It is commonly argued that as more marriages are now likely to end in divorce than ever before, so the idea of marriage for life is increasingly unrealistic. It is true that the number of divorces in the UK has increased from 26 000 a year (1960) to over 170 000 today. Today, one in four of all UK marriages ends in divorce.

The Bible and divorce

In the Old Testament, Moses, the great Jewish law-giver, allowed the Jews to divorce because the people failed to live up to God's ideal of marriage. Yet this was always a compromise and not part of God's original plan.

By the time of Jesus, it was very easy for a man to obtain a divorce, but He taught that a man is only allowed to divorce his wife if she has been unfaithful to him – (Matthew 5.31–32). In Mark's Gospel, however, there were no grounds for divorce (Mark 10.11–12). Jesus said that anyone who leaves their wife and marries someone else commits adultery (Mark 10.11–12) and that was forbidden in the Ten Commandments (Exodus 20.14). A Jewish woman at the time was not able to obtain a divorce under any circumstances.

Paul also had much to say about marriage. He taught that a man must not divorce his wife in any circumstances. A wife should not leave her husband but, if she did, then she was to remain unmarried or return to her husband (1 Corinthians 7.10–11).

> 66 *Haven't you read … that at the beginning, the Creator made them male and female and said, 'For this reason a man will leave his father and mother, and be united with his wife; and the two will become one flesh. So they are no longer two but one. Therefore what God has joined together, let man not separate.'* 99
>
> *(Matthew 19.4–6)*

FROM THE SCRIPTURES

Divorce and the law

1857 For the first time, it became possible in England and Wales for both men and women to obtain a divorce. Men could divorce their partner on grounds of adultery alone, while a woman had to prove the adultery and the cruelty of her husband.

1923 Men and women could obtain a divorce on the same grounds.

1937 Desertion, cruelty and insanity added to adultery as grounds for divorce.

1969 For the first time, it became unnecessary to prove that someone was to 'blame' for the breakdown of a marriage. Instead, divorce was allowed if a 'marriage had irretrievably broken down'. Adultery, cruelty and desertion could be used to prove that this had happened.

Christian Churches and divorce

The Christian Churches have different attitudes to divorce:

1. The Church of England accepts divorce as a social necessity but will not remarry divorced people unless the vicar agrees. Instead, it usually encourages couples to marry in a civil ceremony and then go to church afterwards to receive a blessing from the priest.

2. The Free Churches, such as Baptist and Methodist, allow divorced people to remarry in church, although individual ministers can refuse to conduct the ceremony if it conflicts with their own beliefs about marriage and divorce.

3. The Roman Catholic Church believes that marriage is a sacrament and so cannot be dissolved. Instead, it encourages those whose marriage has broken down either to separate from their partners but remain married or seek an **annulment**. After an annulment has been granted by the Roman Catholic Church, it is as if the marriage never took place. An annulment can be granted if:

- it can be shown that the couple did not fully understand what they were doing when they married;
- one of the partners did not give their full assent to the marriage;
- one of the partners did not intend to have children at any time and the other person did not realise this.

TASK 2

1. State two reasons why many Christians believe that divorce is always wrong.
2. The remarriage of divorced persons is allowed in some churches but not in others. Give one reason for this.
3. How has the law relating to divorce changed since 1857?

4. Christian beliefs about sexual relationships

Because of its ability to hurt others, society and the Christian Church place strict control on sexual behaviour. In the UK, it is illegal for anyone to have sex with someone who is under the age of 16. Surveys show that only 20% of men and women are virgins when they marry, with over 50% losing their virginity before they reach their eighteenth birthday.

Sex and marriage

Although Christians hold different views about sexual relationships, many believe that all sex outside of marriage is wrong. Here we are talking about two different situations:

1. Pre-marital sex. This is sex that takes place between two people who are not married. Pre-marital sex can be between two people who are in a steady relationship with each other or it can be casual sex between two people who hardly know each other. The two situations raise very different moral questions.

2. *Extra-marital sex.* This is sex that takes place between two people, one or both of whom are married – but to someone else. Sex in this situation is adultery. Of course, the marriage may have broken down but the Church doesn't see any difference if this has happened. All sex outside of marriage is a sin.

There are many reasons why sex outside of marriage has become much more common.

- Effective contraception is now freely available for both married and unmarried couples to use.

- If contraception fails, then an **abortion** could be available. With the 'morning-after' pill, which ends conception if taken within four days of sex by aborting the foetus, no one has to go through with a pregnancy they do not want.

- Fewer people expect their partners to be virgins when they marry them.

- Fewer people accept the teaching of the Christian Church which has always been against sex before, and outside, of marriage.

Yet a high price is often paid by many people for their promiscuous sexual activities. Sexually transmitted diseases, such as gonorrhoea and herpes, are increasing steeply. AIDS is spreading, more unwanted and unplanned babies are being born because people often do not use contraception and thousands of marriages are breaking up each year because one, or both, partners have been unfaithful. Christians believe that this goes against God's intention for sex – to cement a marriage relationship and to bless people with the gift of children. Jesus frequently spoke out against fornication (pre-marital sex) and adultery (extra-marital sex). Christians believe that sex is a God-given way for two people to express their love within marriage.

Celibacy

Celibacy is a chosen way of life that excludes marriage and sex. It has been associated with the Roman Catholic Church and its priests for centuries. In the New Testament, Paul was certainly unmarried. He commended the celibate state of those who wished to devote themselves fully to the service of God. In 1139, the Catholic Church decreed that all of its priests should be celibate – the only Church to have made such a demand. Many church members have demanded a change in this rule, particularly in recent years, as the number of men entering the priesthood has gone down dramatically. The rule, however, remains in place. Pope Paul II declared that the rules about priests being celibate would not change.

Christians are bitterly divided on the subject of homosexual behaviour. There are many Christians who are homosexual, including many priests. The Roman Catholic Church is strongly opposed to homosexuality. Although there are many Anglicans who are homosexuals, the Anglican Church in many parts of the world, especially Africa, teaches that such sexual behaviour is a sin.

▲ All Roman Catholic priests have to be celibate and many have left the priesthood as a result, often to marry.

5. Christian beliefs about contraception

The Christian Churches and contraception

The Roman Catholic Church is the only Christian denomination that is strongly opposed to contraception (birth control). It teaches that the love between a husband and a wife leads naturally to having children, since children go to the very heart of that relationship. This is why the Catholic Church teaches that, in the words of Pope Paul VI, '…each and every marriage [sexual] act must remain open to the transmission of life.'

In 1968, he published an encyclical (document) entitled *Humanae Vitae (On the Regulation of Life)*, which outlawed the Pill and the condom as well as sterilisation as methods of contraception for all Roman Catholics. Natural methods of birth control, however, were allowed and encouraged. This means that it is acceptable for a couple to take advantage of those days in the menstrual cycle when a woman may be infertile to have sex. Only 'natural' forms of birth control were said to be in keeping with the purposes of God for married life. Otherwise the couple must abstain from sex if they do not want to have a baby.

Roman Catholics in the USA and Great Britain were deeply upset by this teaching. Surveys suggest that as many as 80% of them ignored the Church's teaching on contraception at the time of the encyclical and continue to do so today. If they do not want to have a baby, they use a reliable method of birth control – against the teaching of the Church.

Most Christians regard sex as one of God's greatest gifts to them and so one to be enjoyed. Sex is for creating new life but it is also to express the depth of love that two people have for each other. Contraception, in removing the fear of an unwanted pregnancy, is to be welcomed. The Protestant Churches, including the Church of England, believe that all forms of contraception are right as long as they are acceptable to both partners. This allows a couple to decide when they would like to have a baby.

TASK 3

1. **a.** Explain the difference between pre-marital sex and extra-marital sex.
    b. Why are many Christians opposed to all sex outside of marriage?
    c. Why is more sex taking place outside of marriage and what are some of the possible consequences?

2. Explain the different attitudes that some Christians have towards contraception.

✳ TO TALK ABOUT

Do you think that children are, in any way, a gift from God? Explain your answer, whatever it is.

HINDUISM

What you will learn about in this section:

1. The roles of men and women within a Hindu family
2. The Hindu marriage ceremony
3. Hindu beliefs about divorce
4. Hindu beliefs about sexual relationships
5. Hindu beliefs about contraception

1. The roles of men and women within a Hindu family

In traditional villages, Hindu men are still seen as the protectors and providers for their family, while women are the childbearers who take the major responsibility for bringing up their children and looking after the home. However, since India gained independence in the 1940s, women have received equality in the eyes of the law and this is very noticeable in the towns and cities. They now have equal voting rights and, for several years, India had a female Prime Minister.

Hindu women are looked after by their fathers until they marry and then their husband takes over this responsibility. This is the reason why the birth of girls is less welcomed in Hindu families than that of boys, as they are a heavier financial responsibility. The education of girls is less thorough than that of boys since boys will need to earn money when they leave school to look after their family and ageing parents. It is comparatively rare for an Indian woman to have a career of her own, although it is beginning to happen more. It is their responsibility to take care of the family puja (worship) and maintain the home shrine. The woman is also expected to make sure that the family carries out its religious responsibilities and observes the religious festivals correctly.

All Hindu men hope that they will have sons. The main reason for this is that the eldest son in the family is responsible for carrying out the correct ritual when their father dies.

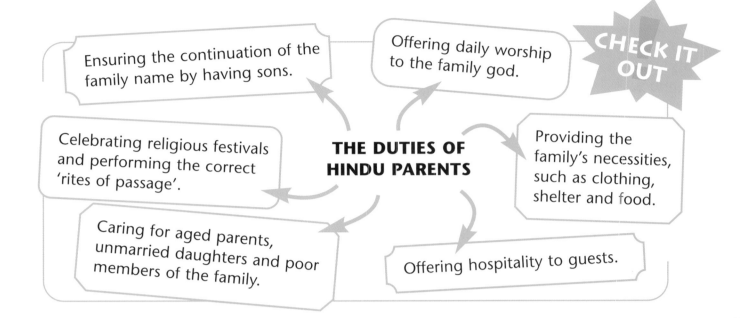

Ensuring the continuation of the family name by having sons.

Offering daily worship to the family god.

CHECK IT OUT

Celebrating religious festivals and performing the correct 'rites of passage'.

THE DUTIES OF HINDU PARENTS

Providing the family's necessities, such as clothing, shelter and food.

Caring for aged parents, unmarried daughters and poor members of the family.

Offering hospitality to guests.

Rama and Sita

The story of Rama and Sita is told in the Ramayana and they are believed by Hindus to be the ideal married couple. Rama is the ideal ruler while Sita gave up her life of riches so that she could look after her husband when he was banished to the forest. Sita remained faithful to her husband and carried out his bidding. Rama protected his wife and placed his life at risk to rescue her when she was captured. Sita showed all the virtues expected of a Hindu woman and is always held up as a shining example to Hindu girls.

2. The Hindu marriage ceremony

In the Hindu faith, a girl may marry at 15 and a boy at 18. A Hindu must marry someone of the same caste and faith – with the marriage being arranged by the parents and relations. Hindus believe that karma destines them to marry a certain person and it is up to their parents to find that person for them.

▶ *A Hindu husband promises that he will look after his wife as her father did before she married.*

A Hindu bride prepares herself carefully for her wedding. Friends rub henna over most of her body and special attention is paid to her eye make-up. A new sari is worn with gold and red bangles and jewellery. A spot of washable powder is placed in the centre of her forehead to show that she is blessed. All married Hindu women wear this spot in public.

The wedding ceremony

The wedding ceremony takes place around the sacred fire, which is a sign of the pure presence of God. The priest, who conducts the service, keeps the fire going throughout the service by pouring ghee (melted butter) on to the flames. He also throws the traditional Indian symbols of rice and spices on the fire to guarantee that the couple will be fertile and have many children. The bride's family 'hands her over' to the groom by placing her hand in his and then her brothers pour fried rice over the clasped hands to show that they agree with the marriage. The couple then take seven steps around the fire, making a promise with every step and offering a separate prayer with each step:

- Step one: to provide for their household
- Step two: to develop physical, mental and spiritual powers
- Step three: to increase wealth by good and proper means
- Step four: for future wisdom and happiness
- Step five: for the blessing of children
- Step six: for self-restraint and a long life
- Step seven: to be true companions and remain life-long partners.

For the last circuit of the fire, the couple's clothes are tied together.

A Hindu marriage is not binding until the couple have taken the last step. Marriage is then a lifetime commitment. The couple go outside to look at the Pole Star together. As they do so, the bride promises her husband that she will be as constant as the Pole Star in her love for him. She also says that she will not stand in the way of any good and righteous actions that he might wish to perform.

1. Read carefully the words that the bride and groom say to each other during the wedding service ('From the Scriptures'). What do you think each of these phrases means?

   a. 'With utmost love to each other may we walk together…'

   b. 'May we make our minds united, of the same vows and the same thoughts.'

   c. 'I am the wind and you are the melody. I am the melody and you are the words.'

   d. 'Let the heart of yours be mine and the heart of mine be yours.'

2. In a Hindu wedding service, what do the seven steps around the sacred fire symbolise?

> *With utmost love to each other may we walk together…*
> *May we make our minds united, of the same vows and the same thoughts.*
> *I am the wind and you are the melody. I am the melody and you are the words.*

On the last step, the couple say to each other:

> *Into my heart I take thy heart*
> *Thy mind shall follow mine,*
> *Let the heart of yours be mine*
> *And the heart of mine be yours.*

✳ TO TALK ABOUT

Arranged marriages are the norm in Hindu societies, but not in the UK. A Hindu woman pointed out recently that in Western countries, couples meet, fall in love and then fall out of love. Hindu couples meanwhile are introduced by their parents, marry and grow into love. Do you think that she had a good point?

3. Hindu beliefs about divorce

Although divorce is not actually forbidden in Hinduism, it is not encouraged either. Many Hindus would not consider applying for a divorce if they follow the Hindu faith seriously. Divorce is possible if a husband is cruel, or if a couple have been unable to have children after 15 years, or more, of married life. Adultery by the husband is not, in itself, grounds for a divorce. The Laws of Manu, a highly respected Hindu holy book, states that a woman should respect and obey her husband even if he has been unfaithful to her. Remarriage after divorce is legally possible, although rare in Hindu society. Some people, however, do advertise in newspapers for new partners.

4. Hindu beliefs about sexual relationships

Hindus regard their sexuality as a positive and natural part of their life – and an important source of pleasure. When they reach the right age, Hindus are expected to marry and have children. Those in the student stage of life and those in the retiring stage are expected to abstain from sex. Sex should be restricted to marriage, the second stage in life. Traditionally, a couple who retire at the age of 50 are expected to stop their sex life and live together as companions. This was the time in the past when the man was expected to go off in search of God. Few Hindus today, however, choose to enter this fourth stage of life.

Many Hindu religious images show sexual activity. The god Krishna is said to have stolen the clothes of the cowgirls while they were bathing so that they had to come out of the water naked. The god Shiva is often represented by the lingam, the upright penis, as a symbol of fertility.

Adultery is not allowed. It is a betrayal of one's partner. It is also a betrayal of one's dharma and so prevents moksha. Hindu marriage is the union of two families and not just two people. Adultery could lead to the breaking of this bond, which could have serious repercussions for all the people involved in Hindu society.

The Hindu Scriptures are largely silent about homosexuality. This may be because homosexuality between men or women would be extremely unusual in a Hindu society. Not to marry and have children appears to most Hindus to be a violation of their dharma. In fact, few Hindus do not marry. Homosexuality is not unknown but it is a taboo subject.

5. Hindu beliefs about contraception

India has a population of over one billion people. Each year, this figure increases by a further 17 million – equivalent to the population of Australia. The vast majority of the world's Hindus live in India. The attitude of Hinduism to contraception must be seen against the background of this population explosion.

With a high level of poverty in India's country areas and many slums in the cities, it is very important that the population growth is controlled. This goes against the advice of the many Hindu holy books. They advise husbands to cohabit with their wives at the right time in the month so that they will have many children. In particular, each traditional Hindu family hopes to have at least one son to perform the funeral rituals for their parents properly. Hindu parents have always wanted many children to look after them when they are old, so as to avoid being very poor and lonely in their old age.

The situation now, however, is very different, especially in the towns. With better food and medical facilities, many more children are surviving beyond their early years. The Indian government has encouraged people to reduce their family size so that their standard of living can go up. Hindu leaders have supported this advice. To reduce the size of their families, most educated Hindus now use contraception. The only condition is that the contraception used should be acceptable to both husband and wife.

▶ *This is a family planning clinic in India. Gradually, more and more people in the country are limiting the size of their families.*

ISLAM

What you will learn about in this section:

1. The roles of men and women within a Muslim family
2. The Muslim marriage ceremony
3. Muslim beliefs about divorce
4. Muslim beliefs about sexual relationships
5. Muslim beliefs about contraception

1. The roles of men and women within a Muslim family

The Qur'an teaches that the main purpose of married life is that the husband and wife should have children and bring them up to be good Muslims. In the home, the husband and wife have their own clear responsibilities. Parents must set their children a good example by respecting the requirements of **halal** – the Muslim food regulations. In the family, parents have several responsibilities to their children. They are expected to teach them:

- to pray (salah);
- to read the Qur'an, including teaching them the Arabic language, if possible;
- the basic beliefs of the faith;
- to observe the fast of Ramadan.

This means that children are gradually introduced to these religious activities as they grow older. Muslim children also attend a religious school, called a madrasa, in which the teaching of their parents is supplemented. For most children, this takes place outside their normal school hours.

The husband and wife have clear roles to play in the family. Men must work hard to provide for their family while women bear and bring up the children.

▲ *Children in madrasa.*

▲ *Muslim parents are expected to take the important decisions for their children until they are old enough to take them for themselves.*

Muslim women have the right to study, own property and conduct business in their own name, whether they are married or not. They can also refuse to marry if they wish. In a Muslim marriage, men and women complement each other. They are not competitors. They are expected to work together for the well-being of their children. The Qur'an, however, emphasises that it is the husband who should have the final word in all family decisions.

2. The Muslim marriage ceremony

The Qur'an encourages Muslims to see marriage as a life-long partnership. Because of this, the Muslim community emphasises the importance of choosing the right partner. In most communities, all members of the close family are involved in making this decision. Although most Muslim marriages are 'arranged', however, they cannot go ahead without the full agreement of both partners. The Qur'an makes it clear that the only genuine marriage in the sight of Allah is one into which the man and woman have entered voluntarily and freely.

The dowry

An essential part of the wedding agreement is the bridal dowry. This is something that still plays an important part in the marriage arrangements of many religions. The size of the dowry usually depends on the social standing of the bride and the customs of her local community. Money or goods are given

4. Muslim beliefs about sexual relationships

Sex, being natural, is accepted by Muslims as good, as long as it is used in the right way. Muhammad ﷺ said that people who had unlawful sex would deserve and receive punishment from Allah. He also said that the right use of sex would bring a reward from Allah on the Day of Judgement.

It is expected that Muslims will marry since they have the right to enjoy sexual fulfilment and marriage is essential for this. Islam has never taught that anything is to be gained by denying oneself sexually. There are no monks or nuns in Islam. Islam seeks what is natural and also that which makes peace between people. For this reason, marriage is the only situation in which sex can be enjoyed. Sex outside of marriage is severely punished. Homosexuality is considered unnatural and forbidden in Muslim countries. Adultery can cause distress and so is against the peace and unity of the Ummah.

When in public, Muslims are expected to cover up certain parts of their body so that they do not tempt others sexually. To do this is a sign of modesty – recognition that the sexual parts of the human body should only be uncovered to one's husband or wife. In many countries, this means that the only parts that can be shown in public are the face and the hands. Every other part is covered. Men are required to cover themselves from the navel to the knees. In private, however, husbands and wives are encouraged to make themselves sexually attractive to each other.

5. Muslim beliefs about contraception

Contraception was allowed by Muhammad ﷺ and is widely used by Muslims. Some Muslims, though, argue that it should only be allowed in three situations:

- where a woman may be harmed or her life put in danger if she were to have more children;
- where having another baby would almost certainly lead to the family living in poverty;
- where there is a real possibility that a baby will be born with a mental or physical disability.

Others argue that contraception is always wrong because it interferes with the natural laws of life.

Many Muslim couples hope to have a son and will not use contraception if they only have daughters. This attitude, however, is more to do with tradition than religion. Muhammad ﷺ condemned those in his day who allowed baby daughters to die because they wanted the economic benefits that only male children could bring.

▲ *In Islam, fatherhood and motherhood are seen as a natural part of being a man and a woman. Muslims believe that parents share in the creativity of Allah.*

1. **a.** Describe what Muslims believe about sexual relationships.
   b. How do Muslims try to make sure that sexual temptation is not presented?
2. What do Muslims believe about contraception?

TASK 2

JUDAISM

What you will learn about in this section:

1. The roles of men and women within a Jewish family
2. The Jewish marriage ceremony
3. Jewish beliefs about divorce
4. Jewish beliefs about sexual relationships
5. Jewish beliefs about contraception

1. The roles of men and women within a Jewish family

Family life is at the very centre of Jewish religion. More religious activities take place at home than in the synagogue. Orthodox and Reform Jews, however, have very different attitudes to the roles that men and women are expected to play in religious and family life:

The Orthodox view

The Jewish laws (mitzvot) are taken by Orthodox Jews to refer mainly to men. Women have always been exempted from the vast majority of them because their supreme obligation is to care for their families. Until fairly recently, Orthodox women married early, had many children and spent most of their lives raising children. They were not even expected to attend the synagogue. In Orthodox Judaism, women cannot form a **minyan** (the number of Jews needed to be present for a service), nor can they say prayers at home or in the synagogue unless a man is present. This is because the role of a Jewish Orthodox woman is to run a kosher home and bring up her family. The role of an Orthodox man is to provide for all his family's needs and keep all the mitzvot that G-d has given. Orthodox Jews believe that it is best to keep to this way of life because it is what G-d demands.

The Reform view

In Reform and Progressive Judaism, there is a very different attitude to women. Women have equality with men:

- They can pray with men.
- They can be part of a minyan.
- They can be rabbis.
- They can initiate a divorce.
- They can be witnesses in court.

These differences with Orthodox Judaism are only possible because Reform Jews do not follow the Torah and the Talmud literally. They believe that some of the laws in the holy books do not apply to life today.

▶ *In Reform Judaism, there are women rabbis, but not in Orthodox Judaism.*

TASK 1

What are the differences between the roles expected of women in an Orthodox and a Reform family?

2. The Jewish marriage ceremony

Although the main purpose of marriage in Judaism is to provide a home for children, it also exists, in the words of one of the marriage blessings, '...to give joy, and gladness, mirth and exultation, pleasure and delight, love, peace and friendship' to the couple.

The marriage service

According to Jewish law, the service must involve a Jewish man and woman and be held in a synagogue. Jewish marriages cannot be held on the Sabbath Day or on any festival day. The service begins with the signing of the wedding document – the **ketubah** – by the groom in front of two witnesses. This document sets out the man's responsibilities towards his wife, but does not contain any promises for the woman to make. The whole intention of the document is to offer the woman future security.

Following the signing of the ketubah, the couple are taken by their parents to stand under the **huppah** – a canopy that symbolises the home that the couple are going to set up together. Following this, there is a blessing over a glass of wine and, as they sip from the same glass, the groom places a simple ring on the bride's right hand. As he does so, he says:

> **Behold thou art consecrated to me by this ring, according to the law of Moses and Israel.**

The ketubah is then read aloud.

A further blessing is made over the wine and seven blessings are then pronounced. Here is a shortened form of the seven blessings:

1. Blessed are You, our G-d, King of the universe, Who has created everything for His glory.
2. Blessed are You, our G-d, King of the universe, Who fashioned the Man.
3. Blessed are You, our G-d, King of the universe, Who fashioned the Man in His image, in the image of His likeness.
4. Blessed are You, Who gladdens Zion (Jerusalem) through her children.
5. Blessed are You, our G-d, King of the universe, Who created joy and gladness, groom and bride, mirth, glad song, pleasure, delight, love, brotherhood, peace and companionship.
6. Blessed are You, Who gladdens the groom with the bride.
7. Blessed are You, our G-d, King of the universe, Who creates the fruit of the vine.

After they are finished, the bride and the groom again sip a glass of wine and the groom then crushes the glass beneath his feet. The purpose of this is to remind the couple on their happy day of the destruction of the Temple in Jerusalem. It is also a reminder that there will be difficult and shattering days as well as happy ones ahead of them in their married life together.

TASK 2

Write a description of a Jewish wedding, placing an emphasis on the different symbolic acts that take place in the service.

3. Jewish beliefs about divorce

Although Jews marry for life, they do accept that some marriages break down. Jewish tradition lays down a procedure for obtaining a divorce without either person having to prove the 'guilt' of the other person. After a divorce has been agreed by the civil courts, the couple appear before the **Beth Din** (the 'House of Judgement'), which is a Jewish court made up of three rabbis. Only the Beth Din can grant a religious and final divorce. As in Islam, a divorce cannot take place for three months to make sure that the woman is not pregnant.

Within the Orthodox community, a man must issue his wife with a **get** (bill of divorcement) before a divorce is finally granted. Without a get, the woman is not free to remarry. Even if a husband has left his wife, he can still refuse to grant her a get and this does happen fairly often. Reform Jews, however, believe that this is unfair and a wife can obtain a get even if the husband refuses to sign it.

4. Jewish beliefs about sexual relationships

Sex within marriage is regarded by Jews as a good and natural thing. It is the duty of every Jewish man to marry and have a family. In the account of creation in Genesis, men and women are told to be fruitful and increase in number. The same account says that it is not good for man to be alone, giving this as the reason for G-d creating Eve. In the Talmud, there is a saying, '…without a wife man is incomplete.' Sex outside of marriage is strongly condemned. Adultery is strongly criticised as it is outlawed by the seventh Commandment and elsewhere in the Torah. This law is very important for religious Jews, as are all of the Commandments.

There are many rules to protect people from sexual temptation. Unmarried men and women should not be together in a closed room or house. Men are warned not to be close to women and they should not have a position of authority over them that would allow them to become too close. Men are also warned not to gaze on the beauty of women, smell their perfume or walk behind them! Although few Jews observe all of these rules, boys and girls are brought up separately in strict Orthodox communities. In Orthodox synagogues, men and women sit separately while worshipping.

These rules are designed to avoid those situations in which people may be sexually tempted.

There are strict rules in the Jewish Scriptures about purity. During her monthly period, and for a week afterwards, a woman is not allowed to have sexual intercourse. She is then expected to take a ritual bath called a **mikveh** after which she can resume normal sexual relationships with her husband.

> A mikveh bath where women have traditionally washed after their period has finished to make themselves clean.

FROM THE SCRIPTURES

> **" You shall not approach a woman in her time of unclean separation, to uncover her nakedness. "**
> *(Leviticus 18.19)*

All homosexual relations were forbidden in the Torah.

5. Jewish beliefs about contraception

There are differences of opinion within the Jewish community about contraception. Some Orthodox Jews think that the only acceptable method of contraception is the rhythm method (natural birth control) because G-d intended sexual intercourse for the procreation of children. There is certainly a strong Jewish tradition that a large family is a happy one. Reform Jews, though, believe that any form of contraception is acceptable since G-d has provided new scientific advances to increase human happiness.

Jews generally are prepared to accept contraception if the following circumstances apply:

- the couple already have at least two children;
- there is a risk to the physical or mental health of the mother if another baby is conceived;
- the family could not afford another baby;
- there is a risk of a new baby inheriting a genetic disease from its parents.

If a couple agrees that using a contraceptive is desirable and necessary, there are two principles that should guide their choice of method used.

1. The contraceptive device should not detract from the pleasure of their sex life.

2. The contraceptive should not work by bringing about an abortion.

1. **a.** What is the generally accepted attitude towards contraception in Judaism?
   b. Make a list of the reasons on which this attitude is based.
   c. Explain why some Jews would disagree with this attitude.

2. What guidance are Jews given about sexual relationships and their dangers?

TASK 3

❊ **TO TALK ABOUT**

'Contraception is a gift of G-d to make life better.' Do you agree? Give reasons for your opinion, showing that you have considered another point of view as well as Judaism's.

EXAM HELP

Make sure that you know about:

CHRISTIANITY

- The role that men and women are expected to play in a Christian family. The two broad attitudes to this – the traditional and the modern. The former linked with the teaching of Paul.
- The Christian wedding ceremony. The three purposes of marriage. Marriage is a lifelong commitment. The Roman Catholic and Orthodox services and their variations. The six beliefs that Christians hold about marriage.
- Christian beliefs about divorce. Teaching of the Bible. Teachings of different Churches.
- Christian teaching about sexual relationships. Pre-marital and extra-marital sex. Sex outside marriage – reasons for and consequences of. Celibacy.
- Christians and contraception. Roman Catholic teaching. Protestant teaching.
  * Important definitions to learn: abortion, adultery.

HINDUISM

- The roles of men and women in Hindu families. Hindu women and their fathers before marriage. Hindu women and their husbands after marriage. Greater equality in town areas.
- The Hindu marriage ceremony. Arranged marriages. The seven steps around the holy fire.
- Hindus and divorce. Divorce not encouraged or forbidden.
- Hindus and sexual relationships. Marriage and sexual pleasure encouraged. The second stage of life.
- Hindu beliefs about contraception. Conflict between India's population problems and teaching of holy books. Encouragement to reduce family size.

ISLAM

- The roles of men and women. Division of responsibilities. Responsibilities of parents to children. Husband, the provider. Wife, the homemaker.
- Muslim wedding ceremonies. The bridal dowry as important protection for wife. Marriage is lifelong. Wedding ceremony civil and not religious.
- Muslim beliefs about divorce. Divorce is the 'most hated of all lawful things'. The three steps before divorce.
- Muslim beliefs about sexual relationships. Sex is important when used properly.
- Marriage and sex always go together. Adultery is strongly condemned. Modesty about the body in public.
- Muslim beliefs about contraception. Most Muslims use contraception without problems. Some teach that it should only be used in certain situations.
  * Important definition to learn: Ummah.

JUDAISM

- The roles of men and women. Family is very important in Judaism. Differences between Orthodox and Reform views.
- The Jewish marriage service. The signing of the Ketubah. The chuppah. The seven blessings. The crushing of the wine glass.
- Jewish beliefs about divorce. The role of the Beth Din. The importance of the get.
- Jews and sexual relationships. Sex within marriage good and natural. Jewish duty to marry and have children. Adultery strongly condemned – seventh commandment.
- Rules to protect against sexual temptation.
- Jews and contraception. Differences of opinion among Jews about contraception. Most Jews use contraception.
  * Important definitions to learn: Beth Din, get, ketubah.

Religion and Medical Ethics

INTRODUCTION

> 66 *It was You who created my conscience; You fashioned me in my mother's womb.* 99
> *(Psalms 139.13)*

Followers of each religion covered in this book believe in a God who created everything in the beginning. The same God continues His creative work in the world today. The religions also agree that all life is a free gift from God. This life is sacred or holy. Religious people who believe that all human life is sacred to God often use the phrase 'the Sanctity of Life'. God creates all new life in His own good time and ends it when He chooses. It is against the will of God to interfere with this process unless it is for a very good, life-giving, reason.

All religions also teach that human beings are free to believe, or not to believe, in God. God has given all human beings the gift of free will. Without this gift, human beings would be little more than puppets or robots. It is possessing free will that makes human beings different from all other animals. This freedom brings with it huge responsibilities. Sometimes the choices that human beings have to make is literally between life and death. These choices are so serious that no human being will take them lightly. This is particularly true in the areas of abortion and **euthanasia**. A study of 'medical ethics' leads us to consider several matters in which a course of action and a person's moral/religious beliefs could come into conflict.

Abortion

'Abortion' means the termination or ending of the life of a foetus in the womb of its mother. Until 1967, all abortions in the UK were illegal and thousands of 'backstreet' abortions were carried out each year. This illegal operation placed the life of the woman at great risk and many women died as a result. The 1967 Abortion Act was amended in 1990 and now abortions are legal as long as they take place before 24 weeks of pregnancy – unless the life of the mother is at risk later than this.

...her life is at risk.

...the doctors agree that an abortion is necessary.

...there is a risk of injury to the woman's physical or mental health.

CHECK IT OUT

A WOMAN CAN HAVE A LEGAL ABORTION IN THE UK AS LONG AS...

...there is a risk that another child in the family would threaten the mental or physical health of existing children.

...there is a substantial risk that the baby might be born physically or mentally disabled.

The crucial question in all discussions about abortion is, 'When does life begin?' There are three possible answers to this question and a person's attitude to abortion depends, to a large degree, on which answer they choose.

Answer 1 Life begins at conception. Many religions believe and many 'Pro–life' groups (those against abortion) are convinced that life begins when the sperm and the ovum fuse in the woman's uterus.

Answer 2 Life begins at some definite point during a pregnancy but no one is quite sure when. Some people think that life begins when the baby starts to move in the womb. People in many religions believe that there is a definite point when God implants the soul so that the foetus becomes a sacred, spiritual life.

Answer 3 Life begins when a baby is capable of living on its own, outside the womb. Until the baby could survive on its own if it were born, the baby remains a part of its mother – dependent on her for its survival. The foetus only has a claim on its mother if she deliberately set out to become pregnant.

There is no clear medical answer to the question, 'When does life begin?' This makes discussion about the ethics of abortion very difficult.

Fertility treatment

Difficulties in conceiving a baby affect 10% of all couples. People in this group would not become parents without help. This is when many of them turn to medical science to help them. There are different ways of assisting conception:

In vitro **fertilisation** 'In vitro' means 'in glass' and people often refer to this method of conception as having a 'test-tube baby'. The technique was developed to help women with blocked fallopian tubes to conceive, since their eggs could not reach their uterus for fertilisation. To solve the problem, the woman is given drugs to help her produce eggs, which are then collected, fertilised with the

CHRISTIANITY

What you will learn about in this section:

1. Christian attitudes to abortion
2. Christian attitudes to fertility treatment
3. Christian attitudes to euthanasia
4. Christian attitudes to suicide
5. Christian beliefs about the use of animals in medical research

1. Christian attitudes to abortion

The Roman Catholic Church and abortion

The majority of Christians feel very unhappy about abortion. The Didache, the oldest known Christian document, goes back to about 70 CE and states:

> *You shall not kill by abortion the fruit of the womb and you shall not murder the infant already born (infanticide).*

The Roman Catholic Church expresses the strongest objection of any Christian Church to abortion. The Second Vatican Council of the Catholic Church stated:

> *God, the Lord of Life, has entrusted to men the noble mission of safeguarding life ... Life must be protected with the utmost care from the moment of conception: abortion and infanticide are abominable crimes.*

It is argued that abortion denies a baby the most fundamental human right of all – the right to life. This life, the Church teaches, begins the moment that a baby is conceived. The destruction of the foetus in the womb is considered to be the same as murder. So important is the life of the unborn baby that, if there is a choice, the life of the baby should be saved ahead of that of the mother. The Catholic Church supports those organisations – such as LIFE and SPUC (Society for the Protection of the Unborn Child) – which oppose abortion in all circumstances.

Protestant Churches and abortion

The Church of England, like other Protestant Churches, believes that abortion is an evil that should be avoided if at all possible. However, it can be justified if:

- there is a risk to the physical health of the mother;
- there is a risk to the mental health of the mother;
- a disabled baby is going to be born;
- the pregnancy is the result of the woman being raped.

The debate about abortion is very important to Christians of all denominations. These are the main arguments that those who support abortion (Pro-choice) and those who oppose abortion (Pro-life) use:

Arguments in favour of abortion (Pro-choice)

The main arguments in favour of giving a woman a free choice about abortion are:

1. Every woman has the right to do as she wishes with her own body.
2. Every baby has the right to be born into a family that can meet its basic needs for food, shelter and love.
3. A disabled baby places an enormous burden of responsibility on those looking after it. Not everyone can carry this very heavy burden.
4. There are far too many unwanted babies in the world at the moment. It would be quite wrong to add to this number.
5. Other members of the family have their own rights as well and these must be respected.
6. A woman who becomes pregnant after a rape should not, in any circumstances, be compelled to have the rapist's baby.

Abortion is never an easy decision for anyone to make. It is a much more difficult choice because it has to be made at a time when the woman is in a very emotional and confused state. The decision demands a sensible and mature choice to be made. This is why a woman in this situation needs help – without any outside pressure being placed on her.

Arguments against abortion (Pro-life)

The main arguments against abortion are:

1. Every child is a gift from God to be loved and cherished. It should be unthinkable for anyone to destroy that gift.
2. Abortion is murder – the killing of another human being.
3. Everyone, especially the most vulnerable, needs special protection – and has the right to expect it.
4. A foetus is a human being from the moment it is conceived. It has a perfect right to live. If the foetus is damaged in any way, it has the same right to life as every other baby.

Aborting a foetus often destroys a woman's peace of mind for a long time and lays heavy on her conscience. Some say it would be far better for someone to offer their baby up for adoption. There is a long line of couples who cannot have their own baby and are waiting to adopt a child.

The Bible and abortion

There is not much in the Bible to help a Christian form an opinion about abortion. There are two comments, however, that might help:

1. The Bible teaches that human beings are made 'in the image of God' (Genesis 1.26) and one of the Ten Commandments states that murder is always wrong (Exodus 20.13). For many Christians, abortion is murder and there are no exceptions to this. For other Christians, however, it depends on when life begins and, as we have seen, that is far from straightforward.

2. When Jeremiah was called by God to be a prophet, he was told:

   ❝ I chose you before I gave you life and before you were born I selected you to be a prophet to the nations. ❞
   (Jeremiah 1.5)

This suggests that God knows everyone from the moment they are conceived. Many would conclude from this that God has actually chosen a person for their life's work before they are born and so abortion is unacceptable.

Many Christians, however, insist that abortion is a very personal decision. They insist that there is a rule which governs every aspect of a Christian's behaviour:

   ❝ In everything do to others as you would have them do to you. ❞
   (Matthew 7.12)

This means treating the decisions of others with great respect – even if you do not agree with the course of action that they take.

TASK 1

1. How do the Roman Catholic Church and many Protestant Churches differ in their attitude to abortion?

2. **a.** Explain why Christians can, and do, disagree about abortion.
   b. Do you think that such disagreement is surprising? Give one reason for your answer.

2. Christian attitudes to fertility treatment

The Bible and infertility

There is no specific teaching in the Bible about fertility treatment. If people were childless in those days, then it was accepted that this was the will of God for them. Nothing could be done about it and it had to be accepted – although childlessness was looked on with disfavour in the Jewish community. Here are three quotations from the Old Testament:

1. Abraham asked of God:

> 66 *What good will your reward do to me since I have no children?* 99
> *(Genesis 15.3)*

2. Rachel cried to her husband, Jacob:

> 66 *Give me children or I will die.* 99
> *(Genesis 30.1)*

3. 66 *Hannah had no children … because the Lord had kept her from having children.* 99
> *(1 Samuel 1.2–5)*

There are two clues here to help you understand how people at that time understood childlessness. Firstly, it was considered to be a disgrace if a couple did not have any children. Secondly, if a couple did not have any children, it was because God had prevented it from happening.

Infertility and the Christian Churches

Today, the attitude towards childlessness is very different. We now understand the causes of infertility. Few people would believe that infertility is the will of God. Within the Christian community, there are two different viewpoints:

Viewpoint 1: Fertility treatment is acceptable as long as it is the husband's sperm and the wife's eggs that are used. This is the view of almost all Christian Churches. Both AIH and IVF are welcomed. This is science making use of its knowledge to make a real difference to the lives of thousands of people. The embryos that are discarded because they are not needed are not foetuses – and so are not yet human beings.

Viewpoint 2: Any form of embryo technology, IVF, AID or AIH, is unacceptable. This is the view of the Roman Catholic Church. IVF involves the fertilisation of some eggs that are not used in the treatment. These eggs are then destroyed or used for scientific experimentation – and both are wrong. AID, AIH and IVF all involve male masturbation and the Catechism of the Catholic Church describes this as, '…an intrinsically and gravely disordered action'.

The Catholic Church also condemns any procedure that involves conception taking place without sexual intercourse. Infertility, then, is a cross that many couples are called on by God to carry. Couples do not have a 'right' to have children. A couple without children can adopt or perform social services to help others instead.

> The promise of new life is treated within the Christian community with great excitement and as a gift from God.

TASK 2

1. How is childlessness explained in the Bible?
2. Which fertility treatments are acceptable to all Christians – apart from Roman Catholics? Why are they accepted?
3. Give three reasons why the Roman Catholic Church is opposed to all forms of fertility treatment.

✳ TO TALK ABOUT

Brainstorm with your group the word 'infertility'. Write down all of the things that the word suggests to you.

3. Christian attitudes to euthanasia

Euthanasia, like abortion, is a very controversial subject among Christians. There is not one united view on the subject. There is, however, general agreement that:

1. Life is a great gift from God and has value in itself.
2. Every person should be able to live, and die, with dignity.

The Churches and euthanasia

Although all of the Christian Churches are against euthanasia, this is for slightly different reasons:

The Nonconformist Churches and euthanasia

The Baptist and Methodist Churches both agree that euthanasia revolves around the same question – who has the right to take human life? The elderly have the right to expect all the support and help they need at the end of their lives. If this is provided, then euthanasia is unnecessary. If a person is brain-dead, however, then there is no duty to keep them alive artificially. The Methodist Conference stated in 1974: 'The argument for euthanasia will be answered if better methods of caring for the dying are developed. Medical skill in terminal care must be improved, pre-death loneliness must be relieved, patients and family must be supported by the statutory services and by the community. The whole of a patient's needs, including the spiritual, must be met.'

The Anglican Church and euthanasia

The Church of England says that all life is sacred and holy. Doctors, though, do not need to keep people 'alive' if they have no quality of life left. When life and death decisions have to be made, then everyone needs to be involved, including doctors and relatives. Elderly people must be treated with great respect.
They must know that they have an important contribution left to make to life.

The Roman Catholic Church and euthanasia

This Church teaches that euthanasia in any form is wrong. Only God can take a person's life – not human beings.

All Churches, however, accept that drugs can be given to relieve pain that may, in the end, shorten life as well. This is the 'law of double effect' and is frequently used.

In recent years, many hospices have been built. They are based on the belief that the last few months and days of a person's life can be made much easier if drugs are used carefully to control the pain. Many of these hospices are founded, and financed, by Christian organisations.

✳ TO TALK ABOUT

The Christian Churches stress that the elderly should be made to feel important members of society. What practical steps could be taken to make this happen?

1. **a.** What is euthanasia?

    b. Give two reasons why most Christians are opposed to euthanasia.

2. Summarise the teaching of the Christian Churches on euthanasia.

3. 'We have the right to choose the moment when we will die.'
    How do you think a Christian might respond to this statement?
    How do you respond?

4. Christian attitudes to suicide

In the past, the Christian Church took a very strong line against suicide.
It believed that suicide was self-murder and murder was wrong. As all life, and
especially human life, was a gift of God, so suicide was a serious sin. The Roman
Catholic Church called it a 'mortal sin' – one serious enough to prevent a
person from entering heaven. People who took their own lives could not be
given a church funeral or be buried in consecrated (holy) ground. They had
to be buried well away from others.

Today, the Christian Church knows that many people live, and die, under great
pressure. If they commit suicide, it is because they are deeply unhappy – not
because they are wicked. They are simply unable to cope with the pressures of
life. Many Christians are among those who volunteer to help with the
Samaritans – in the hope that they can persuade suicidal people that life is
worth living after all.

5. Christian beliefs about the use of animals in medical research

Christians believe that animals are different from human beings. Human beings
alone are made in God's image, while animals are for humans to rule and
control. Human beings have a soul but animals do not. The Christian Scriptures
look forward to a perfect world in which human beings and animals co-exist
side by side. In this world, animals will not be exploited. Jesus said in the New
Testament that the death of a single sparrow does not go unnoticed by God.

> 66 *Wolves and sheep will live together in peace, and leopards will lie down with young goats. Calves and lion cubs will feed together, and little children will take care of them. Cows and bears will eat together, and their calves and cubs will lie down in peace. Lions will eat straw as cattle do. Even a baby will not be harmed if it plays with a poisonous snake.* 99
> (Isaiah 11.6–8)

Christians and vivisection

Most Christians are happy to eat meat for food, although some are vegetarians. They believe that all animals, as part of God's creation, should be respected. God may have given human beings control over them but that control should be exercised very carefully.

Vivisection (the use of animals in scientific experimentation) raises problems. All of the Churches believe that experiments carried out for essential medical research are acceptable. The value of animal life is less than that of human life. Sometimes such experiments are necessary. This does not mean, however, that experiments should be carried out to improve cosmetics or for other trivial reasons. Even if an experiment on an animal is necessary, that animal must be treated humanely.

The Roman Catholic Church warns its members not to give too great an importance to animals. People are still suffering a great deal in the world. We should concentrate on them and their needs. Our approach to animals and pets should be sensible. They should not, however, be treated cruelly. Many Christians are opposed to blood sports, factory farming and the transporting of live animals for great distances. It is almost impossible for any of these to take place without some cruelty being involved.

✳ TO TALK ABOUT

Christians believe that human beings are much more important than animals. What is your opinion of this attitude?

HINDUISM

What you will learn about in this section:

1. Hindu attitudes to abortion
2. Hindu attitudes to fertility treatment
3. Hindu attitudes to euthanasia and suicide
4. Hindu beliefs about the use of animals in medical research

1. Hindu attitudes to abortion

FROM THE SCRIPTURES

> *He is our father, he begat us, (He) the Ordainer: (he all) dwellings (dharma) knows, All worlds (he knows): the gods he named, (Himself) One only: other beings go to question him.*
>
> (Rig Veda X, IXXXII:3)

In India, where over 80% of the population is Hindu, abortion is legal as long as it is carried out in a government clinic. It is supported by many Hindus as a way of ending an unwanted pregnancy and as a means of birth control. About 5 000 000 abortions take place in India each year.

Most Hindus, however, are opposed to abortion for the following reasons.

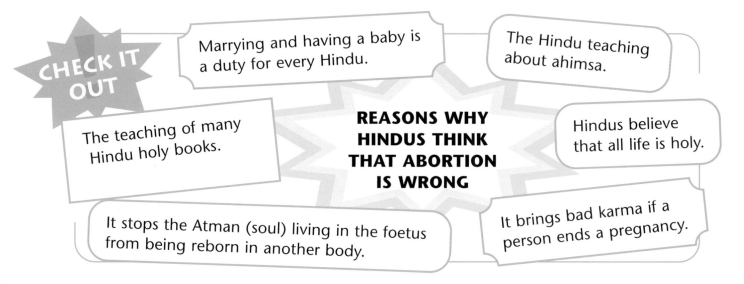

CHECK IT OUT

Marrying and having a baby is a duty for every Hindu.

The Hindu teaching about ahimsa.

The teaching of many Hindu holy books.

REASONS WHY HINDUS THINK THAT ABORTION IS WRONG

Hindus believe that all life is holy.

It stops the Atman (soul) living in the foetus from being reborn in another body.

It brings bad karma if a person ends a pregnancy.

Hinduism teaches that all life is sacred because all life is a part of God. Human beings should not interfere with the natural processes. Since all new life comes from God, so all life is special. Abortion results in bad karma. The amount of bad karma depends on the circumstances. It is very small when carried out to save the life of the mother. It is much greater if there is no good reason for the abortion.

TASK 1

1. Write down three pieces of information about the attitude of Hinduism to abortion.

2. What appears to be the key reason for the Hindu holy books opposing abortion?

2. Hindu attitudes to fertility treatment

FROM THE SCRIPTURES

66 *In all contingent beings the same am I: None do I hate and none do I fondly love.* 99
(Bhagavad Gita 9.29)

Family life is extremely important to Hindu couples. They are anxious, in particular, to have a son to carry out the right ceremonies when they die. It is the son who lights the funeral pyre and carries out other rituals within days of a death to help a soul to find a new home. If this does not happen, then the soul can return to trouble the family.

If a couple do not manage to conceive a baby, under Hindu laws they can divorce. A barren woman is pitied in Hindu society. It is part of life itself that a man should have many children before he reaches old age. The tradition is that he is free to seek God when his children have grown up and left home.

Hindu men and women are happy to use medical science to help them to conceive. They have no problem with either IVF or AIH. AID does, however, cause a problem. A child conceived in this way could not possibly know which caste he or she belonged to. It would be difficult to guarantee that the father and mother belonged to the same caste. Although the caste system has been illegal for over 50 years, it still plays an important role in the choice of a marriage partner and in rural Indian life generally.

1. Why is it important for every Hindu couple to have at least one son?
2. What is the attitude of most Hindus towards treatment for infertility?

3. Hindu attitudes to euthanasia and suicide

Hindus and euthanasia

There are two Hindu viewpoints about euthanasia:

Viewpoint 1: an important Hindu belief is that of ahimsa (non-violence). This includes violence against oneself and this would seem to rule out euthanasia. The teaching of the Bhagavad Gita, a much-loved Hindu holy book, however, would seem to suggest something else. Many Hindus use this book to permit euthanasia. The argument is that the soul survives death and cannot be harmed by anything that happens in this life. It is not harmful to speed up a soul's entry into the next life. A 'willed death' in which an old person refuses to eat and drink as they await death might be right for certain Hindus. In certain situations, it is even greatly admired.

Viewpoint 2: it is always wrong to take life. If someone is suffering, then it is the result of karma – the effect of sinful actions committed in a past life. It is only by dying at the right time that people can wipe out the bad karma. If their end is hastened, then the bad karma will be carried forward into the next life. It is always right to look after dying people very carefully and lovingly but it is never right to end their life early.

Suicide

Some Hindus accept suicide if it is carried out for religious reasons, but the holy books do not support this. Hindu widows used to throw themselves on the burning funeral pyres of their dead husbands but this is now illegal in India. To commit suicide earns bad karma and so Hindus would not do it.

4. Hindu beliefs about the use of animals in medical research

The Laws of Manu, an important holy book, expresses the Hindu belief that all life is sacred – insects, fish, birds, animals and human beings. As a result, all forms of life must be given equal respect. This respect is most usually expressed by placing gods in the company of animals when murtis are built.

- Shiva is often linked with a bull.
- Vishnu frequently took the form of different animals when he visited the earth.
- Ganesha has an elephant head.
- When Krishna came to earth, he looked after cows and spoke to birds in their own language.

▲ *There is often a close link in Hinduism between the murti and the form of an animal.*

Following these examples, most Hindus are vegetarian, since ahimsa is a very important Hindu belief. It extends to animals as well as human beings.

The cow enjoys the respect of all Hindus, largely because of Krishna's fondness for the animal. The cow is never slaughtered. It provides so much that is basic to life – food (milk, cream, cheese), transport and fuel (dung).

Hindus do not feel happy about using animals in medical research. They are opposed to all unnecessary use in such areas as cosmetic testing. They also oppose any testing that causes animals undue pain. At the same time, some Hindus argue that the use of animals in medical research could be acceptable if there is no other alternative. Like other religious people, Hindus believe that human life is more important than animal life.

---

1. What are the two different viewpoints held by Hindus about euthanasia?
2. How do Hindus show the great respect that they hold for animals?
3. What is the Hindu approach to experimentation on animals?

TASK 3

ISLAM

What you will learn about in this section:

1. Muslim attitudes to abortion
2. Muslim attitudes to fertility treatment
3. Muslim attitudes to euthanasia and suicide
4. Muslim beliefs about the use of animals in medical research

1. Muslim attitudes to abortion

The Qur'an teaches that abortion is a sin against Allah and so is forbidden. Many Muslims, however, believe that an abortion can be justified if the life of the mother is at risk. This is because the mother is alive and has greater family responsibilities than an unborn baby. The foetus has not yet developed a human personality. In this situation, an abortion is far from desirable but it is permissible. It must take place within the first four months of pregnancy. Until this time, the mother has more rights than the foetus but, after this time, they have an equal right to live.

Muslims regard all life as a gift from Allah. No one has their life as a right – it is a loan. Like all loans, it must be paid back to the person who lent it. Allah can call in the loan whenever He wishes. The Qur'an reminds women that, on the Day of Judgement, those who were aborted will want to know from their mothers why they were killed.

FROM THE SCRIPTURES

This statement comes from the Qur'an:

> 66 *Kill not your children for fear of want. We shall provide sustenance for them as well as for you. Verily [truly] the killing of them is a great sin.* 99
> *(Surah 17.31)*

2. Muslim attitudes to fertility treatment

IVF and AIH

Most Muslims accept IVF and AIH when a married couple are having trouble conceiving a baby because:

1. The egg and the sperm are taken from the husband and wife. There is no suggestion of adultery being committed – a serious sin in the Qur'an.

2. The couple are using medical science to make family life possible – and all Muslims are expected to enjoy this. Medical science is supported by Muslims when it is used for the betterment of the human race.

3. The discarded embryos in IVF treatment are not foetuses and their destruction can be justified by the law 'of double effect' (the intention is to produce children for childless couples and not to destroy the embryos). Discarded embryos could also be used for 'stem cell' research and Muslims support this.

With these reasons in mind, Muslims see little difference between AID and adultery. **Surrogacy** is also banned because the Qur'an teaches that no one can be a child's mother except the woman who conceived him or her. Muslim men are allowed to have up to four wives and this may happen if a wife is unable to give her husband any children – so making surrogacy less necessary.

3. Muslim attitudes to euthanasia and suicide

Muslims and euthanasia

Islam teaches that it is Allah who creates life for it is He alone who decides when a person should die:

> 66 *But it is to Allah that the End and the Beginning (of all things) belong.* 99
> (Surah 53.25)

To decide when a person should die is to 'play God'. Life is a sacred gift from Allah and He has decided when it should end. Suffering is for a purpose so, if a person is in pain, this is no reason for euthanasia. Ending a person's life is forbidden. If a person suffers, it is the will of Allah. As Allah is the 'Compassionate One', one of His 99 names, so patience is rewarded. He is fully aware of every trial through which a believer passes. Muslims must accept this and not try to find an easy way out – which is what euthanasia would be.

JUDAISM

What you will learn about in this section:

1. Jewish attitudes to abortion
2. Jewish attitudes to fertility treatment
3. Jewish attitudes to euthanasia and suicide
4. Jewish beliefs about the use of animals in medical research

1. Jewish attitudes to abortion

FROM THE SCRIPTURES

The Torah says this:

> *See, now, that I, I am He –*
> *and no god is with Me.*
> *I put to death and I bring to life...*
> *(Deuteronomy 32.39)*

Jews and abortion

For most Jews, there are enough statements in the Torah like the one above to rule out abortion. To Jews, abortion is much more objectionable than contraception. It stands in the way of the will of G-d by destroying a potential human life. At the same time, the life of a foetus is not given the same status in Jewish belief as that of the mother. Most rabbis claim that life does not begin until the foetus is able to exist on its own outside its mother's uterus. This is based on a text from the Jewish Scriptures:

> *If men shall fight and they collide with a pregnant woman and she*
> *miscarries, but there will be no fatality, he shall surely be punished*
> *as the husband of the woman shall cause to be assessed against him,*
> *and he shall pay it by order of judges. But if there shall be a fatality,*
> *then you shall award a life for a life...*
> *(Exodus 21.22–23)*

Abortion is acceptable for a Jewish woman if:

- the pregnancy has become dangerous for her or is likely to become so;
- she would be gravely affected psychologically if the pregnancy were to continue.

Some rabbis also allow an abortion if the baby is likely to be born with a serious mental or physical disability. The earlier an abortion is carried out, the better. The Talmud states that the foetus does not become a human being until the forty-second day of pregnancy, when the soul is planted by G-d in the body.

2. Jewish attitudes to fertility treatment

IVF and AIH are accepted by all Jews and many are also happy with egg donation. Some, however, feel that the egg must be donated by a Jewish woman to make the baby Jewish – the Jewish identity of a person coming through the mother. Others, though, think that if the baby is brought up as Jewish, that is sufficient. There are several reasons for the Jewish attitude to fertility treatment:

1. Having children is extremely important in the Jewish faith.
2. Rabbis are very supportive of couples who are having fertility treatment.
3. Jews believe that G-d intends them to take advantage of medical science.
4. The discarded embryos are not foetuses. Their destruction can be justified by the 'law of double effect' – the intention is to give childless couples a baby and not to destroy embryos.

Most Jews feel unhappy about AID as it can be seen to be a form of adultery and so against the seventh Commandment. They are also concerned about the status of the child who will not know who their father is. Other Jews, however, do accept AID. They argue that, even if the donor remains the biological father in Jewish law, no sin has been committed.

The Jewish attitude towards fertility treatment is a marked difference from the Bible's attitude towards childlessness. In the Bible, it was a stigma for married couples not to have children – a condition put down to the will of G-d:

> ❝ But to Hannah … the LORD had closed her womb. Her rival [Peninnah], provoked her again and again in order to irritate her, for the LORD had closed her womb. ❞
>
> (1 Samuel 1.5–6)

TOPIC 7 Religion and Medical Ethics

EXAM HELP

Make sure that you know about:

CHRISTIANITY

- Abortion. The sharp difference between Roman Catholics and Protestants. The arguments for and against abortion.
- Fertility treatment. Childlessness in the Bible. The different attitudes of the Churches. AIH and IVF welcomed by Protestants. The Roman Catholic Church and fertility treatment.
- Euthanasia. All Churches opposed. Life does not have to be maintained at all costs. Suicide – not wicked but sad.
- Animal experimentation. Animals should not be exploited but not as important as human beings. Only experimentation for essential research acceptable.

HINDUISM

- Abortion. Legal in India. Most Hindus opposed.
- Infertility treatment. Family life very important – especially having a son. Infertility can lead to divorce. Help acceptable but AID causes problems.
- Euthanasia and suicide. Differences of opinion over euthanasia – causes bad karma. Suicide causes problems for same reason.
- Animal experimentation. Close link between animals and Hindu gods. Particular respect given to the cow. Unhappy about use of animals in experiments.

ISLAM

- Abortion. Forbidden but some allow it if mother's life is at risk. All life is a gift from Allah.
- Infertility treatment. Both IVF and AIH acceptable. AID rejected because it is adultery and that is strictly forbidden.
- Euthanasia. Allah alone decides the beginning and end of a person's life. Suffering is sent by Allah and must be accepted. Killing oneself is strictly forbidden.
- Animal experimentation. Humans are allowed to kill animals for food. Experimentation on animals is only allowed if necessary for research. Animals are slaughtered as an offering to Allah during Eid-ul-Adha.
  - * Important definitions to learn: Eid-ul-Adha, Ihram.

JUDAISM

- Abortion. Ruled out for Jews since it destroys a potential human life. The exceptions are when the mother's like or psychological health are at risk.
- Infertility treatment. IVF and AIH are acceptable. Having children is very important. AID not acceptable because it is seen as adultery.
- Euthanasia. Opposed by all Jews. Everything must be done to preserve life. Judaism is understanding about divorce but does not condone it.
- Animal experimentation. The Jewish Scriptures permit the eating of meat. Animals must be killed by shechita and be kosher. Animals must be treated humanely and are governed by the same Sabbath laws as humans. Animal experimentation acceptable if for the benefit of human beings.
  - * Important definition to learn: shechita.

INTRODUCTION

The religious traditions covered in this book believe in the equality of all human beings. There is a good reason for this – God created all human beings to be equal. Since God created all human beings equally, we should also treat them in the same way. As both Christianity and Judaism stress, we should treat others in the way that we want them to treat us.

All four religions emphasise that if everyone is treated equally and fairly, then they should live together in peace and harmony. The Jewish Scriptures look forward to the time when God will set up his kingdom on earth with all the animals living together and being led by a small child – an image of innocence and simplicity. The image is a very powerful one. This harmony stems from the fact that all the peoples of the world are one nation or community, since they are all part of God's creation. Even when differences between the nations of the world do occur, tolerance and harmony should be maintained.

CHRISTIANITY

What you will learn about in this section:

1. The teaching of the Bible about equality

2. Christian attitudes to racism

3. The role of women in Christian society

4. Christian attitudes to other religions

5. Christian beliefs about forgiveness and reconciliation

1. The teaching of the Bible about equality

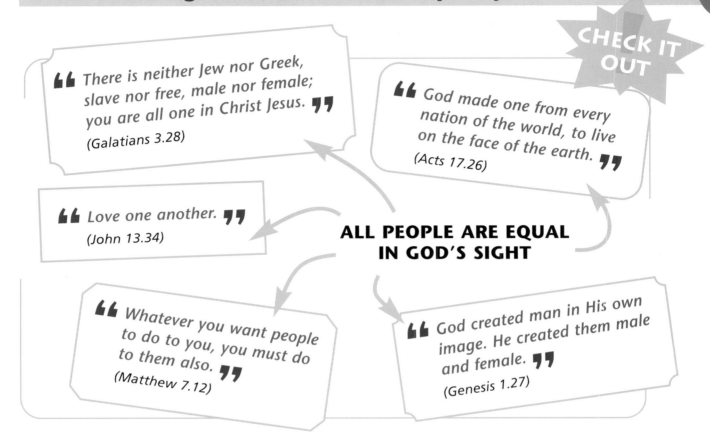

66 *There is neither Jew nor Greek, slave nor free, male nor female; you are all one in Christ Jesus.* **99**
(Galatians 3.28)

66 *God made one from every nation of the world, to live on the face of the earth.* **99**
(Acts 17.26)

66 *Love one another.* **99**
(John 13.34)

ALL PEOPLE ARE EQUAL IN GOD'S SIGHT

66 *Whatever you want people to do to you, you must do to them also.* **99**
(Matthew 7.12)

66 *God created man in His own image. He created them male and female.* **99**
(Genesis 1.27)

CHECK IT OUT

As you will see, the Bible teaches that all people are equal before God. This is how God created them. This was a hard lesson for the early Christian leaders to learn. They were Jews who had always believed that their people were the Chosen People – chosen to enjoy a special relationship with the Almighty. God, however, wanted them to learn that no nation was more favoured by God than any other:

> **66** *Then Peter began to speak: 'I now realise how true it is that God does not show favouritism but accepts men from every nation who fear him and do what is right.'* **99**
> (Acts 10.34–35)

This shows that it does not matter whether a person is a Jew or a Greek, a slave or a free person, male or female. We might also add black or white; straight or gay; young or old; rich or poor. Everyone is equally valuable as a human being to God.

2. Christian attitudes to racism

People who are racially prejudiced believe that some races are superior to others. If this is true, then it also implies, of course, that some races are inferior to others. Someone who holds these views is called a **racist**. Someone who looks down on others from a different race and considers them to be inferior is 'racially prejudiced'. 'Racial discrimination' takes place when a person allows their prejudices to affect the way that they treat others. In other words, racial discrimination is racial prejudice in action.

▲ Racial discrimination becomes a problem for some people as they grow older.

Christians believe in one God who is the Creator and Father of everyone. All people are made in God's image and so are born equal. Jesus demonstrated this truth throughout his life and teaching. Here are three examples from the Gospels:

1. When asked 'Who is my neighbour?', Jesus replied to the question by telling the story of the Good Samaritan (Luke 10.30–37). There had been no contact between the Jews and the Samaritans for centuries. Yet, in the story told by Jesus, it was a Jew who helped a Samaritan when he was in great need. He did this because he recognised the desperate plight of the man and this overcame all of their hostility towards each other. The message of the parable was that all people are neighbours – to be loved and respected for what they are.

2. Jesus healed the servant of a Roman centurion, even though the Romans were an occupying power in Palestine and hated by Jews (Luke 7.1–10).

3. He befriended Zacchaeus, a tax collector, although tax collectors were hated by the Jews because they worked for the occupying power, the Romans (Luke 19.1–10).

All differences between human beings – whether of race or colour – are totally unimportant to God. No person is more favoured than any other. James, in his epistle, made it clear that being prejudiced is sinful.

FROM THE SCRIPTURES

❝ *If you really keep the royal law found in Scripture, 'Love your neighbour as yourself', you are doing right. But if you show favouritism, you sin...* ❞
(James 2.8–9)

The Christian Church has responded in a number of ways to the fight against racial prejudice and discrimination. Its record has been far from perfect. Here are two examples:

- When many black people emigrated to the UK from the Caribbean and elsewhere in the 1950s and 1960s, many of them were Christians. When they tried to join different churches, however, they were given a cool welcome. Many churches showed hostility towards them. Instead, they formed churches of their own which expanded rapidly in the years that followed, while UK churches declined in number.

- In South Africa, from the 1950s onwards, the Dutch Reformed Church was one of the main supporters of the policy of apartheid (the discriminatory policy enforced by the white minority of separate development of the different races) until it finally disintegrated in the early 1990s.

On other occasions, however, Christians have been at the forefront of those fighting for racial justice. Here are two outstanding examples:

Martin Luther King Junior

When Martin Luther King Junior was born in 1929, black people in parts of the USA were persecuted and suffered from oppression. King became a Baptist minister and, in 1955, led a protest when a black woman refused to give her seat up to a white man on a bus. A bus boycott was organised by black people. Because the black people used the buses far more than the whites, the bus company was forced to change its racist policy a year later. Under King's influence, the protest was non-violent from the beginning – following the teaching of Jesus.

▲ The Reverend Martin Luther King Junior believed that his work to improve the lives of black people in America was given to him by God.

The protest grew through campaigns, marches, speeches and demonstrations. Huge crowds of people supported King and his followers. Then, in 1968, when he was only 39 years old, King was shot dead in Memphis, Tennessee. The Civil Rights Movement, however, which King had founded, continued after his death and the rights and the treatment of black people in the USA improved.

Father Trevor Huddleston

Father Trevor Huddleston was a white man who grew up in the UK. In 1943, he was sent as a Christian missionary to South Africa where he worked in a very poor area of the country called Soweto. While he was there, apartheid was made legal and he soon saw how black people were being treated. He began to organise overseas boycotts of South Africa by companies and sporting teams. He became a leading figure in the Anti-Apartheid Movement. Huddleston believed that this was the work that God wanted him to do because he believed that all people were created equally in God's sight. Huddleston lived long enough to see the end of apartheid and the release of Nelson Mandela from his African prison to become President of the country. Trevor Huddleston died in 1998.

▲ *Father Trevor Huddleston believed that the policy of apartheid was contrary to everything that he stood for as a Christian.*

3. The role of women in Christian society

Sexism is prejudice or discrimination against people, especially women, simply because of their sex. There is still a great gulf between the way that men and women are treated worldwide. Although women outnumber men (52% to 48%), they earn just 10% of the world's income and own less than 1% of the property in their own name.

In the UK, it has been illegal since 1975 to discriminate against women in recruitment, promotion and training at work. It also became illegal, at the same time, to dismiss a woman from her employment because she was pregnant. Women, though, still occupy few of the top positions in business because of the problems they have of combining their work with their family responsibilities. Many companies are still far from being 'women-friendly' in their work practices. Few, for example, offer crèches so that women can take their young children to work with them.

There was a great debate in the Church of England in the early 1990s about whether women should be allowed to be priests. The main argument against having women priests was tradition and the fact that Jesus did not include a woman among his disciples. Until this time, all priests were male, although women could do almost every other job in the Church. When the Synod of the

Church of England voted to admit women to the priesthood, many male vicars resigned in protest. Now, years later, the debate is over whether women can be **bishops**.

In the Roman Catholic Church, the debate about women priests has not even begun. In 1994, the **Pope** wrote an apostolic letter stating that women could not become priests – it would be entirely inappropriate and a break with Church tradition. The rule against women priests was said to be part of the 'deposit of faith', going back to Jesus himself.

The Bible and women

Prejudice against women goes back to the Bible. In the Old Testament, men had dominant roles in family and social life. These roles were carried over into the early Christian Church. Paul carried on the tradition in his writings. He wanted older women to teach younger women in the Christian community how they should behave.

Jesus, however, went against the common attitudes of the time towards women. Although he did not have any female disciples, he did have many close friends and supporters who were women. It was some of these women who remained more faithful to him than his male disciples when death approached. There is reason to believe that they supported him strongly during his lifetime – including giving a financial contribution to his work. He also broke a strong taboo when he spoke to a woman in public (John 4) who happened to be a Samaritan.

> **"** *Women should remain silent in the churches. They are not allowed to speak, but they must be in submission, as the Law says. If they want to enquire about something, they should ask their own husbands at home; for it is disgraceful for a woman to speak in the church.* **"**
> *(1 Corinthians 14.34–35)*

FROM THE SCRIPTURES

Some Christians argue that the subservience of women in the Church only reflects the order of creation when God made man first and then the woman. They say that this shows that God has given them different roles to play. The man was always intended by God to work to provide for his wife and family. Women were always intended by God to be the homemakers – having the children and feeding them.

Against this traditional view comes the more modern viewpoint that life has moved on. In the Christian Church, everyone should be equal – and treated as such. To support this, the following arguments are put forward:

- Children benefit most when both parents are involved in their upbringing.
- Women benefit from being challenged by work outside the home.
- Men benefit from being deeply involved on an equal basis with their children.

TASK 1

1. For a man of his time, Jesus broke down many barriers in his dealings with women. Look up the following references and make notes on them.
   a. Mark 12.40   **b.** Mark 10.10–12
   c. Luke 7.36–50   **d.** John 8.1–11

2. How does the Bible reflect prejudice against women?

3. Why do Christians believe that racial prejudice is wrong?

4. Write three sentences about Martin Luther King Junior or Father Trevor Huddleston, explaining how their belief guided them in their actions.

✳ TO TALK ABOUT

Do you believe that men and women, and boys and girls, should be given exactly the same opportunities in life? What are three aspects of life where you think that equal opportunities do not exist at the present time?

4. Christian attitudes to other religions

Within the Christian Church, there are three main approaches to the other major world religions:

Approach 1 Many Christians believe that there is only one way of approaching God and that is through Jesus. They base this on one verse from the New Testament:

> ❝ *Jesus answered, 'I am the way and the truth and the life. No one comes to the Father except through me.'* ❞
> (John 14.6)

In the nineteenth and early twentieth centuries, missionaries were sent to other countries to make converts to Christianity. Those who were not Christian were often referred to as 'pagans'. The Catholic Church expressed the belief that everyone needed to belong to this Church to be saved; its slogan – 'Outside the Church [Catholic] there is no salvation.' This included other Christian Churches as well as other religions. Now, however, things are very different. People still go out to work as missionaries but now they take their skills as doctors, teachers, builders and so on with them to work for the well-being of local communities. Few see their work as being simply one of making converts.

Approach 2 Some Christians believe that there are many different religious paths to God, but only Christianity has the full truth. They base this on an incident in the New Testament when Paul was visiting Athens. He recognised that in their search for the Unknown God, to whom they had built an altar, the Athenians were following a genuine spiritual search (see 'From the Scriptures'). This has encouraged some Christians to believe that good and sincere Hindus, Muslims, Jews and others are really 'anonymous Christians'. They will reach heaven in the end because they are really Christians but they do not know it.

> 66 *Paul stood up in front of the city council and said, 'I see that in every way you Athenians are very religious. For as I walked through your city and looked at the places where you worship, I found an altar on which is written* **To an Unknown God.** *That which you worship, then, even though you do not know it, is what I now proclaim to you.'* 99
> (Acts 17.22–23)

FROM THE SCRIPTURES

Approach 3 All religious people concentrate on spiritual reality – wherever they find it. Some call this spiritual reality God. When people are more centred on spiritual matters, they are less self-centred – and that is a very good thing for themselves and others. All religions are equal to each other and, in their best moments, they help people to find God. The Bible is one of many 'words of God'. The other holy books, however, are also important guides in the spiritual quest.

There are many differences between these three approaches:

- Approach 1 means that Christians and members of other religions have very little to say to each other. The Christian simply waits until other people become Christians.

- Approach 2 sees the good things in other religions but it insists that their followers are really Christians all the time.

- Approach 3 admits that no religion has the complete truth. Each religion is helping followers to worship God but does not have the complete truth.

Religion and Equality

HINDUISM

What you will learn about in this section:

1. Varnashramadharma
2. Hindu attitudes to racism
3. The role of women in Hindu society
4. Hindu attitudes to other religions
5. Hindu beliefs about forgiveness and reconciliation

1. Varnashramadharma

Hindus believe that there are four ashramas (stages) in life:

1. *Brahmacarya (the student stage):* this is the first stage in life when the student is expected to study the Vedas and be taught by a guru. This teaching begins as a Hindu boy receives the Sacred Thread and enters adulthood. He then studies the sacred books under the guidance of his own guru. During this stage, the person should avoid honey, meat, perfumes, garlands, spices, gossip, greed, putting on make-up, playing music, dancing, singing and looking at or touching women. It is the time when study rather than pleasure and comfort should be uppermost.

2. *Grhastha (the householder stage):* this is the most important stage in life because it is the householder who has to work hard to make sure that those in the other three ashramas have the food and the shelter that they need. Most Hindus never go beyond this stage. Dependants are looked after until they die.

3. *Vanaprastha (the retired stage):* when a Hindu man retires from his daily work, he can spend the rest of his life finding out about his religion and searching for God. He can study his favourite holy books. He is highly respected by other Hindus and may be called upon to give advice to others on their spiritual path. In India, he may leave his home to go into the forest to live alone. Few Hindus now do this.

4. *Sannyasa (the stage of the holy man):* a holy man gives up most material things to meditate on the mysteries of birth, life, death and rebirth. He has few belongings and begs for his food.

Traditionally, these ashramas were for men only. Women were expected to work and support their men in all things. Today, however, many Hindu women are students, equal partners in the home, teachers and even holy people.

The soul travels through each of the four stages. It is important that Hindus live according to their position in life and the duties that are expected of them. This is called **Varnashramadharma**.

In Britain today, many people believe that we are all, or should be, equal. Ancient Indians did not hold this belief. They thought that society was meant to be unequal – but fair. The system was based on impurity – most of us are impure by what we do, touch or eat, but the jobs people do make them purer or less pure than others. People live their lives according to their position and carry out their separate duties for the good of all.

All Hindus are born into a varna or social group. They cannot leave this group unless they are reborn. Someone who has lived a very good life could return in a different varna, although if they have lived a bad life they could return in a lower varna.

▲ Some men dedicate their life to a search for God and the meaning of life.

> 66 *By (doing) the work that is proper to him (and) rejoicing (in the doing) a man succeeds, perfects himself.* 99
> (Bhagavad Gita 18:45)

FROM THE SCRIPTURES

The caste system

A caste usually consists of about a thousand families who have a similar trade or profession. So, for example, someone who is in a carpenter caste will marry others in the same caste and bring up his children in that caste.

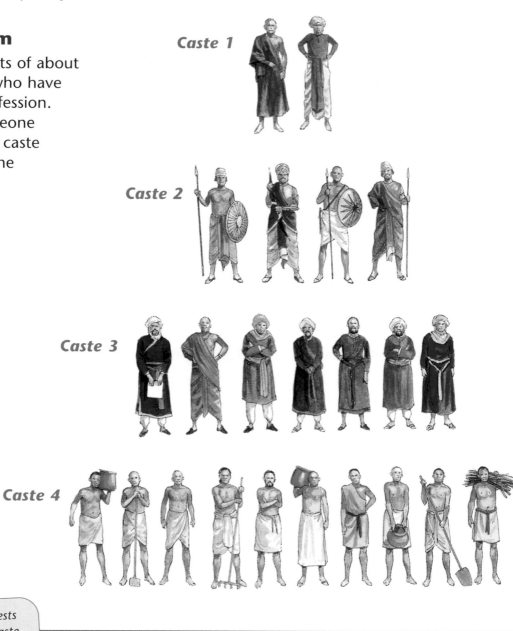

Caste 1

Caste 2

Caste 3

Caste 4

▼ *All Hindu brahmins or priests are members of the top caste.*

Caste 1 The Brahmins are the top caste – the priestly caste. Their task is to maintain the religious traditions of Hinduism and to take a leading part in organising worship in the mandir. They study the Hindu Scriptures and explain them to others.

Caste 2 The Kshatriyas are the warrior group in Indian society. Their main task is to protect and defend other members of the community. They often have top positions in government and help to run the country.

Caste 3 The Vaishyas are the skilled group of tradesmen and craftworkers. These people make most of the money in the community. They run farms and businesses in the community.

In Hindu society, people are still expected to marry a member of the same caste as themselves. In village areas, there are still rules about who can eat with whom. Some varnas are given much greater respect in society. The opportunities given to the different varnas vary. Some, for example, are able to have a good education and travel, while others are not.

Caste 4 The Sudras are the labourers or servants in the community who do the hard, manual work. They provide the services that the other three varnas need.

The Untouchables

There was a class of people below the sudras, which was not even called a varna. Its members became known as the **Untouchables** or **Chandalas**. This group was not allowed to take part in public worship. In some parts of India, its members were not allowed to travel on the same roads as other varnas. They were given such jobs as taking away the dead for cremation and clearing the roads of rubbish. They were often forced to identify themselves as Untouchables so that other varnas could avoid them.

Mahatma **Gandhi** was an Indian reformer who secured independence for his country from the British in the 1940s. He announced that the Untouchables would be given a new name – the **harijans** or 'children of God'. By this simple act, he lifted the status of the Untouchables enormously. It is now illegal in India to treat people as 'untouchable', although they still have a miserable existence.

2. Hindu attitudes to racism

In the past, Hindus suffered from racism at the hands of the Moghuls and the British. For this reason, they find it difficult to be racist in their own attitudes. Although most racial groups in India now reject the caste system, it was based on the interdependence of the different groups.

Mahatma Gandhi provides us with the best example of the Hindu attitude to racism. He fought for equal treatment for all races in South Africa before leading the campaign against British rule in India. He encouraged all the different races and groups in India to live together and treat one another as equals.

3. The role of women in Hindu society

▲ *The religious life of Hindus revolves around the shrine in the home, which is dedicated to a god.*

There are two clear attitudes in Hindu society to the roles that women are expected to play:

The traditional role of women: In traditional Hindu society, there is a clear distinction between the roles of men and women. Men are seen as the protectors and providers for Hindu women. These are the roles carried out by their fathers and taken over by their husbands at the time of marriage. Women are expected to be good wives and mothers – having children, rearing children, looking after the home and supporting their husbands.

The religious life of Hindus revolves around the family shrine at home. This is dedicated to the family god and carries images of the god, together with various offerings. Each member of the family begins the day by praying in front of the shrine. It is the mother's responsibility to make sure that these religious duties are carried out faithfully.

The modern role of women: In the modern world, many Hindu women go to clubs and dance; have important roles in society as businesswomen; train and have careers as doctors, teachers, solicitors and architects and one woman, Indira Gandhi, was recently Prime Minister of India. Hindu women find that they have much more freedom if they live in one of the large cities or towns of India, rather than if they live in a village area.

4. Hindu attitudes to other religions

Hinduism does not have a problem in accepting that everyone has the right to worship freely – whatever their religion. Hinduism does not have a clear-cut view of its own beliefs – so it does not see other religions as offering a threat. God, Hindus believe, is One and is found through the teachings of different religious figures and gurus.

This is why you will often find pictures of leaders, such as Jesus and the Buddha, in Hindu temples. They are there to inspire Hindus in their search for religious truth.

The Ramakrishna Mission

Ramakrishna (1834–86) was possibly the best-known modern Bengali Hindu saint. He spent most of his life as a temple priest and gathered a group of followers around himself. One member of the group began to note down his teachings and sayings. After his death, the Ramakrishna Mission was formed and it engaged in education, disaster relief, preaching and the publication of booklets. At the time, many people were converting to Christianity, but Ramakrishna taught that the religion to which a person belongs is not important and that it was actually better for them to remain with Hinduism since that is the religion in which Indians feel most at home.

1. What are the four ashramas?
2. What is Varnashramadharma?
3. Who are the outcastes and how did Gandhi describe them?
4. What do Hindus believe about the role of women?
5. What is the Hindu approach to other religions – and why?

TASK 1

✳ TO TALK ABOUT

Do you think that Gandhi was right when he suggested that the different religions are simply different roads that converge at the same point? Come up with two arguments in favour of and two against this viewpoint.

5. Hindu beliefs about forgiveness and reconciliation

The Hindu belief about the importance of forgiveness is connected with its belief in reincarnation. It is in the interests of everyone that good and not bad karma should be accumulated. If a person accumulates bad karma through living a bad life, then their next rebirth will be badly affected. If, on the other hand, they accumulate good karma, then they can hope to come back to a better life. Bearing grudges and refusing to forgive someone who has hurt or insulted us results in bad karma. Being ready to forgive others results in good karma – something from which we benefit in the life to come.

ISLAM

What you will learn about in this section:

1. Muslim teachings about equality
2. Muslim attitudes to racism
3. The role of women in Muslim society
4. Muslim attitudes to other religions
5. Muslim beliefs about forgiveness and reconciliation

1. Muslim teachings about equality

The Qur'an makes it very clear that Allah has created everything. He created the heavens and the earth. He created all forms of life, from the animals through to human beings. He even made the variations that we find among humans, such as different languages spoken and skin colours. For those who know about such things, these variations confirm their faith in Allah.

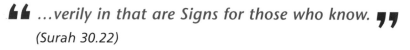 *...verily in that are Signs for those who know.*
(Surah 30.22)

The Qur'an expands upon the theme that Allah made all human beings:

- Allah created the whole of humanity from a single male and female. All human beings come from a single origin.
- Allah divided the human race into separate nations and tribes.
- Allah knows every part of His creation personally.

Since all people have been made by Allah, so all people are equal. This is how Allah sees the human race and how each member of the human race must treat everyone else.

2. Muslim attitudes to racism

The unity of Allah (tawhid) is a basic Muslim belief. It acknowledges that Allah is the architect of all creation and that humanity is one. The different colours, races and languages of the human race are a clear sign of Allah's wonderful work in creating the world. The differences between human beings should enrich everyone. Equal respect should be given to every man and woman.

For their inspiration, Muslims turn to the example of Muhammad ﷺ. He chose Bilal, a former African slave, to be his first muezzin – the man who began the tradition of calling the faithful to prayer five times each day. In his last sermon, which he delivered on his final pilgrimage to Makkah, Muhammad ﷺ told his listeners that they belonged to a community, the Ummah, in which everyone was equal. In the eyes of Allah, no one race, or people, is superior to any other.

Every year, two million Muslim pilgrims, from all parts of the world, follow the example of the Prophet and undertake a pilgrimage (the hajj) to the holy city of Makkah. On the pilgrimage, people of different races and colours treat each other as brothers and sisters – and children of Allah.

◀ This muezzin, calling the faithful to prayer, is following the example of Bilal.

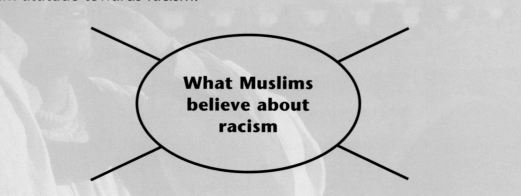

Copy this diagram and complete it to show that you understand the Muslim attitude towards racism.

What Muslims believe about racism

3. The role of women in Muslim society

Islam teaches that men and women have been given different roles to play by Allah. At the same time, they are equal in matters of religion and both sexes have an equal right to education.

The traditional roles of men and women

1. Traditionally, the main roles of a woman in Muslim society have been:

- to have children;
- to create a halal – a good Muslim home;
- to bring up children as good Muslims;
- to worship Allah;
- to fulfil all of the Five Pillars, except the hajj, at home.

Women do have the right to study and to keep their own name and property after they marry.

2. Traditionally, the roles expected of a man in Muslim society have been:

- to support their wife, since Allah has given him a stronger physique;
- to provide for his family;
- to make sure that his children are brought up as good Muslims;
- to send his children to the madrasa, the school attached to the mosque;
- to educate his sons about their religious responsibilities and to worship alongside them in the mosque.

The Qur'an underlines the responsibility of the Muslim man to look after his wife and family. This is because women are the ones designed by Allah to have and look after the children. The Qur'an also says that women should only inherit 50% of what men inherit, showing that men are intended by Allah to look after their family. The Qur'an teaches that men and women should worship separately so that there are no distractions to the males.

The modern roles of women

Some Muslims believe that men and women should have completely equal rights and roles in Islam. They believe that women should be able to have a career as well as a role at home. Women should also be able to pray alongside men in the mosque. This attitude is based on the teaching of the Qur'an that women should be equal in religion and education. There is also some evidence from the life of the Prophet Muhammad ﷺ that men and women used to pray together in the mosque during his lifetime. In the UK, many Muslims combine these two attitudes. Women pursue independent careers of their own but they worship at home because that fits in better with their family obligations.

> The Qur'an says this:
>
> 66 *Husbands are the protectors and maintainers of their wives, because Allah has given the one more (strength) than the other, and because they support them from their means. Therefore the righteous women are devoutly obedient, and guard in (the husband's) absence what Allah would have them guard.* 99
>
> *(Surah 4.34)*

FROM THE SCRIPTURES

4. Muslim attitudes to other religions

Islamic law guarantees the safety of non-Muslims who live in Muslim countries. These people are under the protection of Allah, the Prophet Muhammad ﷺ and the Muslim community. Christians and Jews are given special protection because they are, like Muslims, 'people of the book'. They are promised that Allah will reward them on the Day of Judgement.

Against this, the Qur'an clearly teaches that Islam is the only true religion. The final revelation of Allah was given to Muhammad ﷺ. This revelation was more important than any given to the earlier prophets – including Abraham, Moses and Jesus. This is why Islam is a missionary faith. Muslims believe that they have a God-given responsibility to share their message with everyone. The Muslim who wants to join another religion will find it very difficult – and dangerous (see 'From the Scriptures'). Buddha is accepted as one of the prophets before Muhammad ﷺ, but Hinduism is looked upon as a pagan religion.

> **❝** *If anyone desires a religion other than Islam (submission to Allah), never will it be accepted of him; and in the Hereafter he will be in the ranks of those who have lost (all spiritual good).* **❞**
>
> (Surah 3.85)

TASK 2

1. What are the traditional roles expected of men and women in the Muslim community?

2. What is the Muslim attitude to other religions? Do all Muslims believe this equally?

5. Muslim beliefs about forgiveness and reconciliation

Islam teaches that everyone is equal in the eyes of the law. They must be dealt with in the knowledge that all will stand before Allah – the all-knowing One – on the Day of Judgement. They will have to account for the way they have lived. Islamic law, the **Shari'ah**, outlines how people should be punished for the sins they have committed against others. Four crimes, in particular, are condemned in the Qur'an:

* murder
* adultery
* the making and the drinking of alcohol
* theft.

These crimes are particularly dangerous because they lead to many other undesirable things. Punishments are designed to stop people crossing the boundaries laid down by Allah.

Forgiveness plays a large part in dealing with the law-breaker. Only Allah can forgive. Allah will always do this if a person is genuinely sorry for their actions. Allah will reward those who forgive others on the Day of Judgement.

> **❝** *...but if a person forgives and makes reconciliation, his reward is due from Allah.* **❞**
> *(Surah 42.40)*

What does the Qur'an teach about forgiveness and the way in which it can be obtained?

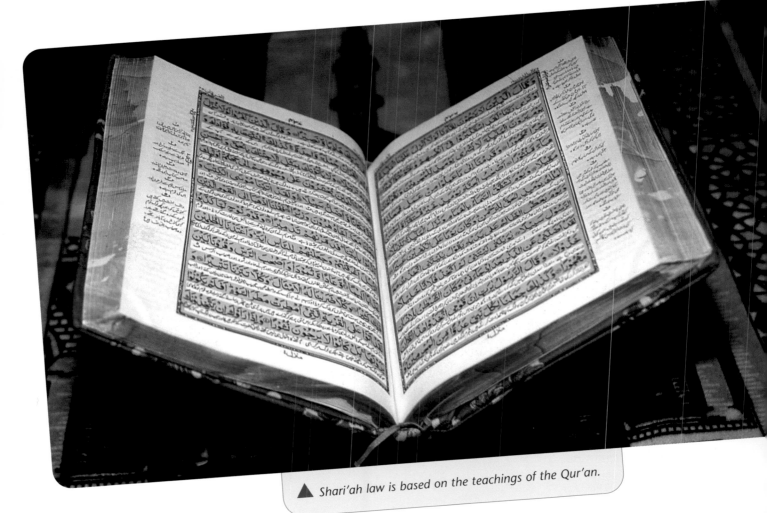

▲ *Shari'ah law is based on the teachings of the Qur'an.*

TOPIC 8 — Religion and Equality

JUDAISM

What you will learn about in this section:

1. The teaching of the Torah about equality
2. Jewish attitudes to racism
3. The role of women in Jewish society
4. Jewish attitudes to other religions
5. Jewish beliefs about forgiveness and reconciliation

1. The teaching of the Torah about equality

Judaism recognises that all people are different and that these differences are from G-d. People who have a different skin colour, a disability or who were born into a different religious community should not be looked down on in any way. It is the duty of every human being to make sure that others are always treated fairly and equally.

The Torah reminds Jews that their ancestors were slaves in Egypt for over 400 years. During this time, they were treated very unfairly. For this reason alone, they should treat any foreigners in their own country with fairness and kindness. The Torah reminds them of this.

FROM THE SCRIPTURES

> **‟** *When a proselyte [stranger] dwells among you in your land, do not taunt him. The proselyte who dwells with you shall be like a native among you, and you shall love him like yourself, for you were aliens in the land of Egypt; I am the LORD, your G-d.* **”**
> (Leviticus 19.33–34)

2. Jewish attitudes to racism

Anti-Semitism

Judaism strongly teaches that any form of racialism or racial discrimination is wrong. There are three reasons for this:

1. The Torah, the most important of holy books, strongly forbids the mistreatment of any foreign people living within Israel's borders – as we saw earlier.

2. Jewish teaching emphasises that we are all children of G-d and have the right to be treated equally.

3. Jews have experienced more than 2000 years of persecution. The Jewish people, more than any other group, have been persecuted over the centuries. Persecution directed against the Jews, because they are Jews, is called anti-Semitism. Much of this persecution came from the Christian Church. Christians held the Jews responsible for the death of Jesus. At different times, Jews were forced to leave many European countries, such as England and Spain.

In the 1930s and the 1940s, Jews were rounded up into ghettoes in Nazi-controlled Europe. They were excluded from jobs and schools. Death camps and concentration camps were built and millions of Jews were put to death – young and old. By 1945, over six million Jews had been killed – including over one million children. Gypsies and homosexuals were also killed in large numbers by the Nazis. Mindful of this experience, Jews have always fought against any form of discrimination and prejudice.

3. The role of women in Jewish society

Orthodox and Reform Jews both accept that men and women are equal. They differ, however, over the roles that they are expected to play in the worshipping community.

Orthodox Jews

There is a clear division of responsibility between men and women in the Orthodox community. Women have supreme authority in an Orthodox home and are mainly responsible for teaching the children, although they are also sent to religion school. Women organise the observance of Sabbath and the annual religious festivals. At the Sabbath evening meal, a Jewish husband tells his wife how valuable she is to him by reading a passage from the Scriptures which begins 'An accomplished woman who can find?' Women cannot form part of a minyan – the minimum of ten people who need to be present before a service is held. They play no part in public worship.

> ▶ *In Orthodox synagogues, there is a gallery where women and children sit during Sabbath worship.*

Reform Jews

Reform Jews are those who believe that the old Scriptural laws and the traditions of Judaism need to be understood in the light of modern life. Reform men and women share in leading public worship. Women rabbis are allowed. Women can read from the Torah in public. In a Reform synagogue, at the age of 12, girls have their own 'coming-of-age' service called a **bat mitzvah**. In an Orthodox synagogue, only boys have a bar mitzvah ceremony.

▲ *Girls in a Reform synagogue have their own bat mitzvah ceremony to mark their coming of age.*

▲ *A boy at his bar mitzvah ceremony.*

4. Jewish attitudes to other religions

Judaism teaches that all religious believers have the right to worship openly and freely. Jews have suffered too much at the hands of other religious believers in the past to persecute believers from other religions. Traditionally, Judaism divides other religions into two groups:

1. *Idolatrous religions* By this, the rabbis of old were referring to religions which taught things that were contrary to the Ten Commandments, in particular, religions that taught there was more than one god. Followers of these religions should not be persecuted. At the same time, they should know that they are far from the truth.

2. *G-d fearing religions* By this, the rabbis meant the other two great religions which believed in one G-d – Christianity and Islam. Both of these religions encourage their followers to live by laws similar to the Ten Commandments. Ironically, Muslims and Christians have mistreated and persecuted Jews many times in history.

Judaism is not a missionary faith. It does not set out to convert others. It does, however, believe that G-d has set Judaism apart from other religions. Jews also hope that they will be left to practise their own faith in their own way without outside interference.

> **❝** *I am the LORD, I have called you with righteousness;*
> *I will strengthen your hand; I will protect you;*
> *I will set you for a covenant to the people, for a light*
> *to the nations; to open blind eyes; to remove a prisoner*
> *from confinement, dwellers in darkness from a dungeon.*
> *I am the LORD; that is My Name; I shall not give My glory*
> *to another, nor My praise to graven idols.* **❞**
>
> (Isaiah 42.6–8)

FROM THE SCRIPTURES

5. Jewish beliefs about forgiveness and reconciliation

Until 70 CE in Israel, a suitable sacrifice was offered by anyone who had broken the law. The sacrifices were usually of grain, oil or incense. Occasionally, however, an animal was offered. In that year, however, the Temple in Jerusalem was destroyed. The offering of sacrifices stopped. They were replaced in Jewish teaching by the 'spiritual offerings' of repentance and prayer.

Nowadays, if Jews do something wrong, three courses of action are open to them to find forgiveness:

1. *Prayer* If a person is really sorry for what they have done, then it is believed that their prayers will be heard and answered by G-d. They must, however, be determined not to commit the same sinful act again. A word of apology is not enough by itself. The repentance must be genuine and heartfelt. The Torah makes this clear:

> 66 *You shall not hate your brother in your heart; you shall reprove your fellow and do not bear a sin because of him. You shall not take revenge and you shall not bear a grudge against the members of your people; you shall love your fellow as yourself – I am the LORD.* 99
> (Leviticus 19.17–18)

▼ Prayer and repentance can lead to forgiveness for a Jew.

2. *Good deeds* Giving to those in need is a spiritual duty for all Jews. It can be part of an action in which a Jew is expressing their sincere repentance for something they have done.

3. *Fasting* In Judaism, fasting involves not eating or drinking for up to 25 hours. Fasting is a traditional religious activity. It shows a person's sorrow for something they have done.

The Day of Atonement

On the Day of Atonement, which falls in either September or October, a Jew must make a total reckoning of their behaviour for the past year. If they have offended or cheated someone, they must put it right. On this day they:

- spend the day in repentance and prayer in the synagogue;
- continue fasting for a full 25 hours;
- give a set amount of money to charity.

This is the day on which G-d decides whether each person will continue to live for the next year. Some are given the gift of life immediately. Others, the wicked, have the gift of life withdrawn from them. A third group are given a short time to show that they are genuinely sorry for their sins. It is important that Jews can only forgive those who have hurt them personally. G-d alone can forgive those who have committed sins against the community.

✳ TO TALK ABOUT

How do you think that belonging to the Jewish faith might affect the way a Jew treats other people?

1. Why do Jews believe that any form of racism is wrong?
2. Explain, in a paragraph of at least six sentences, what anti-Semitism is.
3. Explain four differences between the Orthodox Jewish and the Reform Jewish attitude towards the role of women.
4. Describe the attitude of Judaism towards other religions.

TASK 1

TOPIC 9 Religion, Poverty and Wealth

INTRODUCTION

The causes of hunger, poverty and disease

We live today in a divided world. It is split into two clear parts – by wealth on the one hand and poverty on the other:

1. The Developed World

This part of the world consists of those countries that have a high standard of living and includes:

- North America
- Western Europe
- Australasia.

25% of the world's population lives in the rich, developed world. These countries, however, consume 80% of the world's resources – energy, food and so on.

2. The Developing World

This part of the world consists of those countries that have a very low standard of living compared to the developed world. The developing world includes:

- South America
- India
- Africa.

▲ People living in poverty have little chance of working their way out of it.

These countries, with 75% of the world's population, live off just 20% of the world's resources.

The developing countries of the world share several characteristics.

1. They have a high level of malnutrition. This is brought about by people not having enough food to eat or eating food that has a low nutritional value. The world produces enough grain for every man, woman and child to have 3000 calories a day – more than enough for a healthy life. Yet 600 million people in the world live in absolute poverty with an average intake of around 1800 calories. The Brandt report, published in 1980, reported that just 1.5% of the money that the nations of the world spend on weapons would provide all the farming equipment needed to make developing countries

self-sufficient in food production. This report, although published a quarter of a century ago, is still the best study on world poverty. Other studies show that the situation has not improved since then – it has grown much worse.

2. They have a largely illiterate population. There is a direct link between levels of literacy (the ability to read and write) and poverty. It is almost impossible for illiterate people, about 1000 million of them, to find their way out of poverty.

3. Developing countries lack clean drinking water. Twenty-five million people die each year from water-borne diseases; 2.4 billion people (about 30% of the world's population) do not have adequate sanitation; 2 billion people do not have access to a clean water supply. The effect of all this on the health of the poorest countries is catastrophic.

4. They have poor medical services. Inadequate food and the lack of clean water inevitably bring major health problems. Very young babies and the elderly are the most vulnerable people to these problems. Twenty million people die from malnutrition each year. Three out of every four children do not see their fifth birthday. People in developing countries do not have access to doctors, nurses or dentists. Immunisation programmes against common killer diseases, such as malaria, are scarce. Prenatal and post-natal care of young babies is very poor. Poor medical care leads to a low life expectancy. There are many countries in which life expectancy is around 40 years. In comparison, in the UK, life expectancy is about 75 years for men and 80 years for women.

5. Most people work in agriculture – three out of every four men in some developing countries are employed on the land. This can be compared with 1 in 25 in the UK. Farming in the developing world is largely subsistence – where people grow enough for their own needs without having any left over to sell to others. This leaves them no money to buy other essential goods. They also have no hope of improving their standard of living or that of their family.

In a visual format, summarise some of the characteristics of developed and developing countries.

TASK 1

✳ TO TALK ABOUT

When we talk of living in a divided world, what do we mean?

CHRISTIANITY

What you will learn about in this section:

1. Christian teaching about the poor
2. Christian teaching about money
3. Christian teaching about charity
4. Christianity and moral and immoral occupations

1. Christian teaching about the poor

In the Old Testament and the New Testament, the uneven distribution of wealth is a constant theme. It was strongly believed that everything in the world was provided by God – for everyone to enjoy. The failure to make sure that everyone was fed adequately was usually put down to selfishness and corruption.

The prophets in the Old Testament

There was a great gap between the rich and the poor in ancient Israel. The prophets were very upset about this. The strongest message came from the prophet Amos who lived in about 700 BCE. He attacked the unwillingness of the rich to use their wealth to feed the poor. He spoke of a plumb line being held against a wall to make sure it was built straight. A willingness to look after and feed those in need is God's plumb line. It is the standard by which everyone will be judged. God does not accept the worship of those who do not care for the poor – no matter how much they protest and perform their religious rituals.

Jesus and poverty

Jesus also attacked those who hoarded their wealth. He told his disciples:

> 66 *Blessed are you who are poor, for yours is the kingdom of God. Blessed are those who hunger now, for you will be satisfied.* 99
> (Luke 6.20–21)

He told rich people that they would find that their wealth stood between them and God (see 'From the Scriptures'). On one occasion, a rich young ruler came to Jesus wanting to know how he could enter the kingdom of God. Jesus told him that only one thing stood in his way – his wealth. Only those who shared their wealth with the poor and hungry could expect to have a place in God's kingdom (Matthew 25.31–46).

Jesus told two stories to illustrate this:

- The parable of the bigger barns (Luke 12.13–21). This story shows that the value of a person's life has little to do with their wealth. One year, the ground of a farmer was very fertile and yielded a bumper crop. This overwhelmed the farmer, who realised that he had nowhere to store the extra grain. He decided to build new barns so that the grain could be his security for the future. Jesus pointed out that God demands more of those who have more than their fair share of the earth's resources. He said:

  > 66 *You fool! This night your life will be demanded of you. Then who will get what you have prepared for yourself?* 99
  > (Luke 12.20)

- The parable of the rich man and Lazarus (Luke 16.19–31). Jesus told another story to show that it is the poor and not the rich who will enter God's kingdom. There was a man who dressed in purple and fine linen and lived a life of great luxury. A poor beggar, Lazarus, was covered in sores and lay outside the rich man's gate. The beggar would have been thankful for any of the crumbs that fell from the rich man's table but he received nothing. The beggar eventually died and was carried up into heaven. The rich man died and was carried into the underworld. From there, he envied the poor man's place in heaven but it was too late.

The early Christians

The early Christians sought to put this teaching of Jesus into practice. In the Christian community, we are told that no one claimed that their possessions were their own – they belonged to everyone to share. There were rich and poor in the Christian community. The rich sold their land and brought the proceeds to the apostles (the disciples). The money raised was given to the poor. As a result, we are told that 'there were no needy persons among them'.

In today's world, there is an immense need for food, education and shelter. This can only be met in the long term if there is a massive shift of resources from the rich to the poor. The teachings of Jesus suggest that his followers should set an example. To do this, they must follow a simple lifestyle and share with those in need. That is the kind of lifestyle that Jesus and his early followers pursued.

> 66 *You lack (only) one thing. Sell everything that you have and give to the poor, and you will have treasure in heaven. Then come, follow me.* 99
> (Luke 18.22)

FROM THE SCRIPTURES

TASK 1

1. Describe what Jesus had to say about the poor. In your answer, refer to two parables that he told.

2. How did the early Christians try to put into practice the teaching of Jesus about the poor?

3. What do you think each of these passages in the New Testament is saying about the way that the poor should be treated?
   a. Matthew 25.31–46
   b. Luke 12.22–28
   c. James 5.1–3

✳ TO TALK ABOUT

Do you think it is practical today to follow the advice of Jesus and give all that one has to the poor? If not, how do you think that Christians might follow the spirit of the advice of Jesus?

2. Christian teaching about money

We seem to live in a society in which material goods are all that matter. 'Materialism' is the approach to life that attaches a very great importance to money and possessions. It places a very low importance on spiritual and moral values. Christians believe that materialism is contrary to the teaching of Jesus. They do not suggest that money does not matter – simply that it is not the most important thing in life. Without money, people suffer from poverty, hunger and homelessness.

Money and wealth in the teaching of Jesus

The Bible has more to say about wealth and its dangers than almost any other subject. Wealth certainly figures prominently in the teaching of Jesus. Here are two examples:

1. The Sermon on the Mount (Matthew 5–7). Jesus encouraged the rich to share their wealth with the poor secretly (Matthew 6.1–4). If they did this, he said, then God would reward them openly for their generosity. People were not to spend their lives accumulating wealth, since it is 'treasure in heaven' that matters (Matthew 6.19–24).

2. The Widow's Mite (Mark 12.41–44). On one occasion, Jesus sat down opposite the place where people made their offerings to the Temple in Jerusalem. This was an offering that every Jew was expected to make. After watching many wealthy people put in large sums, Jesus saw a poor widow putting in two small copper coins. Jesus told his disciples that she had put in 'more than all the others since they had given to God out of their wealth but she had made the offering out of her poverty'. To be really God-pleasing, giving must involve sacrifice.

Money and wealth in the teaching of Paul

Paul had much to say about wealth – and its dangers. Writing to Timothy, a young church leader, Paul commented:

> **❝ The love of money is the root of all evil. ❞**
>   *(1 Timothy 6.10)*

Notice that Paul did not trace all evil to money itself, but to the love of money. This fits in perfectly with the teaching of Jesus. He suggested that it is the 'love' of money that prevents a person giving it away to help the poor. Its hold is so strong that it will even prevent someone from entering the kingdom of God. They would rather keep their money – and stay outside that kingdom. Money offers people some kind of security, whereas it is very risky for a person to put their faith in God.

▼ *Both monks and nuns take a vow of poverty, which means that any wealth that they have goes to support the community to which they belong.*

Some Christians believe that Jesus was exaggerating the need to give away everything to shock his listeners. There is probably some truth in this. Others believe that they literally have to give away everything to help the poor. There is probably some truth in this as well. Some Christians decide to become monks and nuns and take on the vow of poverty.

TASK 2

Write four sentences to describe the teaching of the following about money and its dangers:

a. Jesus

b. Paul

3. Christian teaching about charity

All Christians are encouraged to give money to the church to which they belong. In the Old Testament, Jews were expected to give a **tithe** to God. This was 10% of their income each year. Some Christians continue this practice today. In giving money to the Church, they are not only supporting their local church, but are also helping various charities. Other Christians may not give a tithe, but they do give a certain amount each week or month that they place in an envelope. This regular giving is very important because it enables their church or charity to plan its expenditure.

Giving in the New Testament

Writing to the Romans, Paul listed the many gifts that members of the Church have received from God – prophesying, serving, teaching, encouraging and so on. All of these were used in the Church to make them spiritually stronger. He then came to the gift of 'contributing' or 'giving'. To those with this gift, Paul said:

> 66 *...if it is contributing let him give generously...* 99
> *(Romans 12.8)*

In another letter, Paul says that the spirit in which we give is important:

> 66 *Each man should give what he has decided in his heart to give, not reluctantly or under compulsion, for God loves a cheerful giver.* 99
> *(2 Corinthians 9.7)*

This is the advice that Paul gives elsewhere:

> **Now about the collection for God's people... On the first day of every week, each one of you should set aside a sum of money in keeping with his income, saving it up, so that when I come no collections will have to be made.**
> (1 Corinthians 16.2)

Giving in other ways

Of course, giving money is not the only form of giving to charity. Most charities, as with most churches, rely very heavily on the work of volunteers. Christians, and others, give their time and energy to help favourite charities in running flag days, door-to-door collections, bazaars and other activities. The variety of charities in this country alone runs close to 100 000, covering the needs of children, the sick, lifeboatmen, animals, the disabled and many other groups with special needs. Some charities have a more specific Christian aim – such as Tearfund, Christian Aid, CAFOD – and some Christians feel more comfortable supporting these.

4. Christianity and moral and immoral occupations

Christianity does not lay down hard and fast rules about the occupations that its members must follow. At the same time, many Christians have spent their lives working in the caring professions – working as doctors, nurses, teachers, social workers and so on. This gives them the opportunity to express their concern and care for others through the work they do. They also see this as an important way of expressing their Christian faith. So too do others who have gone overseas to work as missionaries.

There are also occupations that some Christians might feel unhappy about working in. They might, for instance, be uncomfortable working in a cigarette factory, or in a job to do with selling alcohol or something connected with gambling. This would be because they know the great damage that such activities as smoking, drinking alcohol and gambling can do to many people. They might feel the same working for a company that does not pay a fair wage to its employees overseas or treats animals badly, such as factory farming or the testing of cosmetics on animals.

TOPIC 9 Religion, Poverty and Wealth

HINDUISM

What you will learn about in this section:

1. Hindu teaching about the poor
2. Hindu teaching about money
3. Hindu teaching about charity
4. Hinduism and moral and immoral occupations

1. Hindu teaching about the poor

> *Puffed up with self-conceit, unbending,*
> *filled with the madness and pride of wealth,*
> *They offer sacrifices that are but sacrifices in name*
> *And not in the way prescribed, – the hypocrites!*
> *(Bhagavad Gita 16:17)*

Hindus believe that there are four basic aims in life for everyone:

Aim 1: Dharma – to keep to one's religious and social duty.

Aim 2: Artha – to gain wealth by any legitimate means.

Aim 3: Kama – to enjoy the good life.

Aim 4: Moksha – to enjoy final freedom or liberation at the end of life.

Hinduism is the only religion that lays down the acquisition of wealth as a worthy aim in life. Although pursuing wealth is one of the four aims in life, however, it must not be allowed to dominate a person's life. It is legitimate because, in the second stage of life, the householder phase, a man must support many people – including his children, his wife and his older relatives.

In recognition of this, each year during the Hindu festival of Divali, Hindu businessmen pray to Lakshmi, the goddess of wealth, for her blessing on them and their business. There is only one restriction placed on this pursuit of wealth – the money must be earned in a righteous way.

In Hinduism, the wealth that a person has does not belong to him alone – it belongs to his whole family. This means four living generations and three generations of ancestors. The present family enjoying the wealth are trustees for other generations to come. They are expected to look after it carefully. After they have met their family obligations, Hindus are expected to give away the wealth

that they do not need. This is why begging is such a strong Hindu tradition. Giving money away means that a person gains merit in the next life.

> ◀ *Hindus are expected to look after members of their own family – especially those who cannot look after themselves – before they try to look after others.*

Write four sentences about the Hindu attitude to wealth. In particular, mention the obligation that having wealth places on a person.

TASK 1

2. Hindu teaching about money

During the Hindu marriage ceremony, the bridegroom promises his father-in-law three times that he will always pursue dharma, artha and kama 'in moderation'. This moderation is important. Hindus must never be greedy. They must not be preoccupied with making money. If they are, then their family will suffer. In the first ashrama, that of the student, Hindus are intended to manage on very little. They learn from this that there are more important things in life than making money. The Hindu holy books speak of three things that should be the main concern of every Hindu:

- to obtain wisdom;
- to love God;
- to carry out family responsibilities to the best of their ability.

All of these are much more important than possessing wealth.

The Mahabharata teaches that the way a person lives is more important than the wealth they have. Having money should lead to generosity and compassion. It should give a person a great desire to observe religious ceremonies. It should result in pleasure, courage, self-confidence, learning and joy. These are all spiritual qualities that make a person better.

3. Hindu teaching about charity

Charity work

Giving to those less fortunate than oneself is very important in Hinduism. It stores up good karma for the giver. Those who are able to spare cash, food or clothes are expected to give to the needy in their area. Before their midday meal, many

Hindu families arrange to give food to at least one needy person locally. Beggars are given cash at railway stations, bus stations and outside temples. This is why the sight of people begging is so common in India.

Many Hindus also support projects to provide jobs, food, healthcare and education for the poor of India. Wealthy people often finance schools and hospitals. All Hindu temples in the UK collect gifts, which are then used to support Hindus locally in their area or projects that are going on in India. Many Hindus in Britain send money directly back to India to support projects that are helping the poor. A major example of this is the Swaminarayan Hindu Mission in the UK, which has a network of volunteers carrying out charity work in India. The Mission often responds when parts of India are struck by natural disasters, such as earthquakes or cyclones.

Reincarnation and charity

As we have seen many times, Hindus blame an individual's suffering on bad karma from a previous life. The needy in society also suffer. Hindus believe that they are paying the price in this life for bad karma in a previous existence. An orphan's karma, for example, is responsible for the death of his or her parents. The poor may have caused someone to starve in a previous life. The mentally ill and the disabled may have inflicted cruelty on someone in a previous existence. This argument is put forward by many Hindus to explain why they do not do more to help and support the poor and needy. If someone is suffering in this life, and they deserve it, there is little point trying to help them.

TASK 2

How may a Hindu justify doing little to help the poor?

4. Hinduism and moral and immoral occupations

Hindus believe that wealth is a good thing, but only if it has been obtained by lawful means. Other people must not be hurt by the way a person earns their money. If people follow their dharma (social duty) in their ashrama (stage in life) and this allows them to become rich, then they should enjoy it. People must do the right job for the caste to which they belong.

In Hindu society in India, however, wealth is not distributed evenly. At one end of the scale are the very wealthy people who can spend money as they wish. At the other end of the scale are people who live in such poverty that a banana or a biscuit would be a luxury. This poverty can lead people to gain money by any means – often dishonestly. If this involves criminal activities, then it is against all that Hinduism believes and teaches.

Artha encourages people to earn money honestly and lawfully. Gaining money dishonestly taints both the money and the people earning it. It is called 'black money'. It will earn them bad karma and this will affect their rebirth – a matter of great concern to every Hindu.

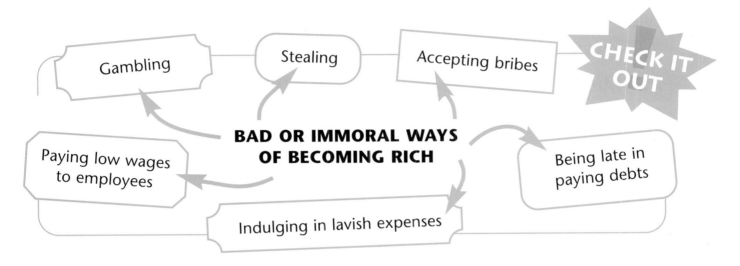

The holy books also make clear what a person can do if they are wealthy.

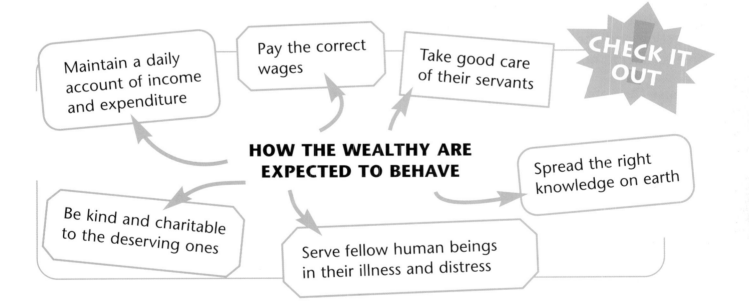

1. Describe some of the bad or immoral ways in which some people might acquire their wealth.
2. Describe how wealthy Hindus are expected to behave.

TASK 3

ISLAM

What you will learn about in this section:

1. Muslim teaching about the poor

2. Muslim teaching about charity

3. Islam and moral and immoral occupations

1. Muslim teaching about the poor

Zakah

Muslims are expected to pay zakah, money that is given to the poor. This is usually set at 2.5% of income and at 10% of the value of jewellery owned. Zakah is not paid as a favour to the poor; it is an act of worship for every Muslim. In some Muslim countries, it is collected as a tax by the State and then distributed to the needy. In other countries, the local mosque organises the collection and then either distributes it to the needy or encourages those who give to decide how the money should be used.

Because they are regarded as precious in the sight of Allah, all people have the right to expect assistance if they are poor. Muslims see it as their duty to provide for the poor. This is because the earth and its resources do not belong to human beings. Everything belongs to Allah. Human beings have been given the wealth of the world to use – as Allah decides. Giving zakah also carries its own reward – whoever helps a needy person in this life will be blessed by Allah, both in this life and in the life to come.

Dealing with poverty

All Muslims are required to fast during the month of Ramadan. This is a spiritual discipline. It is also an act of unity with all Muslims who are hungry and poor. The Muslim who fasts during the hours of daylight can begin to experience a little of what going without food is like. This will make them more sympathetic to those who do not know where their next meal is coming from.

In business, the ideal wage paid to a worker is that which allows someone to have the same standard of living as his or her employer. This ideal, Muslims believe, can be used as a starting point for solving world poverty. Muslims see poverty coming from rulers who are greedy and selfish. By establishing peace and justice,

based on principles in the Qur'an, Muslims believe that world poverty can
be solved.

▶ *These Muslims are giving zakah as part of their obedience to the Five Pillars.*

2. Muslim teaching about charity

We have already seen that zakah is not charity. It is money that each Muslim
can receive as their right, since giving it is one of the Five Pillars of Islam.
Every Muslim believer is obliged to pay it. **Sadaqah**, however, is different. This is
a voluntary gift that should be made secretly to relieve the suffering and poverty
of one's fellow human beings. As the Hadith says:

> **❝** *There is a man who gives charity and conceals it so much that his left
> hand does not know what his right hand spends.* **❞**

In giving sadaqah, no distinction must be made between a Muslim and a non-Muslim. It is given simply because a person is in great need. Generosity in giving brings true happiness and contentment. Much of the money is channelled through Muslim charities, such as Islamic Relief and Muslim Aid. These two charities work extensively in underdeveloped countries. As the Hadith reminds all Muslims:

> **❝** *He is not a believer who eats his fill while his neighbour remains hungry by his side.* **❞**

Because sadaqah is voluntary, it is up to the giver to decide how much to give. There are no guidelines laid down as there are for zakah. Obviously, the more a person gives, the greater will be their reward on the Day of Judgement.

3. Islam and moral and immoral occupations

Muslims are not allowed by their religion to earn money in any way that they choose. The basic rule is that if someone's job hurts someone else or results in a loss to someone, then it is **haram** (forbidden). If it is fair and good for society, then it is halal (acceptable). Obviously, any form of occupation that involves the exploitation of others, dishonesty, corruption, stealing, bribery, fraud, cheating or sexual degradation, is ruled out for a Muslim.

Forbidden professions include:

1. Fighting for any armed force that is involved in fighting a Muslim army.

2. Being involved in the manufacture or sale of alcohol and drugs.

3. Any form of activity that derives money from pornography, prostitution and indecency.

4. Working in a bar, nightclub, dance hall and so on.

5. Drawing, painting or photographing anything that is sexually provocative.

6. Anything connected with gambling.

7. Any lending of money on which interest is to be paid – called 'usury'. It is legitimate, however, to lend money as long as no interest is charged. There are banks in Muslim countries and they do lend money – but do not charge any interest. When a person is in debt, an attempt must be made to help the debtor. As the Qur'an says:

> **❝** *If the debtor is in a difficulty, grant him time till it is easy for him to repay. But if ye remit it by way of charity, that is best for you if ye only knew.* **❞**
> *(Surah 2.280)*

A Muslim is expected to make prayer an important part of his or her occupation. Muslims break from work five times a day to pray – wherever they are. They are expected to stop working on Friday at noon so that they can attend the mosque for prayers. At other times, they can pray where they are.

▲ Praying is a very important part of a Muslim's life. It shows how important Allah is to them because it is making time for Him.

> **❝** It is not poverty that I fear for you, but that you might begin to desire the world as others desired it, and it might destroy you as it destroyed them. **❞**
> (Hadith)

FROM THE SCRIPTURES

JUDAISM

What you will learn about in this section:

1. Jewish teaching about the poor
2. Jewish teaching about money
3. Jewish teaching about charity
4. Judaism and moral and immoral occupations

1. Jewish teaching about the poor

Jews believe that each year, during the festival of Rosh Hashanah, G-d decides how rich a person will be in the year ahead. Jews have to work, however, to provide the means by which G-d can bless them.

Wealth

Judaism discourages materialism, the naked desire for money and possessions. The prophets and the rabbis of old often warned about materialism. At the same time, they recognised that people need to have some material prosperity if they are going to serve G-d. One writer in the Jewish Scriptures asked G-d if he could find himself somewhere in between riches and poverty:

> **"** *Keep vanity and falseness far from me;*
> *give me neither poverty nor wealth,*
> *but allot me my daily bread...* **"**
> (Proverbs 30.8)

Poverty

If wealth has its dangers, then poverty is not something to be welcomed. The Talmud declared that:

> **"** *Poverty is worse than fifty plagues.* **"**

In another place, the same holy book declared that:

> **"** *A poor man is reckoned as dead.* **"**

Jews are expected to give 10% of their wealth to help those who are worse off than themselves. All wealth belongs to G-d. To keep all of one's wealth is to steal from the poor. Jews expect even the very poor to give something to others – although not the full tenth. They believe that everyone has a responsibility to help the poor – even those who are themselves in need.

TASK 1

1. Describe the teaching of the Jewish faith about wealth and riches.
2. What are the main considerations in Judaism about poverty?

2. Jewish teaching about money

The Jewish teaching about the right use of money starts from the belief that everything that we have comes from G-d. If G-d blesses a person and makes them wealthy, then it is right that they enjoy their money. People should be generous with their money, but there is no virtue in making themselves poor. The Talmud declared:

> **It is better to make your Sabbath like a weekday [meaning to eat frugal meals] than to need other people's support.**

The wealthy should always be aware of the needs of those who are poor. The advice given to the farmers in ancient Israel laid down an important principle for every Jew.

FROM THE SCRIPTURES

> **When you reap the harvest of your land, you shall not complete your reaping to the corner of the field, and the gleanings of your harvest you shall not take. You shall not pick the undeveloped twigs of your vineyard; and the fallen fruit of your vineyard you shall not gather; for the poor and the proselyte shall you leave them – I am the LORD your G-d.**
>
> *(Leviticus 19.9–10)*

The Jewish Scriptures are full of warnings that riches and wealth can easily seduce people to leave G-d and worship false gods. Here are two warnings:

1. > **Do not weary yourself to become rich; forbear from your own understanding.**
    >
    > *(Proverbs 23.4)*

2. 🔍 *A lover of money will never be satisfied with money; a lover of abundance has no wheat. This, too, is futility! As goods increase, so do those who consume them; what advantage, then, has the owner except what his eyes see?* 🔍
(Ecclesiastes 5.9–10)

TASK 2

What does the Jewish faith teach about the responsibility and the danger of having money?

3. Jewish teaching about charity

Giving money – tzedaka

It is possible to give directly to a person in need but this could cause the recipient great embarrassment. It is better that money is given in such a way that the giver does not know who the money is going to – and the receiver does not know who has given them the money. Those who give are encouraged to think of their gift as a loan – a loan that they do not expect to be repaid. At the same time, the receiver can hope that they will be able to repay the loan 'some day'.

The problem with this is that after a gift has been given and used, the person is left as poor as they were before it was made. A Jewish thinker who lived in the twelfth century, Moses Maimonides, taught that there were actually eight 'degrees' of charity, each one better than the one that follows:

1. To help people help themselves by giving them a loan or finding them a job.

2. To give anonymously.

3. To give in a way that the donor knows who receives but the recipient does not know who donated the gift.

4. To give in a way that the donor and the recipient do not know who donated or received the gift.

5. To give before being asked.

6. To give only when asked.

7. To give cheerfully – but less than one should.

8. To give grudgingly.

Jews put the same principles into operation with famine-stricken countries.

They prefer to look beyond the emergency and give the help that allows the poor to help themselves in the future.

4. Judaism and moral and immoral occupations

In Jewish teaching, it is necessary for everyone to have a means of earning money. Work, in itself, has always been seen as good.

> **❝** *Great is work. G-d's presence only rested upon the Jewish people when they began occupying themselves with useful work.* **❞**
> *(Midrash)*

This Midrash represents idleness as harmful to the individual. Other Midrash point out that idleness can lead to immoral behaviour and depression. This is supported by the Talmud:

> **❝** *Teach your son a trade or you teach him to become a robber.* **❞**

There is an old Jewish story that tells how Adam was most depressed after being thrown out of the Garden of Eden. He believed that he would have to search for food like any other animal. G-d, however, told him that he would work by the sweat of his brow and feed his family. Adam revived. He knew that he would work and this would set him apart from the rest of creation.

Work, then, is very important for all Jews. There is no place for hermits in Judaism. People have to serve G-d by being active in the world. All of the rabbis of old had an occupation. Jews can take up any occupation that they wish. The only forbidden occupations are those that bring harm to others physically – drug trafficking – or morally – such as prostitution. All work, however, is forbidden on the Sabbath day – unless the life of someone is at risk.

EXAM HELP

Make sure that you know about:

CHRISTIANITY

- The teaching of the Old and New Testaments about the inequality of wealth – the prophets and the teaching of Jesus. The parables of the bigger barns, and the rich man and Lazarus. The teaching of the early Christians about sharing.

- The teaching of Jesus about wealth and its dangers. The Sermon on the Mount and the widow's mite. Paul – the 'love of money' which is spiritually crippling.

- Giving to those in need. The spirit of the giving is as important as the gift. Giving time and effort is as important as giving money.

- Many Christians express their faith through their occupation. Many Christians in the caring professions – nursing, teaching and so on. Christians might feel unhappy in some professions.

  * Important definition to learn: tithe.

HINDUISM

- The four aims of life. One of which is to gain wealth. Divali – a time for businessmen to pray for wealth.

- Wealth must be sought in moderation. Men should also obtain wisdom, love God and carry out family responsibilities. The way a person behaves is more important than wealth. Wealth should be used to help others. The needy suffer because of bad karma.

- Wealth should not be obtained by immoral means. Six immoral ways of earning wealth.

ISLAM

- Muslims help the poor by paying zakah. The poor have a right to this money. The fast of Ramadan is an experience of poverty for all.
- Sadaqah. A voluntary gift. No guidelines.
- Many forbidden occupations. Prayer and work go together.
  * Important definitions to learn: halal, haram, sadaqah.

JUDAISM

- Material prosperity comes from G-d. Materialism is not acceptable. Wealth should be enjoyed but used properly. The dangers of acquiring wealth.
- The different levels of charity. Eight 'degrees' of giving from Moses Maimonides. Good deeds as valuable as giving money.
- Work very important. Idleness is a major issue – leads to many problems.

TOPIC 9　Religion, Poverty and Wealth

EXAM HELP

IN THE EXAMINATION
Here are sample questions for you to try:

CHRISTIANITY
(a)　Describe the major causes of hunger in the world. (8 marks)

(b)　Explain why a Christian might regularly give to charity. (7 marks)

(c)　'It does not matter how you earn your money as long as you make enough to live on.'

　　　Do you agree? Give reasons to support your answer and show that you have thought about different points of view. You must refer to Christianity in your answer. (5 marks)

HINDUISM
(a)　Describe the major causes of hunger in the world. (8 marks)

(b)　Explain why a Hindu might regularly give to charity. (7 marks)

(c)　'It does not matter how you earn your money as long as you make enough to live on.'

　　　Do you agree? Give reasons to support your answer and show that you have thought about different points of view. You must refer to Hinduism in your answer. (5 marks)

ISLAM
(a)　Describe the major causes of hunger in the world. (8 marks)

(b)　Explain why a Muslim might regularly give to charity. (7 marks)

(c)　'It does not matter how you earn your money as long as you make enough to live on.'

　　　Do you agree? Give reasons to support your answer and show that you have thought about different points of view. You must refer to Islam in your answer. (5 marks)

JUDAISM
(a)　Describe the major causes of hunger in the world. (8 marks)

(b)　Explain why a Jew might regularly give to charity. (7 marks)

(c)　'It does not matter how you earn your money as long as you have enough to live on.'

　　　Do you agree? Give reasons to support your answer and show that you have thought about different points of view. You must refer to Judaism in your answer. (5 marks)

Exam hints:

These hints apply to each of the religions:

(a) This question is asking for a list of the reasons why there is hunger in the modern world and some explanation of each reason. The question could ask for your reasons for the presence of poverty or the religious reasons for concern about the dangers of wealth.

(b) All of the religions stress the importance of giving to charity but each of them has their own guidelines. In Islam, for instance, zakah is one of the Five Pillars and lays down the principle that 2.5% of wealth be given each year. There is also voluntary giving in addition to this. In Judaism, the guideline is 10% of wealth.

(c) All of the religions stress that the way in which a person earns their income is very important. Both Islam and Hinduism lay down clear rules about the occupations that are not acceptable. In Christianity, a person's occupation must be acceptable to God. Illegal activities are, of course, ruled out by all religions.

CHRISTIANITY

What you will learn about in this section:

1. Christian attitudes to war
2. Christian attitudes to violence
3. Christian beliefs about the treatment of criminals
4. Christian responses to social injustice

1. Christian attitudes to war

War has always been a fact of life. In the days after the Israelites left their slavery in Egypt, they were only able to enter their Promised Land by conquering it – tribe by tribe. As they did so, they did not hesitate to claim that they were winning victory after victory by the power of God. At the same time, however, they also looked forward to the coming of their Messiah. He was the one anointed and chosen by God to bring in a time of peace across the world. This is why he was called the 'Prince of Peace'. While the Jews are still waiting for the coming of their Messiah, Christians believe that God's promise was fulfilled when Jesus came to earth.

FROM THE SCRIPTURES

> **❝** *I pursue and overtake my enemies; until I have made an end of them I do not turn back. I strike them down and they can rise no more … I wipe out those that hate me.* **❞**
> (Psalms 18.37–39)

> **❝** *They shall beat their swords into ploughshares and their spears into pruning hooks. Nation shall not take up sword against nation; they shall never again know war...* **❞**
> (Micah 4.3)

There is nothing at all in the teaching of Jesus to support war. He encouraged his followers to pursue a **pacifist** approach to life – turning the other cheek to their enemies and putting away their swords forever. He reminded his followers that the law of the Old Testament had said, 'An eye for an eye and a tooth for a tooth', but he taught them that violence should never be returned. In fact, his disciples should even go a step further still. They should meet every act of violence with one of love.

In the Sermon on the Mount, Jesus taught his followers:

> *You have heard that it was said, 'Eye for eye and tooth for tooth'. But I tell you: Do not resist an evil person. If someone strikes you on the right cheek, turn to him the other also. And if someone wants to sue you and take your tunic let him have your cloak as well. If someone forces you to go one mile, go with him two miles. Give to the one who asks you and do not turn away from the one who wants to borrow from you.*
>
> *(Matthew 5.38–42)*

In the light of this teaching, it is very surprising that all Christians are not pacifists (people committed to non-violence). Christians want peace but, over the centuries, have usually been willing to fight in wars. In the thirteenth century, the theologian Thomas Aquinas wrote that three things were necessary for a war to be declared as 'just' and so one that Christians could support (1–3). Two other principles were added later (4–5):

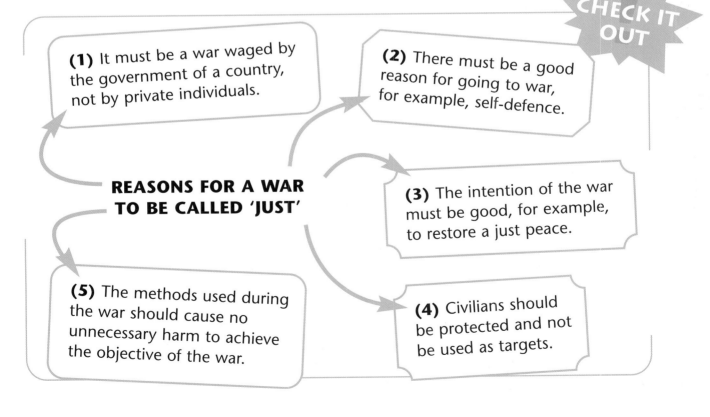

CHECK IT OUT

(1) It must be a war waged by the government of a country, not by private individuals.

(2) There must be a good reason for going to war, for example, self-defence.

REASONS FOR A WAR TO BE CALLED 'JUST'

(3) The intention of the war must be good, for example, to restore a just peace.

(5) The methods used during the war should cause no unnecessary harm to achieve the objective of the war.

(4) Civilians should be protected and not be used as targets.

If a war cannot be avoided, then these rules should make sure that the good done through fighting outweighs the harm.

Conscientious objectors

War is always a very controversial matter for Christians. This is even more true now that nuclear weapons are available and the number of countries possessing them is growing all the time. Many Christians point out that the destruction caused by nuclear weapons to human beings, animals and the whole environment could never be justified – under any circumstances. If they should never be used, what is the point of having them? Others maintain that nuclear weapons do act as a final deterrent and we cannot now pretend that they have never been invented. In any case, the threat that they pose is so frightening that their use by any country is unthinkable.

Many Christians over the centuries have pointed out that the damage that even conventional weapons can cause is so great that they could not possibly fight in a war. People who act on this belief are called **conscientious objectors**. There were many conscientious objectors in the First World War (1914–18) and the Second World War (1939–45). Although they refused to fight, they often carried out 'non-combatant' roles, such as stretcher-bearing and driving ambulances. Some, though, spent a long time in prison because the authority did not accept that their beliefs were genuine. The only Christian Church that is pacifist is the Quakers.

▼ *Christians have tried to make rules for the fighting of a war but without much success.*

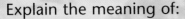

Explain the meaning of:

a. A just war

b. A conscientious objector

✳ TO TALK ABOUT

Some people think that pacifism is unrealistic in the twenty-first century. Do you think that it is unrealistic – or is it a bold approach to adopt? Would you fight in a war, and kill, to defend your country?

---

2. Christian attitudes to violence

This is the most famous Christian declaration against war:

> ❝ *We utterly deny all outward wars and strife; and fightings with outward weapons, for any end or under any pretence whatsoever. And this is our testimony to the whole world. The Spirit of Christ, by which we are guided, is not changeable, so as to command us from a thing as evil and again to move us unto it, and we do certainly know, and so testify to the world, that the Spirit of Christ, which leads us into all truth, will never move us to fight and war against any man with outward weapons, neither for the kingdom of Christ nor for kingdoms of this world.* ❞
>
> (Quaker Declaration 1660)

Anyone reading the Old Testament from start to finish will see that it is full of war and violence. The people of Israel believed on many occasions that God was calling them into battle. They were encouraged to believe that God was on their side. One of the prophets, Joel, encouraged the people to turn their agricultural implements into instruments of war:

> ❝ *Proclaim this among the nations:*
> *Prepare for war!*
> *Rouse the warriors!*
> *Let all the fighting men draw near and attack.*
> *Beat your ploughshares into swords*
> *And your pruning hooks into spears...*
> *Bring down your warriors, O LORD!* ❞
>
> (Joel 3.9–11)

This mood changes, however, in the New Testament. Jesus did not suggest at any time that the killing of people could ever be justified. His teaching was simply:

> ❝ *Blessed are the peacemakers, for they will be called sons of God.* ❞
> (Matthew 5.9)

Are all Christians pacifists? If not, why are so many pacifists Christians?

Pacifism and non-violence

Many Christians have found pacifism to be the only answer to conflict and violence. They have done so for many reasons:

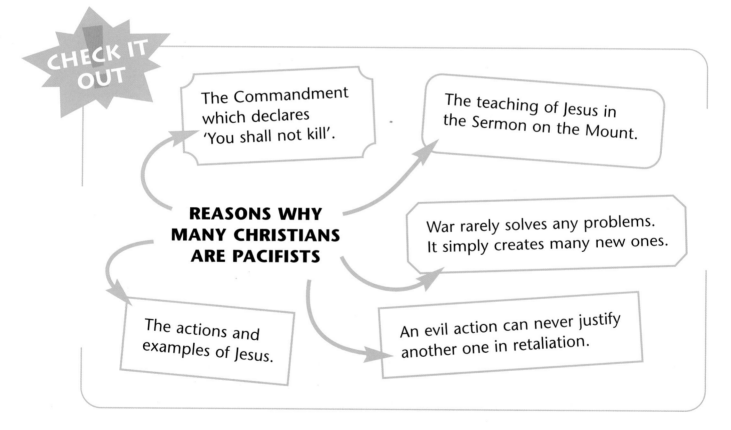

CHECK IT OUT

The Commandment which declares 'You shall not kill'.

The teaching of Jesus in the Sermon on the Mount.

REASONS WHY MANY CHRISTIANS ARE PACIFISTS

War rarely solves any problems. It simply creates many new ones.

The actions and examples of Jesus.

An evil action can never justify another one in retaliation.

Christians believe that there are other ways of solving problems rather than by using violence. In the 1960s, Martin Luther King Junior used non-violent protest as a weapon against those in the USA who denied human rights to black people. It was a very effective weapon. It was a weapon that King learned, partly from the teaching of Jesus and partly from the methods employed by Mahatma Gandhi in India.

3. Christian beliefs about the treatment of criminals

Punishment is the way that society makes criminals pay for their actions. This punishment is likely to involve:

- the loss of a person's freedom – putting them in prison;
- the inconvenience of having their freedom restricted for a time – placing them on probation, making them do community service or tagging them so that they can always be located and then placing them under a curfew;
- the payment of a sum of money – a fine.

The purposes of punishment

There are five clear objectives that most forms of punishment set out to achieve. They are:

Retribution: This means making a person pay for the crime they have committed. The criminal owes society a debt – the bigger the crime, the greater the debt. The person who has been wronged also feels better if he or she sees that the criminal has been punished. The problem is always deciding what punishment fits the crime.

Deterrence: Each punishment is intended to:

- stop the person who has committed the crime from doing so again;
- stop anyone else from committing the same crime.

Punishment is intended to act as a warning. The trouble is that over 80% of people who commit a crime go on to do so again. These people are called 'recidivists'. To be really effective, punishment needs to stop people from re-offending.

Protection: Criminals are a threat to law-abiding citizens. When a person is in prison, they cannot commit another crime and so people feel safer for a time. It is, of course, a different matter when the criminal is released from prison.

Reformation: If someone is locked away, it is very important to make them change their ways before they can do any more harm. In some prisons, education and training for a future career are given a priority, but not in all. This reformative work is very expensive and is often the first thing to be cut back when money needs to be saved.

Vindication: Few people would want to live in a society where everyone broke the law. If people break the law, they must understand what they are doing. They must also know the punishments that are used to uphold (vindicate) the law. Punishment is one of the ways that society lays down its guidelines and shows what are acceptable and unacceptable standards of behaviour. Many people no longer respect the law.

Christians believe that God will judge everyone for the way they have lived. God is the final judge. They also believe that judgement has to be passed on earth and that people must pay the right penalty for their actions. Some people need to be put in prison. Christians believe that the conditions in prison should be humane and that prisoners should be able to keep their dignity while they are there. It was back in the eighteenth and nineteenth centuries that Elizabeth Fry, from a Quaker family, fought for people in prison to have their basic human rights. There are still Christians today working in the prison service with the same ideals that Fry put into practice.

Christians and punishment

It is a very important Christian belief that everyone should be forgiven – if they repent of their sins. This does not mean that there is such a thing as 'easy forgiveness'. It does not mean, either, that they should not be punished, even if they are sorry for their actions. It does mean that the door should never be shut to the possibility of forgiveness for the criminal. This is one of the strongest arguments against **Capital Punishment** for most Christians. It shuts the door to forgiveness totally.

An interesting incident happened in the life of Jesus. It was common at the time for women to be stoned to death if they had been caught committing adultery. Some of his opponents brought a woman to Jesus claiming that the woman had been caught in the very act. What, they wondered, would Jesus do about it? He replied:

> **❝** *If any of you is without sin, let him throw the first stone at her.* **❞**
> *(John 8.7)*

By saying this, Jesus placed his enemies in an impossible position. No one could throw the first stone because none of them was without any sin themselves. The crowd melted away.

4. Christian responses to social injustice

Christians believe that God has created everyone. He intends everyone to be equal and to have equal human rights. If people are denied these rights, they suffer from 'social injustice'. Over the years, Christians have often led the fight to secure these rights – both in this country and elsewhere in the world.

Anyone forced to do without the basic human rights of equality in the eyes of the law and freedom of movement, thought, opinion, conscience, religion and right to marry and have children suffers from social injustice. Christians believe that everyone matters to God. Jesus said this when he told his listeners that the very hairs of their heads were numbered. Even a sparrow that falls dead to the ground is noticed by God (Matthew 10.29). Christians have the responsibility to spread social justice in the world – and to leave it a better place than it was when they were born.

The prophets in the Old Testament preached the same message. You would have expected them to speak mainly about the future, but they were much more concerned about the present time and the way that people were living. They told the people that all the worship in the world was of no interest to God – if there was no social justice. If people continued to cheat the poor and short-change them, then God would judge them. The same message was preached in the letters of the New Testament. James, for example, wrote about the unfairness with which some people treated others.

In some parts of the world, most notably in South America, in recent years many Christians have placed themselves strongly alongside the poorest people in society. This approach is known as liberation theology. It comes from a reading of the teachings of Jesus in which he said that it was the poor and not the rich who would be the first to enter God's kingdom.

Sometimes Christians were even prepared to break the law, and commit violent acts, if they believed that the poor would benefit in the end. It should be remembered, however, that many Christians also felt unhappy with this approach.

> ❝ *Suppose a man comes into your [church] meeting wearing a gold ring and fine clothes and a poor man in shabby clothes also comes in. If you show special attention to the man wearing fine clothes and say, 'Here's a good seat for you' but say to the poor man, 'You stand there' or 'Sit on the floor by my feet', have you not discriminated among yourselves or become judges with evil thoughts?* ❞
>
> (James 2.2–4)

FROM THE SCRIPTURES

1. What is punishment intended to achieve? How does this differ from the legal or social reasons for punishment?
2. What do Christians mean when they speak of 'social justice'?

TASK 3

HINDUISM

What you will learn about in this section:

1. Hindu attitudes to war
2. Hindu attitudes to violence
3. Hindu beliefs about the treatment of criminals
4. Hindu responses to social injustice

1. Hindu attitudes to war

The Bhagavad Gita describes the rivalry between two families – the Kauravas and the Pandavas. Arjuna, the prince of the Pandava family, finds his conscience troubled by the thought of fighting against members of his own family – and possibly killing them. The Bhagavad Gita describes a conversation that takes place between Arjuna and his charioteer, who turns out to be the god Krishna paying a visit to the earth. Krishna tells Arjuna that he must fight because it is his dharma (duty) to do so. He must put to one side his natural feelings towards his own family. He also points out that the true self, the Atman or soul, cannot be killed. The body may be killed but it is the soul that really matters. He goes on to say:

> **Think thou also of thy duty and do not waver. There is no greater good for a warrior than to fight in a righteous war. There is a war that opens the doors of heaven. Arjuna! Happy the warriors whose fate is to fight such a war.**

There is an obvious conflict in Krishna's advice. Arjuna, like all Hindus, believed in ahimsa (non-violence) but against this is the dharma or duty to which every Hindu has to respond. The advice he is given seems to be:

- do your duty and fight, but detach yourself from the result of your actions, being content whatever happens;

- a deeper understanding of the nature of life and death will solve the problem. The soul is much more important than the body.

Although some Hindus are opposed to war in any form, the majority believe that it can be justified, if it is fought in self-defence. In any case, ahimsa really refers to the fight against injustice. This is the fight in which every Hindu should be engaged. Evil should always be overcome by peaceful means, if possible.

In the old holy books, however, the gods were often asked for victory in battle. One of the four varnas in Indian society was that of the kshatriya – the warrior caste – and this caste was given the task of defending others. If violence needs to be used, then fighting in a righteous war is a sacred duty. It opens the gates of heaven to those who are killed, so making a future rebirth unnecessary.

TASK 1

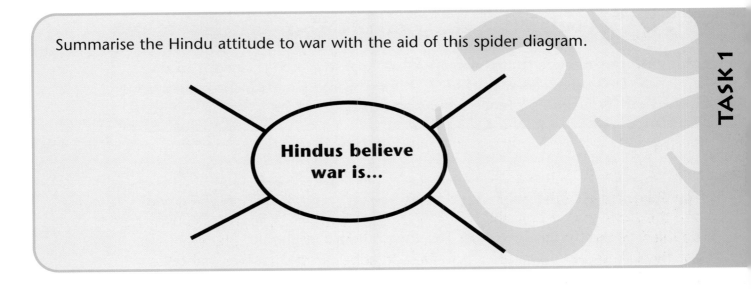

Summarise the Hindu attitude to war with the aid of this spider diagram.

Hindus believe war is...

2. Hindu attitudes to violence

There are two ways of looking at violence in Hinduism:

The way of ahimsa

This is the way of denying oneself comforts to gain spiritual benefit. It is best seen in the life of Mahatma Gandhi. He said that ahimsa should be the basic rule of life. He saw that no one can be totally non-violent since all life must eat – and that involves killing something else. However, a person should live carefully without inflicting pain or suffering on another form of life. Gandhi used ahimsa to wage a campaign against the British in India.

The way of the householder

This accepts non-violence as well, but it allows violence to be used in certain situations. The Laws of Manu says that a person is not guilty if he or she kills an assassin. Killing and other forms of violence are possible in two situations:

- to prevent something worse happening. If someone is about to slaughter a group of people, it is permissible to kill them first;

- if it is necessary to maintain law and order. Should the people be rioting and getting out of control, it may well be necessary to use violence to quell their revolt. That, too, is acceptable.

The rule of non-violence does not include enemies in a war, violent criminals, wicked people and offending animals. It is also possible to kill an animal for one's own work or food.

✳ TO TALK ABOUT

Many Hindus believe that there are situations in which it is right to use violence. Do you agree with them? Think of three situations in which you think that the use of violence would be right.

3. Hindu beliefs about the treatment of criminals

Hindus believe strongly in justice. This means that they should:

- treat all people equally;
- make sure that there is freedom of religion;
- make sure that everyone has equal political rights;
- work for a fairer distribution of the world's resources. Exploiting poor people is a form of violence. The unfairness in the world ignores the truth that a society can only be happy if everyone has a basic standard of living.

Hinduism recognises that some people commit crime because they have been badly treated. Even so, they must be punished. These punishments were originally very severe in Hindu society. Forgers of foreign documents, robbers, thieves, adulterers and those who had sex with members of the lowest caste were treated most severely. The death penalty could be imposed. However, punishments grew more lenient over time. Hindu laws took into account the caste of the criminal and of the one who was hurt. Murderers of a brahmin, the highest caste, committed the most serious crime. No physical punishment, or capital punishment, could be imposed on a brahmin. The most common punishment suggested was that a person should be reduced in caste. As Hindus believe in reincarnation, this could be very serious in the next life.

What does Hinduism teach about the fair and humane treatment of criminals?

4. Hindu responses to social injustice

The rich and the poor

There has always been a great gap between the very rich and the poor in Indian society. The privileges enjoyed by the very rich are enormous. The chances of the very poor to improve themselves, and their standard of living, are non-existent. As we have seen, the different social groups, or varnas, in Indian society are fixed and there is no movement between them. All that a person can hope for is that through good actions in this life, they might come back in a higher state. Everything in a person's life now is the result of past actions. If they are very poor or disabled, then it is because of the way they have lived. If they are very rich and highly respected, it is because of the good life they have led previously. To non-Hindus, this seems to be very unfair. To the Hindu, it is fair because a man or a woman is only receiving what they deserve. This means there is very little incentive to change things.

The Untouchables

The fifth, and lowest, category of Hindu society were the Untouchables. To it belonged those people who had defiling occupations, such as leather-workers and those who moved dead bodies, cleared the streets of rubbish and kept the drains free of rubbish and debris. Until 1950, people avoided all contact with this group but a law was then passed making this illegal. Now members of this group have to be allowed to live in the same houses, to use the same medical facilities and to send their children to the same schools as everyone else. In practice, however, this is not the case in many rural areas of India.

ISLAM

What you will learn about in this section:

1. Muslim attitudes to war

2. Muslim attitudes to violence

3. Muslim beliefs about the treatment of criminals

4. Muslim responses to social injustice

1. Muslim attitudes to war

Jihad

The word 'jihad' means 'striving'. There are two kinds of jihad in Islam:

- The greater jihad. This is the struggle within the Muslim community and within each individual against evil, a form of spiritual discipline. This is the way that every Muslim is expected to live. Life is a constant battle against all that is evil. The Muslim is expected to be deeply involved in the battle against evil within himself or herself.

- The lesser jihad. This is the struggle against an external enemy that is opposed to Allah. This kind of jihad has to be declared by someone of great spiritual authority within the community. It cannot be declared by the political leaders.

There are two reasons for declaring a lesser jihad:

1. A Muslim should always be ready to defend the Ummah (the community of Muslims) when it is challenged by an enemy. A person who takes part in a jihad is called a 'Mujahid'. If a Muslim country, or the Muslim population of a country, is threatened by a non-Muslim enemy, it is always right to respond to that threat.

2. A Muslim must be prepared to take up arms, wherever there is social injustice, on behalf of those who are suffering, whether they are Muslims or not.

There are also two other rules that apply to a lesser jihad:

- It must only happen as a last resort. All peaceful means to protect a society or an individual must be tried first. Only when all else fails can military force be used. Even then, the fighting must be carried out in such a way as to produce the least possible suffering.

- In all situations, when a Muslim is required to kill in war, or to inflict a severe form of punishment, it must be carried out with compassion. It is never part of true Islam simply to inflict pain or to carry out punishment. At the same time, there is no teaching in the Qur'an about 'turning the other cheek' or allowing oppression to continue. There is an obligation on all Muslims to defend themselves and those who depend on them – their relatives and family, the weaker members of the community and so on – to the death, if necessary.

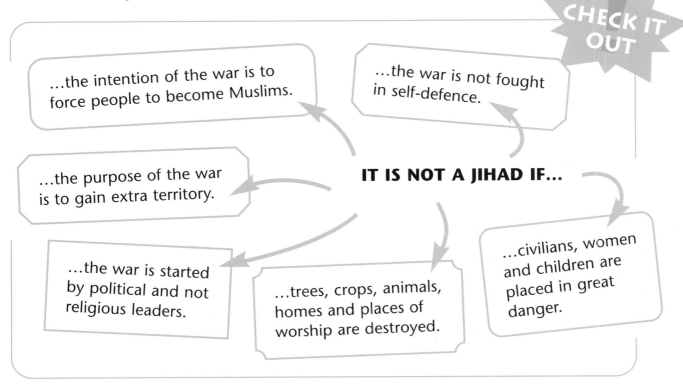

CHECK IT OUT

…the intention of the war is to force people to become Muslims.

…the war is not fought in self-defence.

…the purpose of the war is to gain extra territory.

IT IS NOT A JIHAD IF…

…civilians, women and children are placed in great danger.

…the war is started by political and not religious leaders.

…trees, crops, animals, homes and places of worship are destroyed.

TASK 1

1. What is a jihad and what are the two forms it can take?
2. When can a jihad be declared?
3. When is an armed conflict not a jihad?

2. Muslim attitudes to violence

Islam seeks harmony and peace within the community – the Ummah – and between different communities. This means that it takes the problem of individual violence and hostility very seriously. There is a Muslim tradition which says that putting things right between people is more important than giving to charity, fasting for religious reasons or keeping prayer times faithfully.

This does not mean, however, that Muslim communities that base their laws on the Qur'an do not strongly oppose activities that break those laws. The necessary battles must be fought with understanding and compassion, since this is the way that Allah treats everyone. In every community, people should be able to live without fear. They should not need to worry about lawbreakers.

3. Muslim beliefs about the treatment of criminals

Shari'ah law

The Qur'an says:

> 66 *To each among you have we prescribed a Law and an open way.* 99
> (Surah 5.48)

A Shari'ah was the path to a watering hole. It came to mean the path to life and the laws that Allah revealed to his followers. The Shari'ah is Allah's blueprint for living one's life and organising society. Muslim societies are organised so that they enforce Shari'ah and allow Muslims to live according to it.

Islam teaches that there are different kinds of sin:

1. The sins of idolatry and unbelief in Allah. These are called shirk which means associating anything else with the name of Allah. Many Muslims believe that the two sins of unbelief and idolatry are unforgivable. They earn the person who commits them a stay in hell.

2. The sins against life itself and the family – murder and adultery.

3. Sins such as the drinking of alcohol, the taking of drugs, lying, swearing and envy.

4. An important Muslim writer of the twelfth century added another category of sin – taking property that belongs to someone else.

Only a few countries fully impose the full Shari'ah law – Saudi Arabia and Nigeria among them – although several countries impose part of it. In other countries, Shari'ah law is only used for family matters or civil actions. In Western countries, adultery, fornication and homosexuality are treated as private matters but under Shari'ah law, they are treated with great seriousness. They may involve the death penalty, whipping or imprisonment. The punishment for stealing can involve the amputation of a limb.

Every Muslim believes that human judgements can be wrong. It is only Allah who hears and sees everything and no one can escape His judgement. The Prophet Muhammad ۞ knew that human judgement could be wrong. He said that anyone who accused someone wrongly and allowed them to be punished knowing that a mistake had been made would have to answer to Allah on the Day of Judgement. On that day, we will all stand alone. Allah will have the only true record of our lives and will judge everyone accordingly.

4. **Muslim responses to social injustice**

Throughout his life, Muhammad ⌖ took a special interest in two groups of people:

- Widows. These were women who had lost their husband. Because the property passed through the line of their husbands, these women were left without any real means of support. They were usually very poor. Muhammad ⌖ never knew his father because he had died before Muhammad ⌖ was born and he was, therefore, very sympathetic towards widows.

- Orphans. It was not long after his father died that Muhammad's ⌖ mother also died. He was left as an orphan to be brought up by his grandfather and then his uncle. This had a great impact on the Prophet and he was always aware of the special needs of orphans. He taught his followers that members of their family should take responsibility for any orphans. Those who bring them up must make sure that orphans know as much as possible about their own family when they are old enough. They should also pass on to them any property that is legally theirs (see 'From the Scriptures').

> 66 *To orphans restore their property (when they reach their age), nor substitute (your) worthless things for (their) good ones; and devour not their substance (by mixing it up) with your own. For this is indeed a great sin.* 99
> *(Surah 4.2)*

FROM THE SCRIPTURES

The Qur'an makes it clear that the blind, the lame and the disabled should also be included among the needy who need special help and support. So, too, should the elderly. They are people to whom Islam owes much because of all the things they have done for the religion during their lifetime. A person must look after his or her parents. They must be honoured (see 'From the Scriptures').

> 66 *Thy Lord hath decreed that ye worship none but Him, and that ye be kind to parents. Whether one or both of them attain old age in thy life, say not to them a word of contempt, nor repel them, but address them in terms of honour. And, out of kindness, lower to them the wing of humility, and say: 'My Lord! Bestow on them thy Mercy even as they cherished me in childhood.'* 99
> *(Surah 17.23–24)*

FROM THE SCRIPTURES

JUDAISM

What you will learn about in this section:

1. Jewish attitudes to war
2. Jewish attitudes to violence
3. Jewish beliefs about the treatment of criminals
4. Jewish responses to social injustice

1. Jewish attitudes to war

FROM THE SCRIPTURES

> **"** *The world stands on three things: on justice,
> on truth and on peace.* **"**
> (Ethics of the Fathers)

From the days of the Bible to the present time, Jews have greeted each other with the word 'Shalom' (Peace). This is more than just a simple greeting. Jews have always hated war and shalom expresses the hope that, one day, the whole world will live together in peace. This does not mean, however, that Judaism is a pacifist religion. Although war is evil, it is the teaching of Judaism that there are times when evil needs to be resisted and fought.

Different kinds of war

Jews believe that there are two different kinds of war:

1. *Milchemet mitzvah* (obligatory war): this extract is from the book of Joshua in the Jewish Scriptures:

> **"** *Now, arise, cross this Jordan, you and this entire people...
> Every place upon which the sole of your foot will tread I have
> given to you... Be strong and courageous for it is you who will
> cause this people to inherit the Land that I have sworn to their
> fathers to give them.* **"**
> (Joshua 1.2–6)

These words were said to Joshua, the successor of Moses, as the Israelites were about to enter their Promised Land after leaving the slavery of Egypt. The land, however, was not empty. The people would have to fight for it.

This war was a Milchemet mitzvah – an obligatory war. It was a war that the Jews were commanded by G-d to fight. This makes it similar to a 'holy war'. Such wars are fought when:

- the enemy has struck first. If the enemy has struck first, then Jews consider it to be a religious obligation to strike back;
- a strike is necessary against the enemy to prevent them from striking first. This is a pre-emptive war. In the summer of 1967, Israeli intelligence discovered that Egypt and Syria were about to launch an attack on Israel. The Israeli air force struck at enemy airfields, destroying most of their aircraft when they were still on the ground;
- the people believe that G-d is calling them into battle.

2. *Milchemet reshut* (optional war): this is the just war that can only be undertaken if there are sound reasons for doing so and certain conditions apply:
- all other alternatives to war have been tried – and they have failed;
- care is taken so that few, if any, civilians are harmed;
- damage to the land or to buildings is kept to a minimum.

Fighting any other kind of war is forbidden for Jews. This includes war fought to take over territory or to take revenge on an enemy.

2. Jewish attitudes to violence

The strong Jewish hope, expressed in Isaiah 2–4, is that ultimately nations will beat their swords into ploughshares and war will become a thing of the past. The Jewish attitude towards violence and war must always be seen against the background of this hope for peace.

Lex talionis

The Jewish guideline is that no one should act violently, nor kill another person, unless they are acting in self-defence. There is an old Jewish tradition that says:

> ❝ *He who rises up to slay you, rise up and slay him first.* ❞

If your own life is in danger, then you may kill your attacker, but you should never kill an innocent person – even if your own life is in danger. This comes from the idea that, of the 613 Commandments in the Torah, 610 of them may be broken to save your own life. The three exceptions to this rule are murder, sexual immorality and idolatry. Even in the case of self-defence, many Jews feel that the use of violence is wrong.

At an early stage in their history, Jews felt the need to lay down a standard for using violence on someone who had harmed, or killed, a relative. The original practice was for the closest relative to take the law into their own hands. This was the time, however, when the principle of an eye for an eye and a tooth for a tooth was laid down. The violence used was to be the same as that used in the first place.

3. Jewish beliefs about the treatment of criminals

The fair treatment of the criminal has always been at the heart of Jewish justice. He or she is entitled to have a fair trial at court before the sentence is passed. In Jewish law, no fewer than 36 crimes could carry the death penalty – including witchcraft, adultery, sodomy and murder. In practice, though, the death penalty was rarely passed and carried out in Israel. The reason for this is that the suspected criminal had to be warned of the possible consequences of their actions before they carried them out. Even then, if all of the judges agreed on their verdict, it was thought likely that they were prejudiced – and the verdict was squashed.

There were, of course, other sentences that could be passed for other crimes. For many crimes – including incest and breaking the rule about eating forbidden food – the punishment imposed on those found guilty was 39 lashes with a whip. Even then, the prisoner had to be examined before the penalty to make sure that they could physically bear the punishment.

The emphasis was always on the humane treatment of the criminal. Any suffering involved was always kept to a minimum. The punishments of the Torah and the Talmud have little relevance in Israel today.

TASK 1

1. What is the Jewish attitude towards violence?
2. What is the Jewish attitude towards the treatment of the criminal?

4. Jewish responses to social injustice

Social injustice was a theme that preoccupied the prophets in the Jewish Scriptures. The prophet who was most aware of such injustices in Israel was Amos. He baldly stated that G-d was not interested in hearing the worship of the people unless it was accompanied by a fair and just society.

> ❝ *I hate and loathe your festive offerings, and I will not be appeased by your assemblies. For even if you offer up to Me burnt-offerings and your meal-offerings, I will not be appeased, and I will not regard the peace-offering from your fatlings. Remove from before Me the multitude of your songs, and the music of your lutes I will not hear. Rather, let justice be revealed like water, and righteousness like a mighty stream.* ❞
>
> *(Amos 5.21–24)*

Amos goes on to accuse the Israelites of a whole series of social injustices, including:

- they lie on ivory couches stretched out on their beds in great luxury;
- they eat the best meat;
- they drink wine out of bowls;
- they anoint themselves with the choicest oils.

Yet they refused to fight the very injustices that were going on in front of them.

Jews today would recognise these injustices and seek to fight them. The Talmud and the Midrash tell many stories of people who went to great lengths to help people in need. A nineteenth century rabbi had this to say:

> ❝ *If someone is looking after a sick person and goes away to join the community in prayer, his prayer is no mitzvah at all – it is bloodshed.* ❞

Helping those suffering from social injustice is not just the responsibility of individuals – it is a responsibility for the whole community. This is why, since ancient times, wherever Jews have settled, they have set up organisations to care for those in need.

EXAM HELP

Make sure that you know about:

CHRISTIANITY

- War in the Old Testament, often given God's blessing. Jesus and war, violence. Just War. Conscientious Objectors. Pacifists.
- Five purposes of punishment. Christian approach to punishment.
- The message of the prophets.
  - ＊ Important definition to learn: Capital Punishment.

HINDUISM

- The story of the Kauravas and the Pandavas. Duty and the morality of killing.
- Ahimsa. The way of the householder and acceptable violence.
- Justice and punishment. Criminal and crime in determining punishment.
- The great gulf between rich and poor in Hindu society. The poor can only hope to improve in the next life. Present state is the result of past actions.

ISLAM

- The jihad. The greater jihad. The lesser jihad. The four conditions of the lesser jihad. The greater jihad is continuous.
- Peace within the Ummah. Violence taken very seriously. Unity within Ummah very important. Lawbreaking threatens this unity. Shari'ah law. Human laws fallible – God's laws infallible.
- Widows, orphans and poor singled out for special help.
  - ∗ Important definition to learn: jihad.

JUDAISM

- Two kinds of war.
- Justice built on fair treatment of criminal. Death penalty rarely used.
- Suffering kept to minimum.
- Prophets and social justice. Poor must be cared for.

EXAM HELP

IN THE EXAMINATION

Here are sample questions for you to try:

CHRISTIANITY

(a) Describe what Christians mean by a 'Just War'. (8 marks)

(b) Explain how Christians might respond if they see other people being treated badly by a government. (7 marks)

(c) 'Sometimes using violence is the only way to solve a problem.'

Do you agree? Give reasons to support your answer and show that you have thought about other points of view. You must refer to Christianity in your answer. (5 marks)

HINDUISM

(a) Describe what Hindus mean by 'ahimsa'. (8 marks)

(b) Explain how Hindus might respond if they see other people being treated badly by a government. (7 marks)

(c) 'Sometimes using violence is the only way to solve a problem.'

Do you agree? Give reasons to support your answer and show that you have thought about other points of view. You must refer to Hinduism in your answer. (5 marks)

ISLAM

(a) Describe what Muslims mean by 'jihad'. (8 marks)

(b) Explain how Muslims might respond if they see other people being treated badly by a government. (7 marks)

(c) 'Sometimes using violence may be the only way to solve a problem.'

Do you agree? Give reasons to support your answer and show that you have thought about other points of view. You must refer to Islam in your answer. (5 marks)

JUDAISM

(a) Describe what Jews mean by 'Holy War'. (8 marks)

(b) Explain how Jews might respond if they see other people being treated badly by a government. (7 marks)

(c) 'Sometimes using violence is the only way to solve a problem.'

Do you agree? Give reasons to support your answer and show that you have thought about other points of view. You must refer to Judaism in your answer. (5 marks)

Exam hints:

These hints apply to each of the religions:

(a) Here you need to show your knowledge about the teaching of your chosen religion about war. As you are being tested here about your knowledge, you do not need to give any personal opinions. Try to explain the religious reasons behind the ideas of the just war (Christianity), holy war (Judaism), ahimsa (Hinduism) and jihad (Islam) if you can, as it will gain you higher marks.

(b) Here you are expected to explain the different ways that your chosen religion expects its followers to respond if a government is known to mistreat people. It may be the government of the country in which you live or another government. This may include protest marches, writing of letters to the government or newspapers, joining an organisation like Amnesty International or withdrawing your support from the government.

(c) In this part you will be expected to have, and be able to explain, opinions on such issues as war and the humane treatment of criminals in modern society. You must also try to explain what answer religious believers would give to the question. Notice that while some religions have a pacifist or non-violent element, this is not always found in others.

GLOSSARY

GENERAL

ABORTION The destruction of the foetus in its mother's womb.

ADULTERY Sexual intercourse between a married person and someone who is not their marriage partner.

AGNOSTIC Someone who does not know whether God exists or not.

ATHEIST Someone who does not believe in God.

CAPITAL PUNISHMENT The execution of someone because they have committed a serious crime.

CONSCIENTIOUS OBJECTOR Someone who refuses to fight in a war for religious or moral reasons.

EUTHANASIA 'Easy death'. The choice of a terminally ill person to end their life prematurely.

GENOCIDE An attempt to wipe out the members of any one race or nation.

MONOTHEIST A person who believes in the existence of only one God.

PACIFIST A pacifist is someone who does not believe that violence can be justifiably used against another person, or country, in any circumstances.

RACIST Someone who is antagonistic to someone else because of their race.

SEXISM Discrimination because of a person's sex.

SURROGACY Having a child for someone else.

CHRISTIANITY

ABSOLUTION The forgiveness of a person's sins by a priest.

ABRAHAM The Israelite father figure who, Jews believe, was the father of the Jewish people.

ALTAR The platform at the front of a church behind which the priest stands to conduct Holy Communion.

ANGLICAN CHURCH The worldwide Church that is based on the teachings of the Church of England.

ANNULMENT The dissolving of a marriage between two Roman Catholics.

ASCENSION The Bible says that Jesus was taken up into heaven at the end of his earthly life.

BAPTISM Meaning 'to dip into water'. Used by most Churches to initiate children or adults into church membership.

BAPTIST CHURCH A Nonconformist Church that insists on the baptism of believing adults.

BEATITUDES The series of statements by Jesus about the spiritual qualities necessary to enter the kingdom of God (Matthew 5.3–11).

BIBLE Holy Scriptures sacred to Jews (the Old Testament) and to Christians (Old and New Testaments).

BISHOP A senior priest who oversees all of the churches in his diocese or area.

BREAKING OF BREAD One of the names used by Nonconformist Churches for the service commemorating the death and resurrection of Jesus.

CHRISTMAS The festival that celebrates the birth of Jesus in Bethlehem.

CITADEL A Salvation Army place of worship.

DIVINE LITURGY The name given to the service of Holy Communion in the Orthodox Church.

EASTER The festival at which Christians remember the death and resurrection of Jesus.

EPISTLES Letters written to early Christians and churches by leaders such as Paul and Peter.

EUCHARIST Name used in most Anglican churches for the service commemorating the death and resurrection of Jesus.

GOSPELS The four books at the beginning of the New Testament that contain records of the life and teachings of Jesus.

HOLY COMMUNION One name for the service held in most Christian churches commemorating the death and resurrection of Jesus.

HOLY SPIRIT The third person of the Christian Trinity given by Jesus to the church after his resurrection.

HYMN A communal song that plays a very important part in Christian worship.

ICON A special painting of the Holy Family or a saint, used as an aid to prayer and worship.

ICONOSTASIS The screen that separates the altar from the congregation in an Orthodox church.

INCARNATION The Christian belief that the second person in the Trinity came to earth in the person of Jesus Christ.

INDULGENCE A release from the spiritual penalties payable by a sinner that is granted by the Pope.

LENT The Christian festival that remembers the temptations of Jesus by Satan in the wilderness.

LORD'S PRAYER The prayer that Jesus taught his disciples to use, included in most acts of Christian worship.

LORD'S SUPPER One of the names used by Nonconformist churches for the service commemorating the death and resurrection of Jesus.

MASS The name used in Catholic churches for the service commemorating the death and resurrection of Jesus.

METHODIST CHURCH A Nonconformist Church, formed in the eighteenth century, and based on the teachings of John Wesley.

MINISTER The person responsible for leading worship in a Nonconformist church.

MISSAL The Roman Catholic prayer book.

MOSES Great Jewish leader who led the Israelites out of Egyptian slavery to the verge of the Promised Land.

NEW TESTAMENT The second part of the Bible after the Old Testament. Contains four accounts of the life of Jesus (the Gospels) and letters written by early Christian leaders (the Epistles).

NONCONFORMIST CHURCH A Church that does not 'conform' to the teachings of the Church of England.

NUPTIAL MASS The service held in a Roman Catholic church at the end of a marriage ceremony.

OLD TESTAMENT The title used by the Christian Church for the Jewish Scriptures.

ORTHODOX CHURCH Originally the Church of the Eastern region of the Roman Empire, separated from the Roman Catholic Church in 1054.

PARABLES Stories told by Jesus, carrying a spiritual message.

PAUL Converted to Christianity on the Damascus Road. Became the leader of the early Church.

PENANCE Penalty laid on a Roman Catholic by a priest after he or she has confessed their sins.

PENTECOSTAL CHURCH One of many Nonconformist Churches.

PETER The leading disciple of Jesus, leader of the early Church and believed by Catholics to have been the first Pope.

POPE Leader of the world's billion Roman Catholics.

PRIEST Someone ordained in the Protestant, Orthodox and Roman Catholic Churches and authorised to administer the sacraments.

PULPIT Elevated stand in church from which a sermon is delivered.

PURGATORY The state after death for those not ready to enter heaven.

QUAKERS The Church, also known as the 'Society of Friends', formed in the seventeenth century.

REQUIEM MASS The Mass carried out in a Roman Catholic church for someone who has died.

RESURRECTION Christians believe that Jesus was brought back to life a few days after he was crucified.

ROMAN CATHOLIC CHURCH The worldwide community of believers who follow the leadership of the Pope.

SACRAMENT An outward sign of an inner, spiritual blessing. One of seven special services that are conducted in most churches, including Holy Communion and baptism.

SACRAMENT OF RECONCILIATION The sacrament of the Roman Catholic Church by which a person confesses their sins and receives God's forgiveness from a priest.

SALVATION ARMY A Protestant denomination formed in the nineteenth century by Catherine and William Booth to work in the poorer areas of the inner cities.

SATAN The spiritual force opposed to God.

SERMON ON THE MOUNT A collection of many of the most important teachings of Jesus, brought together in Matthew, chapters 5–7.

SUNDAY The day set aside for Christian worship, the day on which Jesus rose from the dead.

TITHE Practice based on the teaching of the Old Testament of giving 1/10 of one's income to God.

TRINITY The Christian belief that there is only one God who is experienced in three persons (God the Father, God the Son and God the Holy Spirit).

VICAR The minister of an Anglican church.

VIRGIN MARY The Mother of Jesus Christ. Most Christians believe that she gave birth to Jesus without having had sexual intercourse (The 'Virgin Birth').

HINDUISM

ARTI Sacred light or flame in Hindu worship.

ATMAN The soul or principal of life in Hinduism.

AUM The sacred Hindu syllable.

AVATAR One of the nine different forms – including Krishna – in which Hindus believe Vishnu has visited the earth.

BHAVAGAD GITA A Hindu holy book.

BRAHMA The Hindu creator god. Forms a triad with Shiva and Vishnu. Sometimes shown as one figure with many faces in statues.

BRAHMAN The ultimate God in Hinduism. He is the power who is found throughout the whole universe.

BRAHMIN The first of four varnas. Hindu priests are drawn from the Brahmins.

CASTE SYSTEM A division based on a person's occupation within a varna.

CHANDALAS Untouchables.

DHARMA The obligations of belonging to a caste.

DIVALI 'The Festival of Lights', marking the end of the old year and the beginning of the new.

GANDHI A social reformer who used non-violence to achieve his ends.

GURU A teacher or guide who instructs his followers on how to find salvation.

GYATRI MANTRA The most well known part of the Rig Veda, the oldest of the Hindu scriptures.

HARIJANS Name given by Mahatma Gandhi to the Untouchables to indicate that they are really 'children of God'.

KARMA 'Action' or 'Deed'. The actions that a person does and which have a great effect on the state in which they return in the next life.

KSHATRIYAS The Hindu warrior caste.

LAWS OF MANU A Hindu holy book.

MAHABHARATA A Hindu holy book.

MANDIR A Hindu temple.

MANTRA A sacred formula or chant.

MOKSHA The final liberation from the cycle of rebirths, ending in reunion with Brahman.

MURTI The image that acts as a reminder of a god.

PUJA A Hindu act of worship.

SACRED THREAD The Hindu rite of initiation performed on boys between the ages of five and twelve.

SAMSARA The cycle of birth, life, death and rebirth.

SHIVA The destroyer god. Known to Hindus as the 'Lord of the Dance'.

SHRADDHA The daily ceremonies carried out for 11 days after a person has died.

SHRUTI The oldest Hindu Scriptures, the words of God.

SMRITI The words of God remembered by human tradition.

SUDRA The peasant or servant caste.

TRIMURTI The triad of Hindu gods – Brahma, Shiva and Vishnu.

UNTOUCHABLES Old name given to those people who were below the four varnas.

UPANISHADS The second oldest group of Hindu scriptures.

VARNA Means 'colours'. The four categories into which Hindu society is traditionally divided.

VARNASHRAMADHARMA It is important that Hindus live according to their position in life and the responsibilities expected of them as they pass through the four ashramas – passages of life.

VEDAS The ancient scriptures of India. They are regarded as the main scriptures of Hinduism and are said to have been 'heard' by the ancient sages.

VISHNU The preserver god. Has four arms and holds a conch shell in many images.

ISLAM

ADHAN The daily Muslim call to prayer.

AL-FATIHAH The first surah of the Qur'an, which is recited during salah. It is called 'The Opening'.

ALLAH The 'Supreme God' in Islam. Allah is the same God who was proclaimed by Moses and Jesus prior to Muhammad ☻ . The last, and greatest Prophet.

AL-MI'RAJ The ascent of Muhammad ☻ into the heavens where he appeared before Allah.

EID-UL-ADHA The feast commemorating the Prophet Muhammad's ☻ willingness to sacrifice his own son because Allah commanded him to do so.

FIVE PILLARS The five beliefs on which the religion of Islam is built.

HADITH Stories and sayings of Muhammad ☪ , recited by his followers.

HAJJ The pilgrimage to the holy city of Makkah, last of the Five Pillars of Islam.

HALAL Anything that is legal or permitted for Muslims, especially regarding food regulations.

HARAM Anything that is forbidden for a Muslim.

IBLIS The tempter.

IHRAM The term used in Islam for the state of ritual purity required of one taking part in the annual pilgrimage to Makkah.

IMAM The man who leads a prayer in a mosque.

JIHAD A holy war conducted in the name of Allah.

KA'BAH The cube-shaped shrine in Makkah around which pilgrims to the city walk.

MADINAH The town of Yathrib whose inhabitants invited Muhammad ☪ and his friends to join them from Makkah. Now called Madinah.

MADRASA The religion school that Muslim children attend. There they learn the Arabic language and the teachings of the Qur'an.

MAKKAH The birthplace in Saudi Arabia of Muhammad ☪ and the home of the Ka'bah.

MIHRAB The niche in the wall of the mosque that indicates the direction of Makkah (the qiblah).

MINARET The tall tower on a mosque from which the muezzin calls the faithful to prayer five times each day.

MINBAR The platform of steps from which the imam delivers his sermon during Friday prayers.

MISBEHA Beads used by some Muslims to help them to remember the 99 names of Allah.

MOSQUE 'The place of prostration', the Muslim place of prayer.

MUEZZIN Man who calls Muslims to prayer.

MUHAMMAD ☪ The founder of Islam who lived from 570 to 632 CE. Believed by Muslims to be the last and greatest of the prophets sent by Allah.

PROPHET A human being chosen by God to act as His messenger and to make His will known to the people. Muhammad ☪ was the last and the greatest of the prophets sent by Allah.

QUR'AN The Qur'an is the foundation of Islam, the word of God revealed to Muhammad ☪ and the final authority on how Muslims should behave.

RAK'AH Part of the salah, a sequence of recitations and movements that form the foundation of Muslim prayer.

RAMADAN The ninth month of the Islamic calendar, during which all Muslims must fast between sunrise and sunset. Fasting during this month is one of the Five Pillars of Islam.

SADAQAH A voluntary gift given by a Muslim to those in need.

SALAH Prayer, one of the Five Pillars of Islam.

SAWM Fasting, one of the Five Pillars of Islam.

SHAHADAH The Muslim declaration of faith: 'There is no god except Allah, Muhammad ☪ is the Messenger of Allah.' The first of the Five Pillars of Islam.

SHARI'AH The system of law, based on the teachings of the Qur'an, operating in some Muslim countries.

SHIRK The worst sin that a Muslim can commit, namely, to put anything on the same level as Allah, the supreme and only God.

TAWHID The term used in Islam to refer to the belief that there is only one God – Allah.

UMMAH The worldwide community of Islam.

WUDU The ablutions that are carried out before prayer.

ZAKAH One of the Five Pillars of Islam, giving money to the poor. A way of purifying a person's wealth.

JUDAISM

AMIDAH One of the most important Jewish prayers.

ANTI-SEMITISM Hatred directed specifically against Jews because they are Jews.

ARK The cupboard at the front of a synagogue, used to house the scrolls of the Torah.

BAR MITZVAH 'Son of the Commandment'. The name given to a boy who has passed his thirteenth birthday.

BAT MITZVAH Ceremony carried out in Reform Jewish synagogues marking a girl's coming of age at 12.

BETH DIN 'The House of Judgement', a Jewish court of three rabbis, which settles matters of dispute.

BIMAH The ledge at the front of a synagogue that holds the scrolls of the Torah when they are being read.

CHEVRA KADISHAH The group of highly respected Jews who make all the necessary arrangements when someone has died.

COVENANT The agreement that G-d made with the Jews through Abraham to be their G-d.

DAY OF ATONEMENT The holiest day of the Jewish year.

DIASPORA The dispersal of Jews throughout the world after the fall of the Temple in Jerusalem in 70 CE.

EXODUS The journey of the Jews out of Egyptian slavery, celebrated each year at the Passover festival.

GET A Jewish note of divorce signed by a man to allow his wife to remarry.

HAVDALAH 'Separation', the ceremony that separates the holy Shabbat from the rest of the week.

HOLOCAUST The destruction of over six million Jews by the Nazis before and during the Second World War.

HUPPAH The canopy at the front of a synagogue under which a wedding is performed.

KADDISH A Jewish prayer glorifying G-d, which is recited especially by people whose relatives have recently died.

KETUBAH A Jewish wedding certificate.

KOSHER Categories of food that a Jew is allowed to eat.

MESSIAH Meaning 'anointed one'. The spiritual leader for whom the Jews have been waiting since biblical days.

MIKVEH A bath in a Jewish synagogue in which a woman washes after menstruation to make her ritually pure and so able to take part in religious worship.

MINYAN The minimum of ten men who must be present for a service in an Orthodox synagogue to be acceptable.

MITZVOT The obligations or duties required of the Jews by G-d.

ORTHODOX JEW A Jew who tries to keep all the laws as they are contained in the Torah.

PASSOVER The most important Jewish festival celebrating the release of Jews from Egyptian slavery.

RABBI The teacher responsible for teaching and leading a Jewish congregation in their worship.

ROSH HASHANAH Meaning 'head of the year', the name for the Jewish New Year.

SATAN The tempter. The force of evil that is opposed to everything that G-d does.

SHABBAT The Sabbath Day, the holy day of rest for all Jews which starts at sunset on a Friday evening.

SHECHITA The method by which an animal is slaughtered by a single slit across the throat.

SHEMA The Jewish statement of faith in G-d, asserting that G-d is one.

SUKKOT One of the three Jewish pilgrimage festivals for which people in the Diaspora tried to return to the holy city of Jerusalem and the site of the Temple.

SYNAGOGUE The place of Jewish worship and study, and a community centre where Jews meet.

TALLIT A prayer shawl made of white or blue linen with tassels.

TALMUD A collection of teachings from the rabbis, gathered between 70 CE and the end of the fifth century.

TEFILLIN Two black leather boxes containing passages from the Scriptures, worn on the arm and on the forehead.

TEMPLE The building first constructed in Jerusalem by Solomon, destroyed in 586 BCE and then rebuilt later by Herod the Great. Finally destroyed by the Romans in 70 CE.

TENAKH The three initials of this word – TeNaKh – represent the three divisions of the Jewish Bible – the Torah (the Law), the Nevi'im (the Prophets) and the Ketuvim (the Writings).

TEN COMMANDMENTS The ten special laws given by G-d to the Jewish people through Moses on Mount Sinai.

TORAH The five books of the law, given by G-d to Moses on Mount Sinai.

TZEDAKA Giving money to help those in need.

YAD The metal hand pointer used to help someone who is reading from a scroll in public.

YARMULKE A small skullcap worn by Jewish men in the synagogue.

YOM KIPPUR See also the Day of Atonement.

INDEX

A

abortion 167, 192–193, 196–197, 200, 204–205, 208, 212–213, 214

Abraham 10, 20, 25, 26, 154, 199, 239

adultery 135, 165, 174, 180, 185, 194, 209, 213, 240, 282, 286, 290

agnostics 4, 5

ahimsa 204, 206, 207, 284, 285

Anglican Church 35, 37, 43, 161, 201, 229

animal rights 195, 202–203, 207, 211, 215

animals 15, 25, 42, 53, 54, 66, 67, 73, 77, 78, 84, 87, 91, 92, 98, 106, 160, 192, 206, 207, 215, 236, 246, 259, 278, 286

anti-Semitism 151, 152, 153, 243

architecture and design (of religious buildings) 43, 44, 59, 60, 61, 62

atheists 4

atman (soul) 17, 106, 107, 110, 137, 204

authority 10, 11, 18, 22, 26, 28, 140

avatars 15, 16, 84

B

baptism 37, 38

Baptist Church 35, 38, 44, 161, 166, 201

Bible 7, 9, 10, 11, 12, 13, 34, 35, 36, 40, 44, 45, 72, 75, 76, 77, 98, 105, 130, 132, 133, 135, 165, 198, 199, 213, 221, 225, 227, 256, 292

Brahman (the Supreme Spirit/Being) 14, 15, 50, 53, 55, 106, 111, 139

Brahmins (Hindu priests) 49, 50, 51, 139, 232, 286

Buddha/Buddhism 16, 20, 82, 85, 234, 239

C

castes 51, 108, 137, 138, 139, 140, 171, 205, 232–233, 285, 286

charity 112, 144, 148, 247, 258, 259, 261–262, 265--266, 270--271

Christianity/Christians 5, 6–13, 34–47, 50, 72, 73, 75, 76, 77, 78, 79, 80, 81, 88, 98–105, 128–135, 151, 152, 160–169, 196–203, 221–229, 239, 243, 245, 254–259, 276--283

contraception 167, 168–169, 175, 180, 186–187, 212

creation of the world/universe 12, 20, 25, 34, 64, 72, 74, 76, 77, 78, 82, 83, 86, 87, 88, 89, 90, 91, 192, 236

Creator 8, 15, 25, 34, 61, 77, 143, 214, 222

cross/crucifixion 8, 9, 41, 43, 46, 47, 99, 100, 132, 151, 161, 228

D

Day of Atonement (Yom Kippur) 67, 247

Day of Judgement 22, 87, 112, 114, 116, 144, 149, 180, 208, 210, 239, 240, 266, 290

developed/developing world 252–253

dharma (duty) 137, 138, 174, 260, 261, 262, 284

diet/food 14, 22, 41, 42, 53, 54, 58, 64, 66, 67, 84, 91, 203, 207, 211, 215

disciples 9, 37, 38, 41, 42, 120, 161, 224, 225, 257

divorce 23, 135, 165–166, 174, 178, 179, 185, 205

E

environmental issues 79, 80–81, 84–85, 87, 88–89, 92

eternal 8, 9, 18, 25, 55, 78, 106, 113, 120, 136, 143, 163

euthanasia 192, 194–195, 200–201, 206, 209, 214

INDEX

F

family 7, 19, 23, 24, 27, 34, 38, 45, 48, 49, 50, 64, 92, 149, 160, 175, 182, 186, 187, 193, 197, 205, 209, 225, 234, 260, 261, 291

fasting 41, 42, 53, 54, 58, 66, 67, 145, 148, 176, 247, 264

fertility treatment 193–194, 199, 205, 209

Five Pillars of Islam

    general 21, 56, 57, 58, 114, 146, 149, 238, 265

    hajj 58, 148–149, 211, 237

    salah 57, 147, 176

    sawm 58, 148

    Shahadah 21, 56, 115, 146

    zakah 57, 145, 147–148, 264, 265

forgiveness 39, 46, 67, 228, 235, 240, 241, 246–247

free will 132, 144, 192

funerals 104–105, 109–111, 115–117, 120–123, 205

G

Genesis 72, 75, 78, 80, 88, 89, 91, 92, 98, 130, 215

genocide 152

Ghandi, Mahatma 233, 280, 285

Gospels 11, 38, 100, 103, 134, 135, 165, 228

H

halal 176, 238, 266

heaven 22, 23, 38, 55, 87, 100, 101, 102, 109, 112, 113, 114, 116, 120, 130, 143

hell/Gehenna 101, 102, 112, 113, 114, 116, 119, 120, 130

Hinduism 5, 14, 15–18, 48–55, 82–85, 106–111, 119, 136–141, 170–175, 204–207, 230–235, 239, 284–287

Holocaust, the 152, 153

holy books of Hinduism

    Bhagavad Gita 16, 18, 19, 106, 206, 284

    Laws of Manu 18, 174, 206, 260, 285

    Mahabharata (Hindu holy book) 18, 19, 140, 261

    Purusha Sukta 82, 83

    Ramayana 18, 140, 141, 171

    Upanishads 17, 18, 19, 106

    Vedas 17, 18, 55, 139, 140, 230

human rights 282

hymns 18, 35, 36, 45, 52, 105

I

idols 119, 245, 290

Islam/Muslims 5, 20–23, 50, 56--61, 83, 86–87, 112–117, 142--149, 176–181, 208–211, 236–241, 245, 264–267, 288–291

J

Jesus 8, 9, 12, 13, 20, 37, 38, 40, 41, 45, 46, 99, 100, 101, 102, 103, 130, 131, 132, 133, 134, 135, 151, 161, 165, 224, 225, 226, 228, 229, 234, 239, 243, 254, 255, 256, 257, 276, 277, 280, 282, 283

Jewish Scriptures

    Prophets 27, 28

    Talmud 26, 28, 67, 92, 120, 122, 155, 183, 185, 213, 215, 268, 269, 271, 294

    Tenakh 26

    Torah 26, 27, 28, 62, 64, 88, 89, 122, 150, 155, 183, 185, 186, 212, 214, 242, 243, 244, 246, 293, 294

    Writings 28

jihad 210, 288–289

Judaism/Jews 5, 10, 24–29, 41, 50, 62–67, 75, 83, 88–93, 98, 102, 118–123, 134, 150–155, 165, 182–187, 199, 212–215, 221, 239, 242–247, 257, 268–271, 276, 292–295

K

karma 53, 106, 108, 119, 136, 137, 138, 141, 171, 204, 205, 206, 235, 261, 262, 263

kosher 41, 67, 182

L

love 7, 8, 9, 12, 34, 38, 39, 40, 52, 59, 63, 102, 103, 104, 121, 150, 161, 162, 163, 164, 168, 169, 172, 173, 183, 276

loving one's neighbours 34, 39, 222

Luther King, Martin Junior 223, 280

M

Makkah (holy city) 58, 59, 60, 116, 148, 211, 237

mandir (Hindu temple) 17, 48, 50

marriage 23, 49, 162–167, 171–174, 177–178, 179, 180, 183–185, 205, 261

meditation 14, 22, 40, 48, 49, 52, 116

Methodist Church 35, 36, 44, 161, 166, 201

missionary 11, 224, 227, 239, 245, 259

mitzvot (commandments) 26, 27, 63, 155, 182, 214

monotheists 5, 25, 50, 56

Moses 10, 20, 26, 120, 165, 239, 293

mosque 57, 59–61, 143, 147, 178, 238, 239, 264, 267

Muhammad 20, 21, 22, 23, 56, 57, 59, 60, 87, 114, 115, 116, 117, 145, 146, 147, 148, 149, 180, 210, 211, 237, 239, 290, 291

music 18, 36, 40, 44, 45, 54, 64, 122

N

Nazis 55, 151, 152, 243

New Testament 9, 10, 11, 12, 13, 41, 135, 160, 167, 226, 227, 254, 258, 280, 283

Nonconformist churches 37, 38, 44, 105, 201

O

occupations 259, 262–263, 266–267, 271

Old Testament 10, 11, 75, 135, 165, 199, 225, 254, 258, 276, 279, 283

omnipotent, omnipresent, omniscient 8, 25, 63

one God 5, 14, 20, 21, 25, 56, 61, 63, 222, 234

Orthodox churches/faiths 24, 35, 37, 40, 43, 45, 62, 63, 66, 104, 121, 164, 182, 185, 186, 229, 243

P

Passover 64, 151

Paul 11, 98–99, 100, 101, 131, 135, 160, 165, 167, 225, 227, 257, 258, 259

peace 7, 10, 117, 180, 220, 276, 277, 289, 292

perfection 8, 78, 106, 108, 109, 136

pilgrimages 58, 148–149, 237

poverty 252–253, 254–255, 258, 262, 264, 265, 268–269

prayer 7, 12, 14, 16, 21, 22, 23, 24, 34, 35, 36, 38, 39, 40, 41, 49, 50, 56, 57, 59, 60, 63, 64, 65, 66, 101, 104, 115, 116, 121, 132, 142, 144, 145, 147, 148, 176, 182, 183, 237, 239, 246, 247, 260, 267

Protestant Church 100, 104, 105, 169, 197

puja 17, 49, 170

punishment 281–282, 290, 294

purgatory 101, 104

Q

Qur'an 20, 22, 23, 57, 86, 112, 113, 114, 116, 142, 143, 144, 146, 147, 148, 149, 176, 177, 178, 208, 209, 236, 238, 239, 240, 241, 265, 266, 289, 290, 291

INDEX

R

racism 222–224, 233, 243

Ramadan 23, 58, 145, 148, 264

Reform synagogues/Judaism 62, 121, 183, 185, 186, 243, 244

reincarnation/rebirth 83, 84, 85, 100, 106, 107, 108, 111, 136, 137, 141, 230, 231, 235, 262, 263

respect 24, 27, 48, 50, 59, 201, 206, 233, 237

resurrection 9, 99, 100, 102, 104, 120, 131, 161

Roman Catholic Church 9, 13, 35, 37, 43, 101, 104, 164, 166, 167, 168, 169, 196, 199, 200, 201, 202, 203, 225, 227, 229

S

Sacred Thread, the 17, 230

sacrifices 82, 91, 215, 246, 257

Satan/Iblis 67, 77, 130, 143, 144, 150, 151

science/scientists 7, 72–93, 193, 199, 205, 209

Sermon on the Mount 80, 133, 135, 256, 277, 280

sexual relationships 166–169, 174–175, 180, 185, 186

Shabbat/Sabbath 63, 64, 65, 88, 91, 184, 243

Shari'ah (Islamic law) 240, 290

sins 9, 39, 40, 61, 103, 116, 118, 119, 132, 143, 148, 206, 213, 229, 246, 247, 290

suffering 4, 128, 129, 131, 132, 144, 145, 150, 152, 154, 206, 209

suicide 195, 202, 206, 210, 214–215

symbols 46, 47, 50, 55, 64, 65, 131, 172, 174, 229

synagogues 27, 62, 63, 66, 91, 92, 121, 123, 152, 182, 184, 185, 244, 247

T

Temple, the 28, 62, 91, 151, 161, 184, 215, 246

temptation 19, 130, 150

Ten Commandments 26, 62, 91, 119, 133, 150, 155, 165, 185, 198, 213, 215, 245, 280

Trinity, the 8, 9

U

Ummah 87, 180, 237, 288, 289

universe 6, 7, 14, 25, 34, 61, 72, 75, 83, 107

V

varnas 83, 138, 231, 233, 285

W

war 276–280, 284–285, 288–289, 292–293

women, role of 50, 160–161, 165, 170, 171, 176, 177, 182–183, 224–226, 231, 234, 238–239, 243–244

wudu (cleansing) 57, 59, 146